Jerome Kagan and an interested subject in the child
laboratory at Harvard

THE
GROWTH OF THE
child

Other books by the author:

Birth to Maturity
(WITH HOWARD MOSS)

Change and Continuity in Infancy

Understanding Children

Infancy: Its Place in Human Development
(WITH RICHARD KEARSLEY AND PHILIP ZELAZO)

THE

GROWTH OF THE

child

REFLECTIONS ON HUMAN DEVELOPMENT

JEROME KAGAN

W·W· NORTON & COMPANY· INC · NEW YORK

Copyright © 1978 by Jerome Kagan. *All rights reserved.* Published simultaneously in Canada by George J. McLeod Limited, Toronto. Printed in the United States of America.

First Edition

DESIGNER: MARJORIE J. FLOCK

Library of Congress Cataloging in Publication Data
Kagan, Jerome.
  The growth of the child.
  Includes bibliographical references.
    1. Child psychology—Addresses, essays, lectures.
  I. Title.
BF721.K15   155.4   78-16008

ISBN 0 393 01173 9

1 2 3 4 5 6 7 8 9 0

For a modern Penelope

CONTENTS

pREfACE

A BIT OF apprehension is mixed with the satisfaction that accompanies publication of this collection of research papers and theoretical essays. Many of the pieces were written for a small audience that understood the controversies, scientific techniques, and jargon that permeated each manuscript. These tacit understandings between writer and audience embellish the prose with sentences that never have to be written. Moreover, since the audience for most of the papers was professional, it was not necessary to hem every speculation with a caveat. But when these thoughts are taken from their original context, places unclothed alongside one another, and presented to an audience that, although educated, may not appreciate the tacit contracts, the danger exists that the whole will lack coherence.

In order to provide some binding material, I have written a short introduction to the 12 papers in this volume. Two criteria were used in selecting the essays: I avoided the excessively technical manuscripts found in professional journals and chose papers that dealt with a central issue in human development.

The first seven papers discuss the forces that contribute to psychological change—in essence, the mechanisms psychologists call upon to account for growth during different stages of development. This theme requires us to consider the nature of the child and adolescent and how our conception of these phases of development is clouded by ideology. The last five essays examine the presuppositions that support some of our favorite words—intelligence, deprivation, family, love, emotion. These concepts have been with us for so long that we have stopped asking about their origins and accepted the functions they have come to assume as their proper ones—like the remnants of a baby blanket that has been used as a psychic comforter for so long few remember its original shape or purpose. Fortunately, both issues find a common thread in the early years of growth and the assumptions that surround that developmental era.

I am grateful to Edwin Barber of Norton for persuading me to publish these papers and to Doris Simpson and Carole Lawton for help in preparation.

THE
GROWTH OF THE
child

iNTROduCTiON

The Primacy of Early Experience

THE INFANT has a special symbolic meaning in all societies because it marks a beginning. And in the West, where origins are sacred, the infant is awarded a set of unique qualities, the most important of which is the capacity to be changed permanently by experience. Locke's conception of the newborn's mind as a soft wax surface that faithfully retains all marks for an indefinite period is the most popular metaphor for the psychology of the young child. Such a conception leads us to seek explanations of an adolescent's current vitality or apathy in the remote past rather than in more recent history or the current set of problems and opportunities that confronts each person. This premise—which is not yet proven—also implies that the prevention of socially undesirable behavior in adolescents is best accomplished by changing very early experiences rather than by altering the life situation in which the child is growing at the moment. Put plainly, most citizens attribute the high rate of academic failure among youth in urban ghettos to parental treatment of the infant and young child rather than the contemporary values of the neighborhood or the quality of school instruction. Even in pre-Colonial America, clergymen, statesmen, and scholars regularly affirmed that the earliest years of life were critical. In 1796, long before there were any sound empirical data on a child's development, Samuel H. Smith wrote:

> Were man able to trace every effect to its cause, he would probably find that the virtue or the vice of the individual, the happiness or misery of the family, the glory or the infamy of a nation had their sources in the cradle, over which the prejudices of a nurse have presided. The years of infancy are those in which the chains of virtue or vice are generally forged, for in proportion to the length of time any idea occupies the mind so does it acquire strength and produce conviction.

Change the syntax and choice of words a little, and the statement could be from a current issue of the *New York Times Sunday Magazine*. Some pediatricians even claim that if infants are not united with their mother during the first postnatal hours, their development will be impaired by some unknown amount.

There are at least five relatively independent bases for the view that the early experiences of the child cast a special shadow on later development. Perhaps the most obvious is the desire of many Americans to create an egalitarian society. We are a society of classes but wish we were not. Most Americans want to live in a community in which as many youth as possible have the best of health, competence in some technical skill, and equal opportunity. We are saddened by the realization that this goal has not yet been achieved and want to support our political ideal with scientific facts and theories that are most in accord with that prize. John Locke's metaphor of the mind as a blank tablet summarized the desire of many seventeenth-century intellectuals to make experience primary in the molding of the child and, by inference, the adult. To Locke and others who believed in political egalitarianism, the doctrine of innate differences among children was an obstacle to achieving political equality. In order to insure that society would be capable of attaining the egalitarian ideal, it was necessary to hold an epistemology that made all infants equally skilled or unskilled at birth and to place experience in the role of tutor to all. If these premises were valid, the society could arrange for the encounters of all its children to be similar and guarantee that their minds would be equally pure and alert. Citizens who wanted an egalitarian society would be attracted to a psychological theory insisting that experience was the primary determinant of psychological differences among humans.

It is not an accident that both Freud and Piaget, and especially their disciples, emphasized the contribution of infant experience to later development. Erik Erikson, for example, supposed the opening years of life profoundly influenced the psychological profile of adolescents and adults. The infant who did not have a trusting and satisfying relation with the mother, the two-year-old who was harshly punished while being toilet-trained, or the four-year-old who grew up in a house that engendered guilt about masturbation would carry psychological burdens for years.

Piaget argued that the intellectual victories that characterize each stage of development are incorporated into the succeeding stage. The infant's play with a rattle is necessary if the three-year-old is to become symbolic; the rules of categorization gained by the seven-year-old become part of the logical reasoning of the adolescent. Both psychoanalytic and Piagetian theorists assumed a thick cord of connectivity from infancy to adolescence and beyond. These suppositions were neither accidental nor independently invented, for both groups of scholars were products of a society friendly toward the belief in a profound continuity in nature. Had a serious theory of human development been pursued in the East, I suspect it would not have relied so heavily on the notion that one period of growth closely depends on another.

A second reason for the emphasis on early experience comes from the belief that one must prepare for the future. Application of that maxim to childrearing would lead parents to assume that if children are treated optimally during the early years, healthy motives and behaviors established during that first epoch of growth would provide the older child with protection against the traumata of adulthood. Proper early treatment, like vaccination, would inoculate the child against future distress. It was the parents' responsibility to provide the child with the proper environment, the earlier the better—not unlike gathering wood in August to prepare for December's frigid winds. Hence, early Colonial Americans, many of whom were Protestants with an egalitarian ideal, urged mothers to care for their young children in order to obtain a purchase on the future. The effects of early experience were long-lasting and not easily undone, and attention to them would be amply rewarded later.

A third basis for assuming a psychological connectivity between infant and older child comes from our language, which is prejudiced toward continuity of individual qualities. Like the names of colors, the words we use to describe characteristics imply stability over time and location. We regularly choose words like "passive," "labile," "irritable," or "intelligent" to describe infants, children, and adults as if the meanings of those words were not altered by development.

A fourth reason for maintaining a belief in the sustaining power of early experience comes from our tendency to rank children on valued traits. This practice sensitizes parents of young children to the fact that evaluations at school entrance will influence the quality of education the child will receive and therefore the probability of gaining entrance to a good university and achieving future vocational success. Most parents either know this sequence or sense it and therefore want their children to be as high in the rank order as possible when school begins. The child who gets off to a good start in the acquisition of culturally valued qualities is likely, other things being equal, to remain ahead.

Our commitment to a materialistic representation of psychological experience also makes a contribution to a doctrine of infant determinism. Many scientists believe that it is potentially possible to translate psychological experience into sentences that contain words referring only to physiological events. It is true that experiences can affect the structure and biochemistry of the brain. Experimental manipulations of the experiences of young animals can add spinelike growths to nerve cells or alter the sensitivity of the visual cortex to detect vertical lines. These dramatic facts conjure up a view of the brain as a collection of fresh recording tapes. Each experience makes a permanent change in the nerve cells of the brain as a symphony permanently changes the iron filings on a tape. Since recordings are assumed to last indefinitely, each person is supposed to be a complex combination of all his or her experiences. Each act, each emotion, each fantasy is a part of a complicated interaction of all that occurred earlier.

There is reason to question the validity of this extreme view. The cells of the blood are continually being replaced; neurotransmitters in the central nervous system are continually being replenished. Why then do we assume that changes in the central nervous system produced by an experience at 12 months will be permanently protected from transformation or decay? Consider a painter and a canvas as a different metaphor for development. The painter begins to sketch a wooded area near a river; as we pass him he has completed a few small shrubs. We return five years later—he has been painting continuously—and note that the scene is now completely filled. The shrubs have become integrated into a thickly forested vista and can no longer be retrieved. This more synthetic metaphor may be more appropriate for development than that of the tape recorder and its iron filings. It is doubtful if any woman can remember her mother when she was one year old or the first motor habits she used to drive a car. That knowledge was changed as it became integrated with new mental structures. It is probably true that some experiences influence the child from the very first days of its life. But the added conviction that the changes wrought by the first environments are necessarily difficult to alter is not yet proven.

However, since parents and scientists are receptive to the idea that psychological experience is translated into material changes in the neuron, it is easier to assume that the marks are fixed rather than transient. If no one erases the original messages, they will be preserved with fidelity. The assumption that experience produces a permanent change in the central nervous system, combined with the assumption that the brain directs thought and behavior rather than the other way around, leads inevitably to the expectation that early experience must be critical because the first ideas will direct the later ones.

A final basis for a commitment to early experience comes from dramatic empirical data. Our best scientific journals contain many convincing demonstrations of how seemingly trivial events in the early days of an animal's life can have profound effects on the future. If a female rat is given male hormones during the first five days of life, at puberty she is likely to show masculine forms of mating behavior. Experimenters have gently removed the newborn mouse from its mother for a few minutes, placed it in a human hand, and then replaced it with the mother. This simple experience is repeated for several weeks. When the mice are mature, they tend to show less distress than mice who did not receive this gentle handling. Harry Harlow and his colleagues have shown, in well-publicized research, that if monkeys are reared alone either in dark cages or with wire forms rather than with live animals, the adult is hyperfearful and hyperaggressive. If the experimental infant was female, she was usually abusive with her first offspring, although not with the second.

There is no question that modification of early experience can have dramatic, enduring effects. But some of the bizarre products of early experience can be reversed. When a hyperfearful monkey, raised in isolation, is placed in a cage with infant female monkeys for about six months, the patient gradually develops normal reaction patterns, suggesting that major alterations can be obtained by benevolent experience. More to the point, most young children are not raised in small cages but continually encounter new people, new puzzles, and new challenges that require attempts at solution. It is reasonable, therefore, to ask how resilient the child is to new experience. At the moment we do not have a certain answer to that question; the first paper in this volume addresses the issue directly.

The Mechanisms of Change: Interpretation

The bases for psychological change with growth involve themes that attract the deepest curiosity. Why do children begin to fear strangers during the first year, speak during the second, and play reciprocally with a peer during the third? Most societies believe that a mysterious combination of uncontrollable forces and direct experience monitors this universal sequence. But the community's conception of the nature and relative significance of the uncontrollable elements and material encounters varies a great deal among societies of the world. Among the isolated Indians of northwest Guatemala, the uncontrollable forces include demons, fate, and day of birth; the environmental factors are food, illness, and proper instruction by the same-sex parent. In modern America the uncontrollable forces include genes and chance; the environmental elements emphasize special classes of interaction with parents, siblings, peers, and teachers.

Many theorists who have tried to conceptualize the influence of others on the child have assumed fixed consequences of a particular social experience; they did not want to acknowledge that the mind transforms information to fit with the prior knowledge of the receiver. Although the setting sun, the blare of a trumpet, and the pressure of someone's touch are different in external characteristics, all three events are transformed into the same kinds of electrical signals the moment they enter the central nervous system.

Furthermore, the mind is always evaluating the relation between events and exaggerating the differences. If a finger is put in a vial of mercury, one only feels a perception of pressure at the border where the finger meets the outside air. The information is at the locus of change. The mind typically interprets an event relative to the background in which it appears and in relation to other events. Hence a smile, an embrace, or a chastisement gains its meaning from the child's expectations and past experiences. The effect of a spanking is less salient for a child whose mother always straps him than it is for one whose parent rarely punishes physically. Seldom is there a fixed consequence of a particular parental action. The second paper, "On the Need for Relativism," elaborates the idea that the major incentives for psychological change lie not with objective events but with the child's interpretations.

Mechanisms of Change: Maturation

A second force for change emanates from biological maturation. The growth of the central nervous system, which follows a rather strict script for each species, is accompanied by the emergence of psychological qualities, the way a house takes on new functions as it is gradually completed. Certain behaviors, beliefs, and emotions must appear in all children if they grow up with human beings and natural objects and not in a closet. Ernst Mayr has called these *closed systems.* The *open systems* are created by the experiential events that control the variability and the time of appearance of inherited competences as well as the intensity, frequency, and asymptotic level of functioning of these dispositions. The open systems define the profile of psychological characteristics that allow us to detect class, regional, ethnic, and national differences with greater ease than is good for us or for society. The complementary action of closed and open systems is a new way of phrasing the sentence that appears in every textbook on human behavior: The interactions of biological and environmental forces determine the psychological growth of the organism. What does that sentence mean?

There are several reasons why we are unable to answer that question and invent a crisp metaphor for the textbook phrase. One reason derives from the historical debate between science and the church that began almost five centuries ago. The two institutions accommodated to one another following a treaty that awarded material events to science and psychic ones to the church. Each was supposed to honor the intellectual sovereignty of the other. The major philosophical statements of the seventeenth and eighteenth centuries were attempts to keep the truce sturdy as science became stronger and the church weaker. A second reason is less profound but of consequence. Analysis, the preferred mode of science, assumes a special form in psychology. Since psychological phenomena are so variable, social scientists were drawn to statistical techniques that assumed, as an unproven presupposition, that one could analyze a unitary phenomenon—say the child's height, achievement score in reading, or hallucinations—into its separate biological and experiential causes and assign a weight to each. We resist Whitehead's metaphysics, which assumes that the raw materials of science are occasions of experience, each with a duration and an essential unity. The distinguished biologist Waddington writes,

> Any attempt to analyze it into component parts injures it in some way. But we cannot do anything with it unless we do analyze it. A first step toward analysis is to dissect the unity into an experiencing subject and an experienced object. The dividing line between these two is both arbitrary and artificial. It can be drawn through various positions and wherever it is drawn it is never anything more than a convenience.

A favorite model of explanation is the multiple regression equation with its partial coefficients that announce that some factors are more important than others. This model permeates our daily practices and conceptualization of nature and prevents us from viewing an event as a product of a coherence of forces. Consider a Christmas snowfall created by the complementary interaction of humidity and temperature. It seems inappropriate to ask which factor is more critical or to assign different beta weights to temperature and humidity. We seem to have less trouble acknowledging such complementary interactions when both forces are in a material mode than when the names for the forces originate in different metalinguistic domains, like biology and psychology. The power of biological analyses has persuaded us of the utility of treating discrete, material neurological elements as primary and the less discrete psychological events as part of them. But consider the case of a Taiwanese merchant who visits a shaman because of a chronic pain in his chest. The local shaman tells the merchant he has angered an ancestor; if he makes restitution he will be relieved. He leaves the shaman with less distress than when he arrived.

Many Western physicians and psychologists are likely to spend hours arguing whether the symptom was due primarily to psychological or to physiological factors. But suppose there is a synergy between the merchant's physiology and his psychology. Many Taiwanese with his physiology but fewer worries might not develop his somatic symptoms; many with his collection of uncertainties but a different physiology would not have the distress. An infant with potential brain-stem damage due to perinatal anoxia who is raised in a familial environment where no psychological acceleration occurs will display cognitive deficit at age six. A child with the same set of birth conditions growing up in an environment that provides many opportunities for cognitive development will not display the intellectual deficit. A black child in an all-white classroom produces a certain quality of psychological tension; the same child in a black classroom does not. Each of these examples, and we could offer many more, illustrates the general principle that interaction of an element with the larger field in which it exists creates a new entity. The new entity is a part neither of the element nor the field. The sentences that describe the transcendental entity cannot be completely replaced with sentences that describe the original element and field without losing some meaning. A hallucination is neither a part of the brain nor of the structures created by past history. Physics provides the best metaphor in the form of an accelerating electric charge in an electromagnetic field. The charge is described in terms of velocity and energy, the field in terms of strength, and the interaction produces a third, quite different phenomenon—radiation—which is described in terms of frequency. The radiation is neither part of the field nor part of the charge; it is a product of the interaction of charge and field.

Mental phenomena—the perception of red, the ability to recall five numbers, or smiling in response to a face—are analogous to radiation, for they are the result of the interaction of particular neural structures and the larger field we call the psychological state of the central nervous system. The perception of red is no more a part of the cells of the central nervous system than radiation is part of the field or the electric charge that generated it. Biological forces contribute to and are necessary for psychological phenomena, but the characteristics of the phenomena are, like radiation, a product of the interaction. The most detailed knowledge of neural organization, including all the significant synapses in a chicken embryo at a given stage of embryogenesis, would not permit prediction of the actual movements of the embryo at that stage. All we can say is that the state of differentiation of the nervous system at a given stage limits the range of behavioral potentialities.

When maturation monitors a developmental change, certain behaviors, emotions, or cognitions cannot appear until prior changes have occurred in the central nervous system. The biological events permit the psychological function to appear, as long as the proper environmental conditions are present. Maturation does not in any sense cause a psychological function to occur, but it does limit the earliest time of its appearance. The emergence of language provides one of the best examples. The brain of the four-month-old is not sufficiently developed to allow the infant to understand or to speak language, regardless of how much language he or she hears. But a two-year-old whose brain is mature enough for understanding and expressing speech will not talk unless he or she has been exposed to people speaking.

Most of the new reactions that children develop are not influenced by maturation. A one-year-old is frightened by a woman with a green hat and shows fear of green hats for a few weeks thereafter. That temporary change in behavior did not involve maturation. Or a five-year-old watches someone play marbles, acquires an idea of how the game is played, and gradually develops a new skill through practice. These changes in competence are the result of observation and practice, not maturation. The fact that a psychological quality is dependent upon maturation does not mean it must occur; its emergence always requires environmental support. Maturation sets constraints on the mental life of the child while demanding that we see a temporary increase in apprehension in the one-year-old, rough-and-tumble play in the three-year-old, and enhanced sexuality in the adolescent. It is possible, but usually difficult, to prevent those phenomena from appearing at those times.

Perhaps the clearest examples of the consequence of maturation for psychological growth are seen during the period of infancy. Twenty years ago the study of infancy was a wasteland. Today we have a little more understanding of the first 24 months and have come to regard that period both as more dynamic and more transient. Many of the behaviors that appear during infancy may be like the embryo's vanishing yolk-sac or the brain's trellis cells, which remain intact only so long as they are needed as handrails to guide wandering young neurons to their permanent homes. When their mission has been performed, they vanish. A second insight of the recent research on infancy is the discovery that there seems to be a major enhancement of memory between 8 and 12 months of age. These themes are considered in "The Growth of the Infant's Mind."

The view that maturational forces exert an important influence on the period of infancy implies that experiences outside the home might not have the dramatic effect many have suggested. The paper on the effect of day care raises this issue and provides some tentative clarification of the question that surrounds surrogate care of the infant outside the home.

Jean Piaget's theory, which assumes that maturation tethers cognitive growth, offers the profound insight that, at adolescence, quality of thought changes in a serious way. One of the implications of that insight is that the social and emotional stresses seen among Western adolescents might be due as much to changes in cognitive abilities as to the increased flow of hormones. Once adolescents are able to coordinate spontaneously their beliefs on an issue—be it sex, God, career, or family—and detect logical inconsistency among the beliefs, they become vulnerable to a new uncertainty that fuels some of the conflicts so common to American and European youth. The essay on early adolescence elaborates that idea.

The contribution of biology to the psychological differences between the sexes constitutes one of the oldest and most strident debates. Is the intense rough-and-tumble play of four-year-old boys inevitable or the product of a subtle, almost invisible, profile of selective laughters and chastisements to sons and daughters during the early years of development? Most observers have noted that during the first years of life psychological differences between boys and girls are not striking; there is perhaps a little more lability among the boys and slight cognitive precocity among infant girls. But by the end of the second and during the third year, the quality of solitary and social play of boys and girls is clearly different. The boys are more vigorous, more aggressive; the girls are more trusting, more cooperative, and a little more fearful. To what degree are these differences due to socialization, to what degree are they the product of the child's interpretation of the consequences of its biology? The essay on sex differences tries to illuminate those questions.

The Nature of Motivation

Western scholars have always been friendly to explanations of human behavior that assumed some vital force that knew where it wanted to be. Plato assumed that the motion of all objects moved toward the good. Twenty centuries later John Locke substituted pleasure for Plato's good but still insisted that human beings were guided by a desire to attain something positive. This conception of human beings striving to attain absent prizes lies behind the popularity of the term "motivation."

If cognition supplies the architecture of talents, then motivation determines the likelihood that those abilities will be exploited. One question about motivation that has never been answered satisfactorily asks if there is a small set of universal desires that prompt action. Many have suggested that resolution of doubt is one of these universal goals. John Locke and Benjamin Franklin called it "uneasiness." Twentieth-century writers use the term "uncertainty," but the connotations are similar. Uncertainty about the smile of a friend or the day's work seizes the mind and forces it to do something to quiet the tension. But doubt is a generic term that needs a target to give it meaning. The incentives for disquiet change with age, and the profiles of uncertainty of two ten-year-old children are typically not identical. Hence the second question about motivation arises. How can we understand the differences in the arrangement of uncertainties across children and across developmental stages? The child's identification with parents, older siblings, and adults are regarded as one basis for the variation. The essay on motivation, taken from the book *Understanding Children*, examines these ideas more fully.

Modern Ideology

Each language contains its share of unicorns—words that have the illusion of naming a real entity but have no referent in nature. "Intelligence" may be one of these terms. A popular American conception of intelligence holds that human beings possess different amounts of a biologically based quality which permits some to learn new skills and master new ideas easily, others with difficulty. There is a consensus that mathematics is one of the most challenging tasks, conversation one of the least. The continuum of difficulty is correlated with a hidden scale of beauty that runs from rotelike repetition of well-practiced units to the creation of a system of logically coherent propositions. There is, however, reason to doubt the theoretical usefulness of the concept of intelligence, as the essay "The Continuing Enigma of Intelligence" proposes.

A second, related idea with limited utility is cultural deprivation, a term invented to explain why some children from economically disadvantaged families do not do well in school. Children of poverty have always failed to meet the standards set by the more secure elements of the society, but the universality of that fact is still not understood. Why should children from two different families in the same small town who watch the same television programs and attend the same school differ in their ability to read, write, and do arithmetic? (for they do not differ in all qualities). We must preface the analysis by asking about the magnitude of the differences and the changes in magnitude over time. The differences between middle- and lower-class children are minimal during the first year of life, are subtle but measurable by two years, and seem irreversible by adolescence. At two years of age, working- and lower-class children are less attentive and less verbal than middle-class children, but they are attentive and verbal. The statistically significant difference, not always apparent to the naïve eye, becomes important because adults are continually evaluating children and predicting their future usefulness and ability. Consider an analogy. In one florist's rose garden, the gardener treats all roses similarly when he weeds, waters, and sprays because all flowers will attract the same selling price. But in a second garden only roses whose diameters are six inches or greater are commercially valuable. Since years of study have revealed that if a rose has not attained a diameter of three inches by mid-May it is unlikely to grow to six, only the larger ones are cared for. Since no one cares for the smaller flowers, the differences in size and fullness between the small and large roses increase over the long summer.

There is obvious variability in the profiles of psychological qualities among children owing to both temperamental and experiential factors. Middle- and lower-class families and neighborhoods provide different contexts of growth during the opening decade of life. Hence we should not be surprised that adolescents from different classes vary in a way that is in accord with those early environments.

How did these differences, which are of social significance because of their consequences, arise? It is easy to pose a simple answer but difficult to provide the details that make the reply satisfying. The middle-class parent, more aware of the value of linguistic skills, self-confidence, counterphobic defenses to anticipated failure, and autonomy, unconsciously encourages these qualities and discourages their opposite. Lower-class parents march to a somewhat different drummer. They are a bit more concerned with disobedience and more worried about the child's vulnerability to antisocial behavior during adolescence. Hence they are more authoritarian and less permissive of autonomy. The lower-class parent is less likely to subscribe to the belief (or folk theory) that lively play and conversation between parent and young child are likely to facilitate intellectual development. Thus differences in values as well as theories of development inevitably lead the children of the two classes to move in increasingly divergent directions.

But there is more. As the child approaches school age he identifies with his class and assumes that the characteristics of his ethnic or class group belong to him. A school-age child comes to appreciate the attributes the wider society values or derogates. The American child realizes that material wealth, a certain pattern of cognitive abilities, and particular vocations are valued, whereas excessive drinking, an unskilled job, a home in disrepair, and inability to read or write are undesirable, sources of shame. That knowledge produces a sharp change in children's conception of their parents and themselves, for the insight regarding society's evaluation of their family is taken as a diagnosis of the self. Hence the family's social class position and the specific psychological characteristics of parents influence the degree to which the child's self-conceptualization is positive or negative.

The history of experience and pattern of identifications make it a little easier to understand why, by age ten, the lower-class child is less adept than the middle-class child at the tasks of the school. In less frequent but more extreme cases, children have grown up in such unpredictable environments, with more hours of hunger and anxiety than they can understand, that they have an automatic reaction of uncertainty to new challenges. The school environment poses so many new demands that the child becomes frightened; he devotes energy to controlling the distress and has little left for much else. The paper on cultural deprivation attempts to analyze this problem and to suggest some ameliorating actions.

The Family

Modern Americans regard the family as a basic structural unit in the society whose function is to nurture children and to provide the special satisfactions that come only from intimacy.

Whenever citizens and intellectuals become preoccupied with the same topic, an event that has become less common as the academy has become more specialized, one immediately looks for reasons for the consensus. In the case of the sullying of the air and proliferation of destructive weapons the reasons are obvious. It is, however, a little less clear why the family has become of preeminent interest. The White House is planning a conference on the family, private philanthropies and governmental agencies have begun to allocate considerably more support for research on family dynamics and essays on policy, and economists, anthropologists, sociologists, and historians have joined a small cadre of psychologists in attempting to untangle the relations between the home and society on the one hand and the qualities of family members and individual destinies on the other.

It is likely that this effort is energized in part by the deep belief that childhood experiences in the home constitute the most important set of influences on adolescent and adult psychological profiles. The family has become an explanation for many of the problems that plague the community. This is an old idea in our society, although far from universal. John Bowlby's assertion that adult fragility can be traced to the uncertainties of early childhood is explicit both in Rousseau and the sermons of nineteenth-century clergy. Some American parents and journalists have simplistically blamed current adolescent rebellion, delinquency, and dependence on drugs on overly permissive parental practices during early childhood; but even thoughtful citizens place some version of this simple idea on their list of most cherished verities.

In trying to find the reasons for increased alienation, suicide, and gang wars among the young, as well as more prosaic phenomena such as the slide in scholastic aptitude test scores, we can consider several possible explanations: the structure of our schools, class division, the mass media. Although citizens acknowledge the potential relevance of each of these forces, there is a strong preference for assigning primary causality to the family. More intense public emotion is generated over the abuse of infants and the relocation of children from homes to day-care centers than over the size and quality of our schools, the plots of television or movie dramas, or the influence of friends. It is not that Americans believe these latter forces are without potency, only that they are sure that the family has more.

Although that faith may well be justified, neither theory nor empirical data are firm enough to generate propositions that will explain how the family creates these products. For example, many psychologists assume that Scholastic Aptitude Test scores and school failure are influenced by the material encounters between parent and young child—the amount of play, encouragement, punishment, or even the number of embraces that occurred each day. But unfortunately, no one has been able to find a set of parental practices that predicted test scores or grades in school as well as the social class of the child's family, a fact that points to the complementary influence of forces beyond parental practices *qua* practices. Neither maternal behavior nor the child's psychological profile during the first three years of life seems to be related in any serious way to future intellectual talent, after the effects of the child's social class are taken into account.

There are two rational replies to this pessimistic conclusion. First, most existing investigations of the effect of parental practices are insufficiently sensitive. If investigators had better methods of inquiry, they would have found that the material encounters between child and parent provided a commanding explanation of the later phenomena. A second, more reasonable, rebuttal is that the actual practices are less important than the interpretation the child imposes on them. And these interpretations are always colored by the youngster's perception of the parents as human beings. The effect of a father's praise or detachment will always depend on whether he is admired or respected. Since there has been little careful study of the effect of parental actions as they are transduced by the child's evaluation of parental character, one certainly cannot claim that parental behaviors are unimportant.

Let us pose part of the dilemma in a context of a specific empirical fact. The education of a boy's father, at least among working- and middle-class Caucasians in the United States, is as good a predictor of the young adult's occupational and educational attainment as the child's intellectual ability or personality profile during the first five years of life. Is this because the well-educated, professional father behaves in a special way with his son, is a respected role model whom the son tries to emulate, or more simply because the family's affluence permits the child to attend schools whose peer composition and ethos make it likely that the boy will grow to value education and aspire to a professional or managerial vocation? Of course, we do not have to choose among these possibilities; it is likely all are operative. But if they are, we must be willing to acknowledge that factors other than particular parental behaviors are to be awarded a prominent place in the equation that accounts for the adult profile.

There is an odd asymmetry in our statements about the effect of the family, for casual discussions of life histories more often link the family to psychological failure and unhappiness than to a successful career or a happy marriage. We tend to assign chance a more central role in the more positive outcomes.

Recognition of these trends is leading some psychologists to select slightly different constructs to explain the relation between family dynamics and the child's development. The traditional paradigm during most of this century viewed the child as a surface to be shaped by parental manipulation, much as a sculptor forms a lovely statue from a piece of marble. That image contains two salient dimensions. The child is passively worked by the intelligent and loving actions of the parents, and there is a presumed veridicality between what is done by family members and some outcome in the older child. The emergent view, which we owe in part to Piaget's emphasis on the constructive processes of the child's mind, is that many transformations occur between parental communication and the child's inference. The development of a particular talent, motive, or conflict is not analogous to a sculptor chipping at marble but more like the fate of the physical energy produced by a cello sonata as that energy travels from basilar membrane to temporal cortex. At a more speculative level, it is likely that sources of worry are among the major inferences the child extracts from his immersion in the family. Parents indirectly communicate to children what they should fear: parental disfavor, social prejudice, peer rejection, lack of money, exploitation, incompetence, or humiliation for violating social norms. These sources of uncertainty are probably established during the decade from the third to the thirteenth year and are likely to remain sturdy if the child does not have an opportunity to prove them incorrect or to arrange his life so that he is protected from them.

Modern society is characterized by skepticism. The absence of any rule that awards priority to a particular set of behaviors, save the directive to maximize economic gain, has generated a troubled mood. Americans wonder about the meaning of today's actions and the predictability of the future and search for some ritual to deflect the mind from these sources of disquiet. Impatient for an answer, people look for what can be done now and rationalize the choice afterward. We are not receptive to any reply that implies temporary helplessness. In earlier centuries the citizenry were advised to pray away the distress generated by uncertainty. Today most look elsewhere.

Parents, educators, and legislators worry about the large number of academic and social failures among adolescents. If, as modern theory holds, most of these failures were created in the bosom of the family a decade earlier, there is the possibility that at least this vexing problem can be addressed. The belief that parents can initiate special practices with their infants and young children in order to guarantee their future is one reason for the extraordinary interest in child development. The essay "The Child in the Family" summarizes the functions of the family with respect to the child and suggests that the family's influence is mediated less through material parent-child interactions than through the child's interpretations of the experiences and structural relationships in which each child is embedded.

The Meaning of Maturity

Each culture promotes an ideal state that each citizen should try to approach. Life requires too much effort to be without a goal, and a society could not function well if there were no hint of a consensus on purpose. Each community gives the ideal a different name, whether areté, piety, nirvana, or maturity. The choice of words reveals a clue to the essence of what is prized, for each of the desirable qualities has an implied antonym. In America, maturity is set against immaturity. Since "immature" means childish, each person's assignment is to rush from childhood. The most disliked qualities of childhood include dependence, lability of mood, lack of control, power, and autonomy, excessive impulsiveness, narcissism, and a resistance to certain forms of logical argument. (We have in the past regarded women as less mature than men because the local stereotype held that these traits were more characteristic of females.) The West values independence, a restrained mood, control of impulse, autonomy of action, and an alacrity at and willingness to capitulate to logical argument.

Why are control, autonomy, and rationality so precious? The transformation from a fixed, relatively cooperative rural family in an agricultural economy to an entrepreneurial, mobile family in an industrialized economy demanded autonomy among young adults. Youth must leave their family and seek a career that promises economic and psychological independence. If the youth need advice, money, or affection from a family too regularly, they will fail. Since the family cannot support a young adult who returns nothing, if one leaves for the city it is psychologically difficult to turn back.

But this sequence does not explain the repression of sensuality. To seek the sensual is to live in the present, not the future. Keats warned, "Heard melodies are sweet, but those unheard are sweeter." So youth are told to put off temporary enhancement of the present for something better tomorrow. It is difficult to accomplish today's work if one is preparing for an especially sensual delight in the next hour. And sensory experience brings a special quality of relaxation and gentleness of mood that is neither fatigue nor lethargy—a quiet state that is not altogether conducive to invention or work.

The need for work, for individual survival as well as enhanced status, makes it necessary to portion out the moments of pleasure in small pieces— an hour in the evening and maybe all of Sunday afternoon. Children play; they are immature. Adults work; they are mature. "You can play when your homework is done" may be the most common communication from parent to school-age child. Play is a reward for work, not a substitute. And society keeps its promise, for it awards respect as well as material comfort to those who strive to be mature.

Finally, we must consider the insistence on rationality. Why is it not possible to be autonomous and hard-working and still be receptive to intuition? It is not obvious that autonomy and control of the hedonic demand an insistence on fact and logic and the exclusion of intuition as the basis for decision. It is more difficult to account for this aspect of our ego ideal. Rationality involves detecting inconsistency in sets of ideas and a willingness to accept conclusions that are so logically commanding they become obligatory. When a society offers its members little or no choice in decisions, because very few alternatives are available when a person must deal with the press of everyday life, people react to most situations with a ritualized response. But when there is choice, one needs a guide. Although intuition is a potential candidate, it cannot be defended well in debate with others. In a society of strangers with differing values, each of whom is protective of property and freedom of action, rational argument is a useful way to guarantee that all participants will be satisfied. If property is to be justly held and transferred in a society with unequal distribution of property, law is required. Acceptance of and obedience to law demands a respect for rational argument. Since rationality more readily permits disputants to come to a common agreement where intuition would fail, a society of strangers must award rationality more power than intuition. Parents can make decisions about their children on emotional or intuitive grounds, for both parties understand that there was a concerned nurturance behind the decision which guided the selection of an action. But one cannot count on such charitable motives when dealing with nonkin. When strangers differ on basic presuppositions, intuition is not likely to solve disputes. Disputes can best be solved by first agreeing on a set of premises which, when married to factual conditions, force agreement or at least consonance.

The current conception of maturity in Western society has been established gradually. The verbal charge "You are immature" is threatening, for it implies one has failed to meet society's primary standard. The response to that accusation is neither fear nor guilt but embarrassment, since the person does not feel totally responsible for the failure—it is like having a facial scar. The essay, "The Concept of Maturity" tries to deal with these themes.

Emotion

It is often true that the more fundamental the phenomenon the more difficult it is to understand. Endel Tulving has noted that psychologists have not learned very much about forgetting since the time of Aristotle. Almost the same can be said about emotion. The lack of progress may be due, in part, to the incorrect classification of affective phenomena. "Emotion" may be too general a term.

There are at least two phenomena of interest. The first is the experience of a change in internal feeling-tone. The second is the fact that some situations provoke, in most people, a similar class of changed feelings and a similar class of overt behaviors. These are, of course, sharply different issues. It seems wise to explore each separately before inventing names for either of them. The ancient trichotomy of thought, action, and feeling was no doubt invented because these three states have salient qualities, like air, earth, water, and fire. The classification of emotion may have the same theoretical utility. The paper on emotion argues that we should temporarily put the term aside and analyze the relevant phenomena more closely.

Although these essays celebrate the beauty and occasional utility of scientific inquiry, I do not believe that the factual products of research can provide a constructive basis for a community's morality. Science can supply evidence that might undermine the false bases for an ethical premise, but it cannot supply the basis for a moral proposition. Facts prune the tree of morality; they cannot be the seedbed. Our modern community may be too dependent upon the results of science to guide ethical decisions. No absolute moral imperative is demanded by any fact of nature. Morality springs usually from changing social conditions, not from principles of animal behavior or propositions that describe the functioning of the central nervous system. Modern Americans believe that all citizens have a right to private religious beliefs. That value is necessary because our society contains so much divergence; it must be upheld if we are to avoid quarreling with one another. Modern Americans also hold that competition is a morally good quality. That belief is based, in part, on the nature of our economy, not on the fact that animals compete for resources. Legislators, physicians, parents, and teachers, sensing that the young discipline of psychology might ease the burden of moral choice, seek any fact or reasonable hypothesis that rationalizes an action that must be issued or defends one that must be replaced because it is obviously not working. Piagetian theory is corrupted to serve the curriculum expert, Freudian theory transformed to serve the counselor, behavior theory exploited to serve the prison psychologist, ethological theory quoted to rationalize the daily blizzard of aggression and competitiveness.

It seems reasonable to expect psychologists to supply relevant and even therapeutic information. And on occasion they have. A decade of research on the effect of day care on young children suggests that attendance at a good day-care center during infancy and early childhood does not possess hidden dangers. But the community wants more than psychologists are able to deliver. That pressure forces overly eager respondents to answer the impatient citizen with advice that bubbles up from a loose combination of intuition and a sense of what the community wants to hear, rather than firm empirical fact or a logically coherent argument. Science can supply ways to implement value decisions made by others. Having decided that alcoholism is bad, we can ask science to supply information on cures. Having decided that reading is good, we can expect science to tell us how to teach that skill better or to discover the cause of reading disability. Those are useful facts. Science is valuable but not strong enough to give birth to a morality. Morality lies in the sentiment of a community, and sentiment is not logical.

These essays are to be enjoyed. If they enhance the reader's understanding of the child, they will have served their purpose.

ONE

RESiliENCE ANd CONTiNUiTY iN psyCHOLOGiCAL devELOpMENT

ACH SCIENTIFIC discipline, during successive eras in its growth, is loyal to one member of a set of opposed assumptions that typically form the axioms of the discipline. Holton (1973) has called these polarized premises *themata*. Debate over whether matter is particulate or wavelike, whether the universe is steady-state or expanding, or whether growth is continuous or discontinuous are among the themes that scientists have debated in the past and will continue to discuss in the future because, as Bohr wisely noted, the propositions are likely to be complementary rather than incompatible.

This paper considers the evidence bearing on a pair of opposed themata that have given direction to the empirical study of human psychological development. One proposition holds that the experiences of infancy produce a set of dispositions that have a continuous influence throughout life, implying that some of the effects of early experience are not malleable to change. The opposed position is that the infant is resilient and the effects of early experience—which can be dramatic—are reversible under proper environmental conditions. The debate centers on the degree of modifiability of psychological structures established early in life. There is unequivocal support for the view that the experiences of young infants have a powerful contemporary effect on their behavior, temperament, and knowledge. This hypothesis is

Adapted from A. M. Clarke and A. D. B. Clarke, *Early Experience: Myth and Evidence* (London: Open Books, 1976); Emergent themes in human development, *American Scientist* 64 (1976):186–96, and The baby's elastic mind, *Human Nature* 1 (1978).

unchallenged. But it is less clear how stable these early structures are, especially if the environment should change in a serious way. Stated in the interrogative, how resilient—or responsive to change—are the cognitive structures and behavioral dispositions shaped during the first three years of life?

Two centuries ago clergy and statesmen regularly affirmed the critical importance of the child's early years, urging mothers to stay at home with their infants and to treat them tenderly.

John Locke's metaphor of the infant's mind as a blank tablet and the desire of many seventeenth-century intellectuals to make experience primary in the creation of knowledge are among the fundamental sources of this idea. For Locke and others who believed in egalitarianism, it was useful to assume that political equality among all citizens was more easily attained if infants were relatively similar at birth. If experience were the primary—but not the sole—determinant of differences among human beings, society could arrange for all of its children to have equivalent experiences, thereby guaranteeing that they would all become free, equal, and independent as adults. Since four-year-olds are so different, many wanted to conclude that early experience was the main cause of the variation.

There are many reasons why a majority has continued to favor the view that the products of early experience are difficult to alter. The influence of psychoanalytic theory and data from animal laboratories form the modern scientific basis for the belief. Comparative psychologists and ethologists alerted the scientific community with demonstrations of dramatic and apparently irreversible effects of early experience. The most impressive examples came from the experiments on imprinting and the production of abnormal behavior in rhesus monkeys raised with inanimate wire "mothers." These provocative findings made Freud's theoretical position persuasive and strengthened the psychologist's belief that the events of infancy could seriously constrain future functioning.

Darwinian theory also made a contribution. Darwin created a paradox by positing a continuum between animal and man. Since animal behavior was regarded by nineteenth-century scientists as instinctive and resistant to change, how was it possible for man to be so varied, flexible, and progressive?

One way to resolve the dilemma was to award a special function to what appeared to be a prolonged period of infant helplessness in humans as compared with animals. Since evolutionary theory made scholars sensitive to the idea that all qualities of living things had a purpose, it was reasonable to ask about the purpose of man's prolonged infancy. Most concluded that infancy was the period of maximal plasticity, the time when adults were to teach children skills, habits, and ideas they would carry with them throughout life. In a lecture at Harvard in 1871, Fiske argued that the power to control the environment and to make progress was due to our educability. The purpose of infancy was to educate and to train the child, because he or she was most malleable to training during the early years (Fiske 1883). That assumption was congruent with a belief in continuity from infancy to later childhood; it served to keep parents affectively concerned with their actions toward their babies; and it was an argument for creating good schools.

Additionally, each of us feels a compelling sense of continuity when we reflect on the experiences of our own childhood. The sense of the past's contribution to the present derives from our need to regard our life as coherent and past decisions as a part of a rationally causal chain. More speculatively, faith in the permanent effects of early experience may be a derivative of one of the central maxims of Protestantism, namely, preparation for the future. Application of that principle to childrearing would lead parents to believe that if children were treated optimally during the early years, healthy attitudes, talents, and behaviors established then would provide protection against trauma during adolescence and adulthood. Proper early experience, like vaccination, was expected to inoculate a child against vulnerability to future psychic distress.

The doctrine of early infant determinism also owes some of its popularity to the biological materialism of modern psychology. Psychological experience presumably causes changes in the neurons and their synapses, like marks on a tablet, and it is easier to assume that the marks are fixed rather than transient. The modern metaphor for the mind becomes reels of tape in a tape recorder. The iron filings on the fresh tape are permanently altered by a baby's early experiences, and if no one erases the message, it will be preserved with fidelity for an indefinite period.

Faith in the stability of early experience rests, in part, with the words we use to describe human behavior. We use adjectives like "passive," "irritable," "intelligent," or "emotional" for infants, children, and adults as if the age of the person described were irrelevant to the meaning of the terms. A child is labeled "dependent," "labile," or "alert" whether six days, six months, or six years old and regardless of the setting. This is not true in many other languages. In Japanese, for example, different terms are used to ascribe intelligence to an infant and an older child.

The permanence rooted so deeply in our descriptive language may contribute to the belief that early experience sculpts attitudes, fears, and behaviors that are extremely resistant to change.

A final, less legitimate, reason for believing in the permanent effect of early experience comes from investigations of the academic performance of children. Studies of economically disadvantaged American children, most often black but occasionally Mexican-American, Puerto Rican, and white, reveal that children from poverty families perform differently from middle-class children on tests of language, memory, reasoning, and problem solving before school entrance. Less adequate, but not wholly unsatisfactory, observations in the homes of poor and middle-class preschool children reveal that each group is exposed to different patterns of encounters with their parents. This information was interpreted as indicating that the intellectual development of poor children had been impaired by their home experience during the first three years of life. Since the children of the poor consistently remained behind their middle-class peers on standardized tests of academic skills and intelligence, it was suggested that their intellectual retardation (compared with middle-class youngsters) was irreversible.

There is a serious difference, however, between this basis for positing irreversibility and the data derived from the animal work. In the latter case the investigator had some absolute reference for the behavior of a species reared in the natural environment. If a rhesus monkey raised on a wire surrogate-mother did not, after months or years in a rehabilitating context, display any substantial change in self-mutilation, fearfulness, or avoidance of mating behavior, it was reasonable to entertain the hypothesis of irreversibility. By contrast there is no absolute norm or reference that informs us of the expected level of competence at reading, writing, or arithmetic. Those norms change each 20 to 50 years as children acquire more and different words, facts, and skills. Half of the words that a Boston first-grader was supposed to know in 1900 would be unfamiliar to a middle-class Boston child in 1976. The poverty child remained behind the middle-class youngster only in relative rank on particular tests. Actually he was acquiring more facts and improving his skills each day. Although the average seven-year-old child of poverty was less proficient than the seven-year-old middle-class child on reading or reasoning skills, the typical fifteen-year-old of poverty was not less competent than the seven-year-old middle-class youngster.

All parents know that their children will be evaluated for ability and character at the end of kindergarten. Those evaluations will influence the quality of education the child will receive through elementary and high school, the probability of admission to a good college, and by implication, future success, happiness, wealth, and dignity.

Few societies practice severe grading of young children with such efficiency and zeal. In most communities, children receive responsibility when they are ready, not when they attain a particular age. Moreover, children usually are given assignments they can master, such as carrying water or caring for younger children. Their status in the community is attained in adulthood by hard work, loyalty to the village, and the acquisition of land or livestock. Relative competence in motor or language skills at five years has little effect on their lives.

But because the industrialized West needs less than a third of its youth to assume positions of high responsibility or to master complex skills, we send the best-trained adolescents to professional schools. Selection usually occurs when the child is 10 or 11, and once made, the child's motivations become relatively fixed and his place in the rank order becomes relatively stable.

Most parents either know or sense this sequence and try to make sure their children are as talented and motivated as possible when schooling begins. They assume that the obvious differences among five-year-olds are the result of what happened earlier in the family. Hence parents want to guarantee that their children have the richest set of early experiences. The belief that early experience was the primary determinant of adult success was satisfying because it resolved uncertainty, provided parents with anxiety-reducing rituals, made material encounters between the child and the environment the basis for both positive and negative results, and above all, was rational.

One reason why it is difficult to disconfirm this view is that the vast majority of children remain with their families in similar environmental contexts from birth until late adolescence. As a result differences in intellectual competence, social behavior, and psychopathology among sixteen-year-olds from different families could just as well be due to events that occurred during the years six to twelve or twelve to sixteen as to experiences during the first two years of life. Consider two 16-year-old boys from the same town, one of whom is successful in school and the other failing. There is a strong temptation to attribute primary causality to motivational and intellectual structures established during the first half-decade rather than to dispositions that developed later. A Gedanken experiment suggests the potential usefulness of questioning that assumption. Imagine a happy, social, alert, secure, curious, creative and spontaneous three-year-old who is transferred to an environment in which he is punished inconsistently and regularly exposed to violence, cynicism, failure, and derogation. If we return ten years later we might not see most of the strengths that were present at age three. This 13-year-old might resemble the other children in that family who had been continually exposed to the same regime. Now imagine removing a three-year-old from a toxic environment to a benevolent one and returning ten years later. Intuition suggests that the transferred adolescent will be substantially different from a sibling who had remained in the destructive family context.

During the last decade some evidence has accumulated that permits us to at least begin to question the strong version of the doctrine of irreversibility. The most persuasive data come, oddly enough, from the animal laboratory. Suomi and Harlow (1972) have reported that even the stereotyped and bizarre social behaviors shown by six-month-old macaque isolates can be altered by placing them with female monkeys three months younger than themselves over a 26-week therapeutic period.

Generally, investigators have reported that, although the isolate-reared animal is initially inhibited and deficient on test performance, after continued exposure to the test situation his behavior approaches that of the normally reared animal, often in a short time. Wild-born or isolate chimpanzees were placed with a passive human for 10 minutes a day for 13 days. Each day, after the initial 10 minutes, the person spent 50 minutes encouraging the chimpanzee to socialize by making gentle social contacts. The wild-born chimps contacted the human throughout the 13 days. The isolates were initially inhibited but by the last session made as much contact as the wild-born animals (Mason, Davenport, and Menzel 1968).

Even imprinting toward a nonnatural object in a laboratory context seems to be reversible. Hess, in an attempt to imprint ducklings to human beings in the laboratory, exposed newly hatched ducklings to adults for 20 continuous hours; before long, they followed the adults. The ducks were then given to a female mallard that had hatched a clutch of ducklings several hours before. After only an hour and a half of exposure to the female, the human-imprinted ducklings followed her on her first exodus from the nest (Hess 1972).

This phenomenon is analogous to changes in the object of primary attachment among primates. Rhesus monkeys were raised from birth with cloth surrogates, their mothers, or a peer monkey for three to ten months. All the monkeys were then separated from these objects of primary attachment and gradually exposed to spayed adult female dogs. Initially most of the monkeys were fearful, but this behavior disappeared quickly, and after seven hours all monkeys approached the dogs and eventually clung to them. Soon the monkeys displayed the classic signs of attachment—clinging and following. The initial attachment had been changed (Mason and Kenney 1974; see Elias lecture MS and Ader 1970 for additional support for the rehabilitative properties of proper experience following early insult).

Although it is difficult to find as dramatic evidence for changes in human development, individual strands of evidence, each too weak to bear the burden of proof, can be woven into a fabric with some persuasive power. After World War II, for example, American families adopted homeless children, most of them from Greece and Korea, who had led uncertain lives during the war. When 38 of these children, whose ages ranged from five months to ten years, arrived in the United States, their progress was followed by a team from the Judge Baker Guidance Center in Boston.

Soon after the children came to their new homes, they showed signs of many problems: overeating, sleep disturbances, nightmares, and of course, excessive clinging to their new parents. But eventually these symptoms vanished, the vast majority made good progress in school, and there was not one case of serious learning disability among them. When Constance Rathbun, Letitia Di Virgilio, and Samuel Waldfogel assessed the children, they wrote: "The degree of recovery observed in most cases could not have been predicted from the writings of those researchers who have studied the effects of separation most carefully. The present results indicate that for the child suffering extreme loss, the chances for recovery are far better than had previously been expected."

A study of 141 Korean orphans by Myron Winick, Knarig Meyer, and Ruth Harris produced similar results. These girls were adopted when they were between two and three years old by middle-class American families. After six years in their foster homes all were in elementary school, and their scores on IQ and school-achievement tests were comparable to scores made by the average American child.

Several years ago I interviewed a 14½-year-old girl who spent most of the first 30 months of her life in a crib in a small bedroom with no toys and a sister one year older than herself. She was removed to a foster home at 2½ years of age, severely retarded in both weight and height, without language, and, of course, completely untestable. She had remained with the same foster family for 12 years. Her full-scale IQ was 88, and she performed normatively on a wide battery of standard and nonstandard cognitive tests. Koluchova (1972) has reported a similar history for twin Czechoslovakian boys who were isolated from 18 months until 7 years of age, when they were sent to a foster home. Their full-scale Wechsler IQs at age 11 were 95 and 93, and the clinician noted that they appeared psychologically normal for their age.

Recently, linguists at the University of California and psychologists at the Los Angeles Children's Hospital have been following the development of a girl named Genie who was taken from her home when she was 13½ years old. Genie had been immobilized and isolated from contact with others for most of her life. When she was discovered she was malnourished, unable to stand erect, and without language—a victim of unprecedented deprivation.

After only six years in a normal family environment, Genie has developed some language, learned social skills, can take a bus to school, and has begun to express some of the basic human emotions. Surprisingly, on some of the performance scales of the Wechsler Intelligence Scale for Children she obtained scores that approached average ability. Although Genie is still like a child in many ways and markedly different from an average California 20-year-old, she has grown remarkably in a relatively short time. These results suggest that the mind may have some of the qualities of an elastic surface, easily deformed by shearing forces, but able to rebound when those forces are removed.

These clinical data are affirmed by two recent follow-up studies of institutionalized infants. Dennis (1973) assessed 16 children who had been adopted from institutions in Lebanon by middle-class families when the children were between 12 and 24 months of age and had an average developmental quotient of 50 on the Cattell scale. The average Stanford-Binet IQ obtained when these children were between 4 and 12 years of age was 101, and 13 of the 16 children had IQ scores of 90 or above. Tizard and Rees (1974) assessed 65 4½-year-olds who had spent their first two to four years in an institution in which an exclusive relation between an infant and one caretaker was actively discouraged. Of the original group of 65, 15 were now living with their natural mothers, 24 had been adopted, and 26 were still living in the institution. There was no difference in Wechsler IQ scores among the three groups at 4½ years of age (means ranged from 100 to 115). Although the institutionalized children had been retarded in language development when they were 2 years old, they were not retarded with respect to British norms at 4½ years (Tizard and Rees 1974; see also Dennis 1938; Rheingold and Bayley 1959).

The results of long-term longitudinal studies of children raised under more normal conditions also fail to support the view that the infant previews the future. With Howard Moss, I assessed a large number of working- and middle-class adults who had grown up in intact homes in southwestern Ohio. The results of this project, summarized in *Birth to Maturity*, related evaluations of the children at various periods during their first 14 years to their psychological status as adults. With few exceptions, we could find little relation between psychological qualities during the first three years of life—fearfulness, irritability, or activity—and any aspect of behavior in adulthood.

Not until a child was six to ten years old was there any firm evidence that his or her behavior foretold the kind of adult the child would become. At that time, predictions began to approach correlations of 0.5, a figure that indicates a moderate but not stunning degree of continuity.

In a subsequent investigation we followed 140 Caucasian firstborn infants, assessing them at 4, 8, 13, and 27 months. We evaluated the attentiveness of the babies, their vocalizations, smiling, irritability to a variety of sights and sounds, and the tempo of their play. Variation on any of these qualities observed at 4 or 8 months bore little relation to the child's display of similar qualities at 27 months.

We recently retested 65 of these children when they were ten years old. There was no relation between behavioral differences in the first year of life and differences in either reading ability or IQ. There was a suggestive relation, but only among girls, between a four-month-old's tendency to smile at masks of human faces and a reflective disposition at ten years.

Most recently, Richard Kearsley, Philip R. Zelazo, and I studied children who were either attending a day-care center or being reared only at home. We evaluated them on eight occasions, first when they were 3½ months old and the last time at 29 months. We found even less stability over the first 2½ years of life than in the earlier project.

A baby's reactions—attentiveness, vocalizations, smiling, or fretfulness—to interesting events during the first year predicted no significant behavior at 2½. Although there was great variation among the infants, who came from both working- and middle-class homes, their behavior from seven months to 2½ years showed little continuity. For example, a baby who showed anxiety with an unfamiliar child at 13 months might or might not be fearful a year and a half later.

Nor was there any long-term stability in a baby's tendency to protest when his mother left the room. We found no evidence that a child carried a generalized disposition one might call fearfulness across the first 2½ years of life—a finding that is in accord with the results of other investigators.

In an extensive study of the stability of temperament, known as the New York Study and carried out by the N.Y.U. School of Medicine, researchers used interviews and observations to evaluate such qualities as passivity, adaptability, responsiveness, intensity of reaction, and mood. Data were gathered continually during the infancy of 136 children and again during their preschool and early school years. Although preliminary data suggested some threads of continuity, more recent reports reveal no relation between ratings of temperament during the first year of life and a variety of behavior at age five. According to Michael Rutter and his colleagues at the University of London, who conducted the follow-up study, "Behavioral ratings in the first six months of life are of no predictive value in relation to the child's temperamental characteristics as shown during the school years."

A final and more controversial source of support for resilience in growth comes from our investigation of children growing up in small, isolated, subsistence-farming villages in western Guatemala. In one of these villages, San Marcos La Laguna, infants typically spend their first year confined to a small, dark hut. They are not played with, rarely spoken to, poorly nourished, and they suffer from respiratory and gastrointestinal distress for much of the year. Thus their experience is limited, their opportunity to practice maturing skills restricted, and their health poor.

When compared to American babies of the same age, the Guatemalan infants are retarded. Some of the major developmental milestones, such as the ability to recall past events, the belief that objects continue to exist when they are out of sight (object permanence), symbolic play, and language appear from two to twelve months later than they do in American infants.

For example, a baby is given a toy and allowed to play with it for 20 to 30 seconds. The toy is taken away, and a few seconds later the baby is shown two toys—the one he has just handled and a new one. By six to seven months, the typical American infant will shift his gaze back and forth between the toys several times before he chooses one of them. This action suggests he is comparing the two objects and indicates he remembers the earlier toy. A typical San Marcos infant does not behave in this way until he is 10 or 11 months old.

In a test of object permanence, the examiner, an Indian woman, hides an attractive toy under a cloth. If the baby searches for the toy, we infer he remembered its being hidden and could coordinate that knowledge with action. If he does not search, we assume he "forgot" the event; some psychologists would conclude the toy no longer exists for him. American infants usually solve this problem by the age of eight months; the San Marcos child does not retrieve the toy until he is 11 months old.

Pretend play with objects usually appears in American children around 12 months, but such imaginative play is delayed several months among San Marcos children. Finally, American children begin to speak their first words about the middle of their second year; San Marcos children do not begin to speak until the middle or end of their third year.

By the second year, life changes for San Marcos children. They are allowed to wander outside the hut and encounter the rich variety of the world. By the time they are four or five, they play with other children, and by eight or nine the boys and girls have adult responsibilities, which include working in the fields, caring for infants, cooking, and cleaning.

Our research team has made two separate assessments of the intellectual abilities of San Marcos children. In the first, we found that before age ten, the performance of San Marcos children on special tests of perceptual analysis, memory, and reasoning is clearly inferior to that of children in the United States. What is more, their performance is also inferior to that of children living in a nearby village who are not so severely restricted during their first year. However, by adolescence, San Marcos children perform nearly as well as American children on these tests.

Recently we returned to San Marcos and administered more difficult memory tests. For example, in one procedure we presented a series of 12 pictures that illustrate familiar objects. The child tries to recall the 12 pictures in the order in which they are presented. All of our middle-class Cambridge children were able to remember the order of all 12 pictures by the time they were 11 years old. Only 10 percent of the San Marcos 11-year-old children performed as well. But by late adolescence 58 percent could recall the order of all the pictures. Thus San Marcos adolescents can handle some difficult intellectual tasks at a level that approaches that of children who have grown up in more varied and challenging settings.

The retardation of the San Marcos infant does not preclude the continuous enhancement of his mental talents. Although the ten-year-old San Marcos child is not as proficient as the typical American ten-year-old, this difference is as likely to result from continued cultural isolation and poor schooling as from the lack of varied experience and good nutrition during the first year. As in the case histories discussed earlier, change and growth seem to be characteristic of psychological functions.

One reason for the weak support for continuity from infancy to later childhood is that the behaviors displayed during the first year or two are particularly suited to the problems of that developmental era and not to those of later childhood. It would be maladaptive for a child to retain for too long a time the hierarchical organization of cognitive and behavioral structures that are characteristic of the first year. And nature will not permit him that luxury, for maturational forces replace old behaviors with new abilities that permit, indeed demand, a different interaction with the world.

Each phase of development is marked by changing clusters of dominant reactions toward objects and people. As cognitive and motor systems mature, early behaviors are replaced by more mature ones. Mouthing of other monkeys is an act frequently displayed by macaque rhesus during the early weeks of life. By four months, rough-and-tumble play has replaced this initial class of simpler behaviors. This sequence is analogous to the human progression from the display of crying in distress, seen at 6 months, to requests for help at 18 months, as speech replaces fretting in a frustrating context. We do not know why the new behavior appears. Some assume, I think gratuitously, that greater variety, efficiency, and pleasantness accompany display of the new form. But it is not clear that a motivational interpretation is helpful. Although the butterfly inevitably follows the caterpillar, each form seems equally efficient, happy, or distressed. It is not obvious that adding a statement about pleasure to explain the emergent response enhances understanding, especially since the macaque displays a decrease in rough-and-tumble play—an act that appears to be such great fun—after his first birthday and begins to spend more time sitting and grooming—acts which appear, at least to a human observer, to contain less variety, vigor, and excitement. Observations of early behavioral development in both monkey and man suggest that, during the early years, the frequent changes in response classes are based, in part, on changing cognitive and motor competences.

A useful metaphor for early development is waves of emerging, plateauing, and declining behavioral systems which dominate the scene for a time until they are displaced by a new set. This view suggests that there will be, at any one age, two important sources of individual differences in behavior. One source is individual variation in rates of development; the other, experience combined with temperamental factors that make one class of action prepotent over another. In general, the older the child, the longer the period between the emergence of new sets of cognitive competences; hence, the more likely it is that individual differences will be experiential in origin. But during the first few years of life, when there are frequent maturational changes in basic competences, individual differences are just as likely to be the result of differences in rates of development as they are to be a product of experience. Perhaps that is why there is so little predictive validity for most behaviors from infancy to later childhood.

The total corpus of information implies that the young mammal retains an enormous capacity for change and, therefore, for resilience in the growth of psychological competences *if environments change;* if an initial environment that does not support psychological development becomes more beneficial. The existing data—clinical, longitudinal, institutional, cross-cultural, and animal—do not support the belief that certain events during the first year can produce irreversible consequences in either human or infrahuman infants. For most of this century many parents and some developmental psychologists have favored the irreversibility pole of the irreversibility-reversibility theme. The extreme form of that position is as likely to be incorrect as its opposite, which assumes complete capacity for alteration of any disposition at any age.

Available knowledge is certainly not firm enough to assert that there is no relation between structures established during infancy and the victories of the next three, five, or ten years. Further, the data do not imply that caretakers need not be concerned with the experiences of their infants. Infants recover from colds, but we still try to protect them from this distress. Rather, these data invite a slightly more critical attitude toward the strong version of the tape-recorder view of development. We should entertain the possibility that there is less inevitability between infancy and later childhood than has been traditionally assumed.

Young sciences suffer the combined disadvantages of ambiguous propositions and weak methodology—a condition that makes it likely that original suppositions, usually loose metaphors taken from the philosophy of the larger culture, will be difficult to disconfirm. As a result these suppositions live longer than they should. It is useful to remain critically skeptical of the unexamined premises of an emergent discipline. We should expect that many of psychology's early advances will be disconfirmations of old prejudices, and it is wise, therefore, to heed Parmenides' prophecy:

> But you also shall learn how it was that elusive opinion
> Forcing its way through all things was destined to pass for the real.

TWO

ON tHE NEEd foR RElATiVISM

HE PSYCHOLOGY of the first half of this century was absolutistic, outer directed, and intolerant of ambiguity. When a college student carries this unholy trio of traits he is called authoritarian, and such has been the temperament of the behavioral sciences. But the era of authoritarian psychology may be nearing its dotage, and the decades ahead may nurture a discipline that is relativistic, oriented to internal processes, and accepting of the idea that behavior is necessarily ambiguous.

Like her elder sisters, psychology began her dialogue with nature using a vocabulary of absolutes. Stimulus, response, rejection, affection, emotion, reward, and punishment were labels for classes of phenomena that were believed to have a fixed reality. We believed we could write a definition of these constructs that would fix them permanently and allow us to know them unequivocally at any time in any place.

Less than 75 years ago biology began to drift from the constraints of an absolute view of events and processes when she acknowledged that the fate of a small slice of ectodermal tissue depended on whether it was placed near the area of the eye or the toe. Acceptance of the simple notion that whether an object moves or not depends on where you are standing is a little more than a half-century old in a science that has five centuries of formalization. With physics as the referent in time, one might expect a relativistic attitude to influence psychology by the latter part of the twenty-third century. But

Adapted from *American Psychologist* 22 (1967): 131–42. Copyright 1967 by the American Psychological Association. Reprinted by permission.

Preparation of this paper was supported in part by research Grant MH-8792 from the National Institute of Mental Health, United States Public Health Service. This paper is an abridged version of a lecture presented at the Educational Testing Service, Princeton, New Jersey, January 1966.

philosophical upheavals in one science catalyze change in other disciplines, and one can see signs of budding relativism in the intellectual foundations of the social sciences.

The basic theme of this paper turns on the need for more relativistic definitions of selected theoretical constructs. "Relativistic" refers to a definition in which context and the state of the individual are part of the defining statement. Relativism does not preclude the development of operational definitions but makes that task more difficult. Nineteenth-century physics viewed mass as an absolute value; twentieth-century physics made the definition of mass relative to the speed of light. Similarly, some of psychology's popular constructs have to be defined in relation to the state and belief structure of the organism, rather than in terms of an invariant set of external events. Closely related to this need is the suggestion that some of the energy devoted to a search for absolute, stimulus characteristics of reinforcement be redirected to a search for the determinants of attention in the individual.

It is neither possible nor wise to assign responsibility to one person or event for major changes in conceptual posture, but work of the last 15 years contains three messages.

1. If a stimulus is to be regarded as an event to which a person responds or is likely to respond, then it is impossible to describe a stimulus without describing simultaneously the expectancy and preparation of the organism for that stimulus. Effective stimuli must be distinct from the person's original adaptation level. Contrast and distinctiveness, which are relative, are part and parcel of the definition of a stimulus. If infants are allowed to look at a red sphere until they become bored, they will show a dramatic increase in attentiveness if they are shown a red cylinder but not so large an increase in attentiveness if shown an ellipse, for the ellipse is too similar to the sphere they had looked at for so long. But if infants are first shown a cylinder until they tire of it, then they will show a great deal of interest in the ellipse, for its contrast with the cylinder is far greater than the contrast between the sphere and ellipse. There are many examples of this basic principle. Infants, children, and adults react to change, contrast, and the unexpected.

2. The failure of one individual to respond to an event that is an effective stimulus for a second individual is not always the result of central selection after all the information is in, but can be due to various forms of peripheral inhibition. Some stimuli within inches of the face do not ever reach the interpretive cortex and, therefore, do not exist psychologically.

3. Human beings react less to the objective quality of external stimuli than to categorizations of those stimuli.

These new generalizations strip the phrase "physical stimulus" of much of its power and certainty and transfer the scepter of control—in humans at least—to cognitive interpretations. The interpretation of contrast and the unexpected becomes an important key to understanding the incentives for human behavior. Since contrast depends so intimately on context and expectancy, it must be defined relativistically.

The issue of relativism can be discussed in many contexts. Many existing constructs are already defined in terms of contextual relations. The concept of authority only has meaning if there are fiefs to rule. The role of father has no meaning without a child. The concept of noun, verb, or adjective is defined by context—by the relation of the word to other constituents. We shall consider in some detail the ways in which a relativistic orientation touches two other issues in psychology: the learning of self-descriptive statements (the hoary idea of the self-concept), and, even more fundamentally, some of the mechanisms that define the learning process.

The Concept of the Self

The development and establishment of a self-concept is often framed in absolute terms. The classic form of the statement assumes that direct social reinforcements and identification models have fixed, invariant effects on the child. Praise and love from valued caretakers are assumed to lead the child to develop positive self-evaluations; whereas criticism and rejection presumably cause self-derogatory beliefs. The presumed cause-effect sequences imply that there is a something—a definable set of behaviors—that can be labeled social rejection, and that the essence of these rejecting acts leads to invariant changes in the self-concept of the child. Let us examine the concept of rejection under higher magnification.

The concept of rejection—peer or parental—has been biased toward an absolute definition. Witness the enormous degree of commonality in conceptualization of this concept by investigators who have studied a mother's behavior with her child (Baldwin, Kalhorn, and Breese 1945; Becker 1964; Kagan and Moss 1962; Schaefer 1959; Schaefer and Bayley 1963; Sears, Maccoby, and Levin 1957). These investigators typically decide that harsh physical punishment and absence of social contact or physical affection are the essential indexes of an attitude called maternal rejection. It would be close to impossible for an American rater to categorize a mother as high on both harsh beating of her child and on a loving attitude. A conventionally trained psychologist observing a mother who did not talk to her child for five hours would probably view the mother as rejecting. This may be a high form of provincialism. Alfred Baldwin (personal communication) reports that in the rural areas of northern Norway, where homes are five to ten miles apart and the population constant for generations, one often sees maternal behaviors which an American observer would regard as pathognomonically rejecting in an American mother. The Norwegian mother sees her four-year-old sitting in the doorway blocking the passage to the next room. She does not ask her to move but bends down, silently picks her up and moves her away before she passes into the next room. Our middle-class observer would be tempted to view this indifference as a sign of dislike. However, most mothers in this Arctic outpost behave this way, and the children do not behave the way rejected children should by our current theoretical propositions.

An uneducated Negro mother from North Carolina typically slaps her four-year-old across the face when he does not come to the table on time. The intensity of the mother's act tempts our observer to conclude that the mother hates or at best does not like her child. However, during a half-hour conversation the mother says she loves her child and wants to guarantee that he does not grow up to be a bad boy or a delinquent. And she believes firmly that physical punishment is the most effective way to socialize him. Now her behavior seems to be issued in the service of affection rather than hostility. Determination of whether a parent is rejecting or not cannot be answered by focusing primarily on the behaviors of the parents. Rejection is not a fixed, invariant quality of behavior *qua* behavior. Like pleasure, pain, or beauty, rejection is in the mind of the rejectee. It is a belief held by the child; not an action by a parent.

We must acknowledge, first, a discontinuity in the meaning of an acceptance-rejection dimension before drawing further implications. We must distinguish between children prior to 30 or 36 months of age, before they symbolically evaluate the actions of others, and the child thereafter.

We require, first a concept to deal with the child's belief in his or her value in the eyes of others. The child of four or five years is conceptually mature enough to have recognized that certain resources parents possess are difficult for the child to obtain. They view these resources as sacrifices and interpret their receipt as signs that the parents value them. The child constructs a tote board of the differential value of parental gifts—be they psychological or material. The value of the gift depends on its scarcity. A ten-dollar toy from a busy executive father is not a valued resource; the same toy from a father out of work is much valued. The value depends on the child's personal weightings. This position would lead to solipsism were it not for the fact that most parents are essentially narcissistic and do not readily give the child long periods of uninterrupted companionship. Thus, most children place high premium on this act. Similarly, parents are generally reluctant to proffer unusually expensive gifts to children, and this act acquires value for most youngsters. Finally, children learn from the public media that physical affection means positive evaluation, and they are persuaded to assign premium worth to this set of acts. There is, therefore, some uniformity across children in a culture in the evaluation of parental acts. But the anchor point lies within the child, not with the particular parental behaviors.

This definition of acceptance or rejection is not appropriate during the opening year. The one-year-old does not place differential symbolic worth on varied parental acts, and their psychological significance derives from the overt responses they elict and strengthen. A heavy dose of vocalization and smiling to an infant is traditionally regarded as indicative of maternal affection and acceptance. This bias exists because we have accepted the myth that "affection" is the essential nutrient that produces socially adjusted children, adolescents, and adults. The bias maintains itself because we observe a positive association between degree of parental smiling and laughing to the infant and prosocial behavior in the child during the early years. The responses of smiling, laughing, and approaching people are learned in the opening months of life on the basis of standard conditioning principles. This conclusion is supported by the work of Rheingold and Gewirtz (1959) and Brackbill (1958). However, phenotypically similar behaviors in a 10- or 20-year-old may have a different set of antecedents. The argument that different definitions of rejection-acceptance must be written for the pre- and postsymbolic child gains persuasive power from the fact that there are no data indicating that degree of prosocial behavior in the child is stable from 6 months to 16 years. Indeed, the longitudinal material from the Fels Research Institute study of behavior stability (Kagan and Moss 1962) showed no evidence of any relation between joy or anxiety in the presence of adults during the first two to three years of life and phenotypically similar behaviors at 6, 12, or 24 years of age. The child behaviors that are presumed, by theory, to be the consequences of low or high parental rejection do not show stability from infancy through adolescence. This may be because the childhood responses, though phenotypically similar to the adult acts, may be acquired and maintained through different experiences at different periods.

It seems reasonable to suggest, therefore, that different theoretical words are necessary for the following three classes of phenomena: (a) an attitude on the part of the parent, (b) the quality and frequency of acts of parental care and social stimulation directed toward the infant, and (c) a child's assessment of his value in the eyes of another. All three classes are currently viewed as of the same cloth. The latter meaning of "rejection" (i.e., a belief held by a child) is obviously relativistic, for it grows out of different experiences in different children.

Self-Descriptive Labels

Let us probe further into the ideas surrounding the learning of self-evaluation statements, beyond the belief, "I am not valued." The notion of a self-concept has a long and spotted history, and although it has masqueraded by many names in different theoretical costumes, its intrinsic meaning has changed only a little. A child presumably learns self-descriptive statements whose contents touch the salient attributes of the culture. The mechanisms classically invoked to explain how these attributes are learned have stressed the invariant effects of direct social reinforcement and identification. The girl who is told she is attractive, annoying, or inventive comes to believe these appellations and to apply these qualifiers to herself. We have assumed that the laws governing the learning of self-descriptive labels resemble the learning of other verbal habits, with frequency and contiguity of events being the shapers of the habit. Identification as a source of self-labels involves a different mechanism, but retains an absolutistic frame of reference. The child assumes that she shares attributes with particular models. If the model is viewed as subject to violent rages, the child concludes that she, too, shares this tendency.

Theory and data persuade us to retain some faith in these propositions. But relativistic factors also seem to sculpt the acquisition of self-descriptive labels, for the child evaluates himself on many psychological dimensions by inferring his rank order from a delineated reference group. The ten-year-old does not have absolute measuring rods to help him decide how bright, handsome, or likable he is. He naturally and spontaneously uses his immediate peer group as the reference for these evaluations. An immediate corollary of this statement is that the child's evaluation is dependent upon the size and psychological quality of the reference group and cannot be defined absolutely. Specifically, the larger the peer group, the less likely a child will conclude she is high in the rank order, the less likely she will decide she is unusually smart, pretty, or capable of leadership. Consider two boys with IQs of 130 and similar intellectual profiles. One lives in a small town, the other in a large city. It is likely that the former child will be the most competent in his peer group while the latter is likely to regard himself as fifth or sixth best. This difference in perceived rank order has obvious action consequences since we acknowledge that expectancies govern behavior. In sum, aspects of the self-descriptive process appear to develop in relativistic soil.

Learning and Attention

A second issue that touches relativistic definitions deals with a shift from external definitions of reinforcement—that is, reward or pleasure—to definitions that are based more directly on internal processes involving the concept of attention. Failure to understand the nature of learning is one of the major intellectual frustrations for many psychologists. The query, "What is learning?" has the same profound ring that the question, "What is a gene?" had a decade ago. Our biological colleagues have recently had a major insight while psychology is still searching. The murky question, "What is learning?" usually reduces to an attempt to discover the laws relating stimuli, pain, and pleasure, on the one hand, with habit acquisition and performance, on the other. Pain, pleasure, and reinforcement are usually defined in terms of events that are external to the organism and have an invariant flavor. Miller (1951) suggested that reinforcement was isomorphic with stimulus reduction; Leuba (1955) argued for an optimal level of stimulation; but both implied that there was a level that could be specified and measured. We should like to argue first that sources of pleasure and, therefore of reinforcement, are often relative, and second, that the essence of learning is more dependent on attentional involvement by the learner than on specific qualities of particular external events.

The joint ideas that humans are pleasure seekers and that one can designate specific forms of stimulation as sources of pleasure are central postulates in every person's theory of behavior. Yet we find confusion when we seek a definition of pleasure. The fact that humans begin life with a small core-set of capacities for experience that they wish to repeat cannot be disputed. This is a pragmatic view of pleasure, and we can add a dash of phenomenology to bolster the intuitive validity of this point of view. A sweet taste and a light touch in selected places are usually pleasant. Recently, we have added an important new source of pleasure. It is better to say we have rediscovered a source of pleasure, for Herbert Spencer suggested that *change in stimulation* is a source of pleasure for rats, cats, monkeys, or men. But, change is short-lived, quickly digested, and transformed to monotony. Popping up in front of an infant and saying peek-a-boo is pleasant for a 3-month-old infant for about 15 minutes, for a 10-month-old infant for 3 minutes and for a 30-month-old child for a few seconds. This pleasant experience, like most events that elicit their repetition a few times before dying, is usually conceptualized as a change in stimulation. The source of the pleasure is sought in the environment. Why should change in external stimulation be pleasant? The understanding of pleasure and reinforcement in man is difficult enough without having to worry about infrahuman considerations. Let us restrict the argument to the human. The human is a cognitive creature who is attempting to create schema for incoming stimulation. Children and adults try to generate a representation of what is happening and a rule to predict what might happen in the future. When one recognizes an event that happened in the past, after a little effort, or one is able to predict the future, a special state is created. In the young child this state is often, but not always, accompanied by a smile. A twenty-month-old, on five separate monthly visits, has watched a woman sit down, pick up three animals, make them walk on the carpet, and say, "These animals are going for a walk." The child smiles for the first time in five months because on this day, finally, the child recognized what was happening and was able to predict what was about to occur.

The peek-a-boo game works for 15 minutes with a 12-week-old, for it takes him that long to be able to predict the event—the "peek-a-boo." Charlesworth (1965) has demonstrated the reinforcing value of "uncertainty" in an experiment in which the peek-a-boo face appeared either in the same locus every trial, alternated between two loci, or appeared randomly in one of two loci. The children persisted in searching for the face for a much longer time under the random condition than under the other two conditions. The random presentation was reinforcing for a longer period of time, not because it possessed a more optimum level of external stimulation than the other reinforcement schedules, but because it took longer for the child to create a schema for the random presentation, and the process of creating a schema is a source of pleasure.

Display of a smile or laugh is one common index of pleasure. Indeed, Tomkins' (1962) scheme for affect demands that pleasure be experienced if these responses appear. Consider two studies that bear on the relation between pleasure and the creation of schema. We studied the same infants at 4, 8, and 13 months of age and showed them a variety of visual patterns representative of human faces and human forms. In one episode, the four-month-old infants are shown achromatic slides of a photograph of a regular male face, a schematic outline of a male face, and two disarranged, disordered faces. The frequency of occurrence of smiling to the photograph of the regular face is more than *twice* the frequency observed to the regular schematic face—although looking time is identical—and more than *four times* the frequency shown to the disordered faces. In another, more realistic episode, the four-month-old infants see a regular, flesh-colored sculptured face in three dimensions and a distorted version of that face in which the eyes, nose, and mouth are rearranged. At four months of age the occurrence of smiling to the regular face is over three times the frequency displayed to the distorted version, but looking time is identical. There are two interpretations of this difference (Kagan, Henker, Hen-Tov, Levine, and Lewis 1966). One explanation argues that the mother's face has become a secondary reward; the regular face stands for pleasure because it has been associated with care and affection from the mother. As a result, it elicits more smiles. An alternative interpretation is that the smile response has become conditioned to the human face via reciprocal contact between mother and infant. A third interpretation, not necessarily exclusive of these, is that the smile can be elicited when the infant matches stimulus to schema—when he has an "aha" reaction; when he makes a cognitive discovery. The four-month-old infant is cognitively close to establishing a relatively firm schema of a human face. When a regular representation of a face is presented, there is a short period during which the stimulus is assimilated to the schema, and then, after several seconds, a smile may occur. The smile is released following the perceptual recognition of the face, and reflects the assimilation of the stimulus to the infant's schema—a small but significant act of creation. This hypothesis is supported by the fact that the typical latency between the onset of looking at the regular face (in the four-month-old) and the onset of smiling is about three to five seconds. The smile usually does not occur immediately but only after the infant has studied the stimulus. It is difficult to avoid the conclusion that the smile is released following an act of perceptual recognition of matching event to knowledge.

Additional data on these and other children at eight months of age support this idea. At eight months, frequency of smiling to both the regular and distorted faces is *reduced dramatically,* indicating that smiling does not convary with the reward value of the face. The face presumably has acquired more reward value by eight months than it had at four months. However, the face is now a much firmer schema, and recognition of it is immediate. There is no effortful act of recognition necessary for most infants. As a result, smiling is less likely to occur. Although smiling is much less frequent at eight than four months to all faces, the frequency of smiling to the distorted face now *equals* the frequency displayed to the regular face. We interpret this to mean that the distorted face is sufficiently similar to the child's schema of a regular face that it can be recognized as such.

At 13 months of age these infants are shown six three-dimensional representations of a male human form and a free form matched for area, coloration, and texture with the human form. The stimuli include a faithful representation of a regular man, that same man with his head placed between his legs, the same man with all limbs and head collaged in an unsual and scrambled pattern, the man's body with a mule's head, and the mule's head on the man's body, the man's body with three identical heads, and a free form.

More than 70 percent of the smiles occurred to the animal head on the human body and the three-headed man, forms that were moderate transformations of the regular man, and stimuli that required active assimilation. The free form and the scrambled man rarely elicited smiles from these infants. These stimuli are too difficult to assimilate to the schema of a human form possessed by a 13-month-old infant. It is interesting to note that the regular human form sometimes elicited the verbal response "daddy" or a hand waving from the child. These instrumental social reactions typically did not occur to the transformations. The occurrence of decreases in heart rate (indicative of a brisk orientation to an event) to these patterns agrees with this hypothesis. At 13 months of age, the man with his head between his legs, the man with the animal head, or the three-headed man each elicited the largest cardiac decelerations more frequently than the regular man, the scrambled man, or the free form ($p < .05$ for each comparison). Thus, large cardiac decelerations and smiles were most likely to occur to stimuli that seemed to require tiny, quiet cognitive discoveries—miniaturized versions of Archimedes' "Eureka."

It appears that the act of matching stimulus to schema when the match is close but not yet perfect is a dynamic event. Stimuli that deviate a critical amount from the child's schema for a pattern are capable of eliciting an active process of recognition, and this process seems to be a source of pleasure. Events that are easily assimilable or too difficult to assimilate do not elicit these reactions. This dynamic also operates to influence the child's reaction to what he witnesses. After one year the child has a representation of his ability to perform a particular action he may have witnessed in the past. If the act is beyond the child's competence, from his perspective, he or she will become anxious and perhaps cry. If the act is too easy to implement, the child will not reproduce it. If, however, the child is moderately uncertain, he or she is most likely to display the action. Consider the following persuasive demonstration of this suggestion.

A 22-month-old infant plays happily with some toys for ten minutes. A familiar woman then leaves the couch on which she was sitting and invites the child to watch her play. If she executes a simple act, well within the competence of the child, like putting a baby bottle to a doll, it is unlikely that the child will imitate her. If, on the other hand, she initiates an act that is too complicated—she takes out two plates, puts a doll by each plate, and says the mother and father have to eat supper—the child will begin to fret, run to the mother in an obvious display of apprehension because the actions were too difficult to comprehend. The child felt an obligation to execute the act but recognized she was unable to do it. If, however, the act modeled by the woman is of moderate difficulty and the child has only a little uncertainty over its execution—for example, the model picks up a telephone and puts it to the head of a toy doll and says, "Hello," the child is most likely to duplicate that action and perhaps smile when the woman returns to the couch.

One-year-old children faced with a set of toys like balls, blocks, cloths, dolls, and bottles will spend some time banging and throwing and some time displaying pretend symbolic actions. But after 20 months the same child faced with the same toys may suddenly show an instance of spontaneous categorization. The child will put all the wooden balls on one part of the carpet and perhaps all the small animals in another location. These acts are neither imitative of any event witnessed nor instrumental in attaining any goal. We must assume that as the child becomes capable of detecting similar dimensions among events, he will, during the period when the competence is maturing, implement that knowledge in action, as if Plato's "To know the good is to do the good" were guiding the child's behavior. It does not seem fruitful to ask why the child grouped all the wooden balls. The proper question seems to be, "What conditions occasioned the behavior?" The conditions were the emergence of a new competence that was not yet mastered. The capacity for simple metaphor, which usually appears by the third year, leads a child to express her new talent in language. A girl notes that her dresses are closely packed in a closet and comments, "Look, all my dresses are friends." This sentence was not issued to acquire any praise or to reduce dissonance. The sentence was created and displayed just because it was possible to do so. After a few months, when that expression no longer has any aura of uncertainty, one may never hear it again. Observations of young children require acknowledgment of the fact that some important classes of behavior dominate the stage of performance for a while just because the child is somewhat capable of their display—a condition reminiscent of Sartre's recognition in his later years that he wrote simply because he was capable of writing.

A study by Edward Zigler adds important support to the notion that the smile indicates the pleasure of an assimilation. Children in grades 2, 3, 4, and 5 looked at cartoons that required little or no reading. The children were asked to explain the cartoon while an observer coded the spontaneous occurrence of laughing and smiling while the children were studying the cartoons. It should come as no surprise that verbal comprehension of the cartoons increased in a linear fashion with age. But laughing and smiling increased through grade 4 and then declined markedly among the fifth-grade children. The fifth graders understood the cartoons too well. There was no gap between stimulus and schema and no smiling. Sixteen-week-old infants and eight-year-old children smile spontaneously at events that seem to have one thing in common—the event is a partial match to an existing schema and an active process of recognitory assimilation must occur.

The fact that a moderate amount of mismatch between event and schema is one source of pleasure demands the conclusion that it is not always possible to say that a specific event will always be a source of pleasure. The organism's state and structure must be in the equation. This conclusion parallels the current interest in complexity and information uncertainty. The psychologist with an information-theory prejudice classifies a stimulus as uncertain and often assumes that he does not have to be too concerned with the attributes of the viewer. This error of the absolute resembles the nineteenth-century error in physics and biology. This is not a titillating or pedantic, philosophical issue. Psychology rests on a motive-reinforcement foundation which regards pleasure and pain as pivotal ideas in the grand theory. These constructs have tended to generate absolute definitions. We have been obsessed with finding a fixed and invariant characterization of pleasure, pain, and reinforcement. Melzack and Wall (1965) point out that although the empirical data do not support the notion of a fixed place in the brain that mediates pain, many scientists resist shedding this comfortable idea. Olds' (1958, 1962) famous discovery of brain-reinforcing areas generated excitement because many wanted to believe that pleasure had a fixed and absolute locus. The suspicious element in this discovery of pleasure spots is that there is no habituation of responses maintained by electrical stimulation to hypothalamic or septal nuclei, and minimal resistance to extinction of habits acquired via this event. Yet, every source of pleasure known to phenomenal man does satiate—for a while or forever—and habits that lead to pleasant events do persist for a while after the pleasure is gone. These observations are troubling, and additional inquiry is necessary if we are to decide whether these cells are indeed the bed where pleasure lies.

We are convinced that contiguity alone does not always lead to learning. Something must ordinarily be added to contiguity in order to produce a new bond. Psychology has chosen to call this extra added mysterious something "reinforcement," much as eighteenth-century chemists chose to label their unknown substance "phlogiston." If one examines the variety of external events that go by the name of reinforcement, it soon becomes clear that this word is infamously inexact. A shock to an animal's paw is a reinforcement, a verbal chastisement is a reinforcement, an examiner's smile is a reinforcement, a pellet of food is a reinforcement, and a sigh indicating tension reduction after watching a killer caught in a Hitchcock movie is a reinforcement. These events have little, if any, phenotypic similarity. What, then, do they have in common? For if they have nothing in common it is misleading to call them by the same name. Learning theorists have acknowledged their failure to supply an independent a priori definition of reinforcement, and the definition they use is purely pragmatic. A reinforcement is anything that helps learning. And so, we ask: What has to be added to contiguity in order to obtain learning? A good candidate for the missing ingredient is the phrase "attentional involvement." Let us consider again the events called reinforcements: a shock, food, a smile, each of these acts to attract the attention of the organism to some agent or object. They capture the organism's attention, and maybe that is why they facilitate learning. Consider the idea that what makes an event reinforcing is the fact that it (a) elicits the organism's attention to the feedback from the response he has just made and to the mosaic of stimuli in the learning situation and (b) acts as an incentive for a subsequent response. The latter quality is what ties the word "reinforcement" to the concepts of motivation and need, but much learning occurs without the obvious presence of motives or needs. Ask any satiated adult to attend carefully and remember the bond syzygy-aardvark. It is likely that learning will occur in one trial. It is not unreasonable to argue that a critical component of events that have historically been called reinforcement is their ability to attract the organism's attention. They have been distinctive cues in a context; they have been events discrepant from the individual's adaptation level. If attention is acknowledged as critical in new mental acquisitions, it is appropriate to ask if attention is also bedded in relativistic soil. The answer appears to be "Yes." Attention investment is not always distributed to many channels at once. One has to know the state of the organism. Knowledge of the organism's distribution of attention in a learning situation may clarify many controversial theoretical polemics that range from imprinting in chickens to emotion in college undergraduates. For example, comparative psychologists quarrel about which set of external conditions allow imprinting to occur with maximal effect. Some say the decoy should move; others argue that the young chick should move; still others urge that the decoy be brightly colored (e.g., Bateson 1964a, 1964b; Hess 1959; Klopfer 1965; Thompson and Dubanoski 1964). The quarrel centers around the use of phenotypically different observable conditions. Perhaps all these suggestions are valid. Moving the decoy, or active following by the infant chick, or a distinctively colored decoy all maximize the organism's level of attention to the decoy. The genotypic event may remain the same across all of these manipulations.

Distinctiveness of Events

The above examples suggest that the organism's distribution of attention is a critical process that should guide our search for the bases of many diverse phenomena. One of the critical bases for recruitment of attention pivots on the idea of distinctiveness of the signal. Jakobson and Halle (1956) argue that the chronology of acquisition of phonemes proceeds according to a principle of distinctive elements. Distinctive elements capture the child's attention and give direction to the order of learning.

The personality differences ascribed to children in different ordinal positions are the result, in part, of differences in relative distinctiveness of social agents. For the firstborn, the adult is the distinctive stimulus to whom to attend; for the second-born the older sibling has distinctive value and competes for the attention of the younger child. Only children lie alone for long periods of uninterrupted play. A parent who enters the room and speaks to the infant is necessarily a distinctive stimulus. For a fifth-born whose four older siblings continually poke, fuss, and vocalize into the crib, the caretaking adult, is, of necessity, less distinctive, and, as a result, less attention will be paid to the adult. The importance of distinctiveness with respect to adaptation level engages the heated controversy surrounding the role of stimulus enrichment with infants and young children from deprived milieux. The pouring on of visual, auditory, and tactile stimulation willy-nilly should be less effective than a single distinctive stimulus presented in a context of quiet so it will be discrepant from the infant's adaptation level. If one takes this hypothesis seriously, a palpable change in enrichment strategies is implied. The theme of this change involves a shifting from a concern with increasing absolute level of stimulation to focusing on distinctiveness of stimulation. Culturally disadvantaged children are not deprived of stimulation; they are deprived of distinctive stimulation.

The early learning of sex-role standards and the dramatic concern of school children with sex differences and their own sex-role identity becomes reasonable when one considers that the differences between the sexes are highly distinctive. Voice, size, posture, dress, and usual locus of behavior are distinctive attributes that focus the child's attention on them.

One of the reasons why the relation between tutor and learner is important is that some tutors elicit greater attention than others. They are more distinctive. Those of us who contend that learning will be facilitated if the child is identified with or wants to identify with a tutor believe that one of the bases for the facilitation is the greater attention that is directed at a model with whom the child wishes to identify. A recent experiment touches on this issue.

The hypothesis can be simply stated. An individual will attend more closely to an initial stranger with whom he feels he shares attributes than to a stranger with whom he feels he does not share attributes, other things equal. The former model is more distinctive, for a typical adult ordinarily feels he does not share basic personality traits with most of the strangers that he meets.

The subjects in this study were 56 Radcliffe freshmen and sophomores preselected for the following pair of traits. One group, the academics, were rated by four judges—all roommates—as being intensely involved in studies much more than they were in dating, clubs, or social activities. The second group, the social types, were rated as being much more involved in dating and social activities than they were in courses or grades. No subject was admitted into the study unless all four judges agreed that she fit one of these groups.

Each subject was seen individually by a Radcliffe senior and told that each was participating in a study of creativity. The subject was told that Radcliffe seniors had written poems and that two of the poets were selected by the Harvard faculty as being the best candidates. The faculty could not decide which girl was the more creative and the student was going to be asked to judge the creativity of each of two poems that the girls had written. The subjects were told that creativity is independent of IQ for bright people, and they were told that since the faculty knew the personality traits of the girls, the student would be given that information also. The experimenter then described one of the poets as an academic grind and the other as a social activist. Each subject listened to two different girls recite two different poems on a tape. Order of presentation and voice of the reader were counterbalanced in an appropriate design. After the two poems were read, the subject was asked for a verbatim recall of each poem, asked to judge its creativity, and finally, asked which girl she felt most similar to. Incidentally, more than 95 percent of the subjects said they felt more similar to the model that they indeed matched in reality. Results supported the original hypothesis. Recall was best when a girl listened to a communicator with whom she shared personality traits. The academic subjects recalled more of the poem when it was read by the academic model than by the social model; whereas, the social subjects recalled more of the poem when it was read by the social model than the academic model. This study indicates that an individual will pay more attention to a model who possesses similar personality attributes than to one who is not similar to the subject. Distinctiveness of tutor is enhanced by a perceived relation between learner and tutor.

Myths and superstitions are established around the kinds of experimental manipulations teachers or psychologists should perform in order to maximize the probability that learning will occur. When one focuses on the kind of manipulation—providing a model, giving a reinforcement, labeling the situation, punishing without delay—there is a strong push to establish superstitions about how behavioral change is produced. Recipes are written and adopted. If one believes, on the other hand, that a critical level of attention to incoming information is the essential variable, then one is free to mix up manipulations, to keep the recipe open, as long as one centers the subject's attention on the new material.

The most speculative prediction from this general argument is that behavioral therapy techniques will work for some symptoms—for about 20 years. A violation of an expectancy is a distinctive stimulus that attracts attention. The use of operant shaping techniques to alleviate phobias is a dramatic violation of an expectancy for both child and adult, and attention is magnetized and focused on the therapeutic agent and his paraphernalia. As a result, learning is facilitated. But each day's use of this strategy may bring its demise closer. In time, a large segment of the populace will have adapted to this event; it will be a surprise no more, and its attention-getting and therapeutic value will be attenuated. Much of the power of psychoanalytic techniques began to wane when the therapist's secrets became public knowledge. If therapy is accomplished by teaching new responses, and if the learning of new responses is most likely to occur when attention to the teacher is maximal, it is safe to expect that we may need a new strategy of teaching patients new tricks by about 1984.

Let us weave the threads closer in an attempt at final closure. The psychology of the first half of this century was the product of a defensively sudden rupture from philosophy to natural science. The young discipline needed roots, and like a child, attached itself to an absolute description of nature, much as a five-year-old clings to an absolute conception of morality. We now approach the latency years and can afford to relax and learn something from developments in our sister sciences. The message implicit in the recent work in psychology, biology, and physics contains a directive to abandon absolutism in selected theoretical areas. Conceptual ideas for mental processes must be invented, and this task demands a relativistic orientation. Learning is one of the central problems in psychology, and understanding of the mechanisms of learning requires elucidation and measurement of the concept of attention. Existing data indicate that attention is under the control of distinctive stimuli, and distinctiveness depends intimately on adaptation level of subject and context and cannot be designated in absolute terms.

These comments are not to be regarded as a plea to return to undisciplined philosophical introspection. Psychology does possess some beginning clues as to how it might begin to measure elusive, relative concepts like "attention." Autonomic variables such as cardiac and respiratory rate appear to be useful indexes, and careful studies of subtle motor-discharge patterns may provide initial operational bases for this construct.

Neurophysiologists have been conceptualizing their data in terms of attention distribution for years, and they are uncovering some unusually provocative phenomena. For example, amplitude of evoked potentials from the association areas of the cortex are regarded as a partial index of attention. Thompson and Shaw (1965) recorded evoked potentials from the association area of the cat's cortex—the middle suprasylvian gyrus—to a click, a light, or a shock to the forepaw. After they established base level response to each of these "standard" stimuli, the investigators presented these standard stimuli when the cat was active or when novel stimuli were introduced. The novel events were a rat in a bell jar, an air jet, or a growling sound. The results were unequivocal. Any one of these novel stimuli or activity by the cat produced reduced cortical evoked responses to the click, light, or shock. The authors suggest that the "amplitude of the evoked responses are inversely proportional to attention to a particular event [p. 338]." Psychology is beginning to develop promising strategies of measurement for the murky concept of attention and should begin to focus its theorizing and burgeoning measurement technology on variables having to do with the state of the organism, not just the quality of the external stimulus. The latter events can be currently objectified with greater elegance, but the former events seem to be of more significance. Mannheim once chastised the social sciences for seeming to be obsessed with studying what they could measure without error, rather than measuring what they thought to be important with the highest precision possible. It is threatening to abandon the security of the doctrine of absolutism of the stimulus event. Such a reorientation demands new measurement procedures, novel strategies of inquiry, and a greater tolerance for ambiguity. But let us direct our inquiry to where the pot of gold seems to shimmer and not fear to venture out from cozy laboratories where well-practiced habits have persuaded us to rationalize a faith in absolute monarchy.

THREE

THE GROWTH OF THE INFANT'S MIND

THE WORDS used to describe the young child are seriously influenced by the preoccupations of the adults who do the describing. The world of the baby is probably not a blooming, buzzing confusion; William James may have projected that state onto the infant because of the popular belief that infants were passive, helpless creatures with little power to deal with their environment. It would be reasonable for a harassed university professor to assume that if the day's events intruded so disruptively into his psychological space, they must be overwhelming for the more vulnerable infant. The ease with which James and other scholars attributed qualities to infants they may not possess reflects a more general tendency to ascribe to young children qualities that are either the opposite or the undeveloped beginnings of the characteristics prized by adults. For example, Americans value independent behavior and emphasize the dependence of the baby; they celebrate individuality and describe the infant as undifferentiated and unable to separate self from other.

In these instances the adjectives used to describe infants are the undesirable opposite of the qualities the Western adult is supposed to attain. Adults from other cultures see the infant through different lenses. The Japanese, who prize a close interdependence between persons, regard the infant as autonomous. The Japanese mother rushes to soothe the infant when he cries, responds quietly to the baby's babbling, and sleeps with her infant at night in order to encourage the mutual bonding that is so valued among adults.

Historical shifts in the traits theorists ascribe to infants can reveal secu-

Adapted from Emergent themes in human development, *American Scientist* 64 (1976): 186–96.

lar changes in the ego ideal. During the 1930s, when control of childhood aggression was regarded both as highly desirable and attainable, the British psychoanalyst Melanie Klein awarded the infant unrestrained aggressive impulses and sought to explain the nursing infant's clamping on the mother's nipple as an expression of that primitive instinct. Since the Second World War, childhood aggression has become both more acceptable and inevitable and, accordingly, Klein's description has become obsolete. When conformity to parents and to other benevolent authority was the ideal in the nineteenth century, American children were described as willful. The goal of socialization was to teach children the mature attitude of obedience to adults. As the roll of events during the last 20 years tainted moral imperatives given by authority, regardless of their status, some scholars have felt it necessary to promote a personalized conscience to a more prominent position. As a result, children who regularly conform to the commands of adults because of fear of punishment have been reclassified as immature.

The selection of words to describe the young child is so pervasively influenced by the preoccupations of adults that it is impossible for any writer to be completely free of this disturbing prejudice. But I shall try to describe the infant as impartially as possible in terms of his or her competences rather than strain to decide whether the baby has more or less of some adult quality.

The Infant

The newborn is ready to experience the basic sensations of the species from the moment he or she is born. The infant can see, hear, smell and is sensitive to pain, touch, and changes in bodily position. Additionally, the infant can display a variety of complex reflexes, some of which are necessary for survival. The infant will track a moving light if the speed is not too fast, will suck on a nipple inserted into the mouth, and turn in the direction in which the corner of his or her mouth is touched. Newborns can cry, cough, turn away, lift their chins from a prone position, grasp objects placed in their palms, and be startled by loud sounds or sudden bright lights.

Many years ago, a magazine printed a photograph of a room as the photographer imagined it might have appeared to an infant. The photo was blurred at the edges and in perfect focus only at the center. Scientific research suggests that the photographer distorted the infant's perceptual experience, for the young child has remarkable visual acuity. As early as two weeks of age infants can detect the difference between a gray patch and a square composed of stripes that are only one-eighth of an inch wide at a distance of nine inches from the face. Sensitivity is also excellent in the auditory mode; infants can detect the difference between C and C-sharp or between the syllables "Pa" and "Ba."

The major principle that governs the distribution of attention in very young infants is attention to change. One of the most convincing illustrations of this principle is seen in the fact that young infants will attend for long periods of time to stimulus events that move and those that have a great deal of black and white contour. Hence they will look longer at a hexagon with one-inch sides than a square with one-inch sides because the former has more contour. During the first four to five weeks of life infants are unlikely to scan the eyes, nose, and mouth of the mother's face, but rather look at the edge where the hairline meets the forehead. But after two months of age, they begin to scan the internal parts of the face, focusing especially on the eyes.

Infants attend longer to wavelengths corresponding to red and blue than to other hues. And the young infant's pattern of attention suggests categorical perception for wavelengths that correspond to blue, green, yellow, and red—a finding that confirms the earlier, elegant work of sensory physiologists.

It also appears the infant is more excited by circularity than by linearity. Ruff and Birch (1974) showed pairs of stimuli to infants 13 weeks old and quantified their attentional preferences (see Fig. 3.1). Concentric patterns were studied longer than nonconcentric ones, and when pattern was similar, forms constructed of arcs were looked at longer than identical patterns constructed of straight-line segments.

In our laboratory Hopkins (1974) permitted ten-month-old infants to view one of four simple three-dimensional segments each time they pressed a bar in front of them. When they became habituated to one of these simple stimuli (i.e., the rate of operant barpressing fell below an a priori criterion), children in nine experimental groups were shown a different stimulus while control children continued to see the same event. Infants who were familiarized on the straight-line segment and dishabituated on a curved one showed the greatest recovery of both bar-pressing and attention. Infants who experienced the opposite change, from a curve to a straight-line segment, showed some recovery but significantly less than that displayed by the former group.

This special effect of curvature on attention is present in the newborn but in less sturdy form (Fantz and Miranda 1975). By two months of age, however, following maturation of acuity and scanning patterns, the infant displays a more consistent attraction to circularity and attends longer to a bull's-eye than to a checkerboard (Fantz 1965). Since the spiral is one of nature's favorite and most versatile forms, it is not unreasonable to suppose that evolution would have prepared each of us to be sensitive to this pattern.

Figure 3 · 1   When 13-week-old infants were shown pairs of patterns composed of curves and straight-line segments, they were found to prefer forms constructed of arcs to forms constructed of straight lines and they studied concentric patterns longer than nonconcentric ones. The numbers below each pattern refer to the relative power of that stimulus to maintain the infant's attention; stimulus 1 elicited the most attention, stimulus 10 the least (from Ruff and Birch 1974).

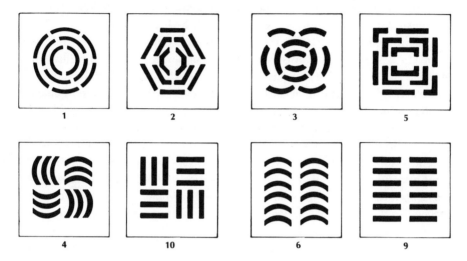

Contour, curvature, color and movement have a claim on the infant's attention, especially when these events represent a change in the immediate perceptual field. The earlier belief that the infant was insensitive to the world around him has been clearly refuted by psychological research.

The Reaction to Information

Infants scan the environment and extract a representation of what they see, hear, feel, touch, or smell. The representation is called a *schema* and is the child's first knowledge. The infant also possesses the capacity to detect a similarity between a new event and a previously acquired schema and to form a new schema or to alter an old one in a way that preserves the relation between the ongoing perception and prior knowledge. In simple terms, infants can recognize the relation between past knowledge and the present. This capacity may even exist in fragile form in the newborn. If newborns are shown a checkerboard pattern composed of 16 black and white squares until they become bored and then are shown a new pattern with, let us say, 9 squares, they show renewed interest, indicating they are able to recognize that the total amount of black and white contour had been altered. By ten weeks of age the ability to recognize an event as related to one experienced in the past is firm.

As the child acquires schemata, these new elements of knowledge gradually compete with the power of contour, movement, color, and curvature to hold a child's attention. The original attraction to physical characteristics of events, which led to the acquisition of the first schemata, becomes subdued by a new force that permits different schemata to develop. This principle is common in development. One mechanism dominates the functioning of the organism for a while until its task is accomplished; then it is replaced. This generalization is illustrated in the embryogenesis of the central nervous system. Early in embryonic development a set of nerve cells called trellis cells help to guide migrating neurons to their final destination. After the neurons have arrived at their proper locations in the cortex of the developing mammalian brain, the trellis cells disappear.

By two months infants are most likely to study events that are related to but a little different from those encountered in the past—called discrepant events—and attend far less to very familiar or very novel events. This important principle suggests that the infant's attention will be maximal to those experiences that have some relation to his or her knowledge. Children must recognize the potential relation between an event and what they know and perform some mental work to attain a more complete understanding. If the event is too quickly understood or there is minimal relation to their knowledge, the children will not invest much attention in the new experience and will not learn very much from it.

Maturation of New Competences at Eight Months

The Western conception of psychological events has been plagued by an inability to regard body and mind as components of one idea. We do not want to believe in two different life processes but cannot seem to find the right set of sentences that will pierce the semantic barrier separating the two constructs and permit each to nestle alongside the other. Although many historical forces have contributed to this epistemological tension, the most obvious was the need of Renaissance scholars to accommodate to both the new science of matter and the still powerful church. Despite half a millennium of debate, we continue to struggle with that conceptual issue, which has taken a specific form in developmental psychology.

Because the development of muscle, bone, and myelinization of the nervous system are guided by a maturational program, we acknowledge that the motor behaviors of reaching, sitting, standing, and walking must be under rather strict maturational control. But because mental phenomena are supposed to be of a different quality—not part of soma—we have supposed that they are under the stewardship of experience. As a result we have looked to Locke rather than Darwin to explain the development of perception, thought, and emotion in the young child. Hence many parents and developmental psychologists believe that the probability of a one-year-old's crying as he watches his mother leave him alone in a strange room is a function of his past nurturant experience with her—his attachment to his mother. But whether or not he walks to her as she enters his bedroom with a toy is regarded as a function of whether he is motorically mature enough to locomote.

THE ENHANCEMENT OF MEMORY AND COMPARISON

Soon after the eighth month infants begin to display some new capacities that seem to be part of a maturational timetable. One of these new competences is increased attention to discrepant events. If a mask of a human face is shown to infants 4 through 36 months old, infants younger than 7 and older than 10 months look longer than those between 7 and 10 months of age. This U-shaped function holds for nonsocial visual events and for attentiveness to human speech.

A second phenomenon that emerges in the middle of the first year is inhibition to the unexpected. Prior to 7 months the infant typically reaches at once for a novel object that is presented after repeated presentation of a familiarized standard, while an 11-month-old shows a short, but obvious, delay before reaching for the novel object.

There is also a dramatic increase in the likelihood of facial wariness, inhibition of play, and, occasionally, crying to events that are discrepant transformations of earlier experience. Infants 2 to 23 months of age were exposed to a series of unusual events—a stranger approaching the child, a visual cliff, a jack-in-the-box, a mechanical dog that moved, or facial masks. Infants younger than seven months rarely showed signs of wariness toward any of these events. The peak display of apprehension usually occurred between 11 and 18 months for most of the episodes and then declined. Similarly, inhibition, facial wariness, or overt crying to an unfamiliar adult is rare prior to seven months, increases dramatically between that time and the end of the first year, and then declines.

Finally, the growth function for separation distress, the tendency to cry and show inhibition of play following departure of a primary caretaker, is similar among children being raised at home or in day-care centers in the United States, barrios in urban Guatemala, subsistence farming villages in the Guatemalan highlands, Israeli kibbutzim, and Kung San bands in the Kalahari Desert. The distress to maternal departure emerges about 8 months, rises to a peak at 13 to 15 months, and then begins to decline.

Perhaps the most significant ability to mature at this time is the increased capacity to remember past events, even though there are no clues available in the infant's immediate environment. Four-month-olds can recognize that a face or picture is or is not similar to one they have seen before, but they are less able to retrieve a schema of an event spontaneously without some incentive present. Psychologists make a distinction between recognition memory and recall memory. It is the latter capacity that is enhanced after eight months of age. Consider two experiments that document this point. In the first, ten infants were seen monthly from 8 to 12 months of age. The infants had to retrieve a toy that they saw being hidden under one of two identical cloths in front of them. Sometimes there was a delay of one, three, or seven seconds before the child was permitted to reach for the toy, and there was either no screen, a transparent screen, or an opaque screen lowered during the delay interval. There was a steady improvement in the infant's capacity to remember the location of the toy across the four months of observation. No eight-month-olds were able to remember the toy's location when there was a one-second delay and an opaque screen was lowered during that interval. By one year, all infants were able to find the toy when the opaque screen was lowered for three seconds, and seven of the ten infants solved the problem when the opaque screen was lowered for as long as seven seconds.

In a similar investigation, eight- and twelve-month-olds sat in front of a board on which were mounted two faces. One of the faces would light up briefly, then go off, and the infants had to learn to touch the face that had been lit earlier. The delay between the offset of the lighted face and the child's touching the face varied from zero to nine seconds. Additionally, for some infants a clear screen separated the child from the faces during the delays. For others, the separating screen was opaque. One-year-olds, but not eight-month-olds, could remember which face had been lit even at the nine-second delay with the opaque screen. The eight-month-olds were unable to remember which face had been lit when the opaque screen was lowered or when the screen was transparent, but the delay lasted as long as nine seconds.

Similar investigations with infants from other cultures affirm the conclusion that the ability to retrieve schemata from past experience, despite delay and intereference, is amplified during the last third of the first year. Since the three-month-old, and perhaps the newborn, will show renewed interest to some events that are transformations of a familiar one, even after a 24-hour delay, very young infants can, under some conditions, retrieve a representation of a prior experience. But establishment of the schema is often slow and the retrieval competence vulnerable to long delays. I believe that the major differences between the functioning of the ten- and three-month-old are that the older infant can establish a schema more quickly, can retrieve a representation of past events with minimal stimulus incentives in the field, after a longer temporal delay, and can hold the representations of past and present in active memory for a longer period of time.

Before considering the psychological implications of this new competence, one additional assumption must be made explicit. When older children and adults read a sentence or listen to a conversation, they are able to integrate the incoming information with their knowledge over a period of time that can last as long as 20 seconds. Suppose adults read or hear the sentence, "The Senegalese woman whose father had fought against the French decided before the end of colonialism to live in Nigeria." Most would be able to understand and rephrase the sentence, despite its length, because adults are able to hold all the information in a temporary memory while retrieving their knowledge of Senegal, its relation to France, and the location of Nigeria. Psychologists call the hypothetical process that permits this integration to occur "active memory." Others might call it consciousness. Active memory becomes a more sturdy phenomenon after eight months of age.

It is difficult to find the proper language to describe these processes in preverbal infants. Although metaphors can be misleading, if regarded as heuristics, they can help to communicate the theorist's working assumptions. Suppose we liken active memory to a temporary stage on which information is placed for recognition, organization, and comparison. The stage collapses and the information is lost if it is not rehearsed or an interfering or distracting event occurs. We suggest that with age there is a steady increase in the duration of time the stage can remain intact, despite interfering events, and the ease with which information in long-term memory can be retrieved and transferred to this stage for comparison with the present. The cognitive functioning of senile adults provides an analogy. Some adults after 75 years of age experience extraordinary difficulty in retrieving information they have recently seen or heard; they cannot hold the information on the stage of active memory for mental work. These phenomena are believed to be the consequence of irreversible changes in the central nervous system and not epiphenomenal to lowered motivation or interest. We suggest that the human infant, prior to seven months of age, has a similar difficulty, which is a result of the fact that certain changes in the central nervous system that appear by the end of the first year have not yet matured. As a result, the younger infant easily forgets new events if the delay between their presentation and the occasion of their recall (not their recognition) is more than a few seconds or an interfering event occurs between the original experience and the retrieval.

These ideas might explain the increased attentiveness to transformations of familiarized events seen after seven months of age. Four-month-olds are highly attentive to discrepant events because they maintain attention until they assimilate the event to a relevant schema or fail to do so. With growth, the reservoir of schemata is amplified, and the infant's ability to assimilate the event to a schema becomes more efficient; therefore, the seven-month-old looks less than the four-month-old. But that principle predicts that 12-month-olds should study the same event even less than 7-month-olds. However, they do quite the opposite; they are more attentive. We can account for the increased attention after seven months if we assume that older infants are able to retrieve a representation of the repeated experience, hold it in memory, and, additionally, relate it to the discrepant event in their perceptual field. If the event is a mask of a human face, they retrieve their representations of faces and try to generate the relation between their knowledge of normal faces and the mask in front of them. As long as a trace of the past event remains articulated and the infants continue to relate it to their present experience in the service of understanding, they remain attentive.

I believe the eight-month-old infant's ability to compare information with past knowledge and the inclination to attempt a resolution of inconsistent information help to explain the universal appearance of particular fears that normally appear during the last third of the first year. The two most popular fears have been called stranger and separation anxiety. In the first, the child of eight months wrinkles her face as a stranger approaches. She looks back and forth between the stranger and the mother and, after a few seconds, cries. In separation anxiety, the mother gets up, tells her one-year-old daughter who is playing that she will be returning shortly, and leaves the child. If the setting is not familiar, the child will gaze at the door where the mother was last seen and then begin to cry. These two reactions typically appear between 8 and 15 months in infants living in different cultural settings.

I believe the enhanced memory and comparison competences just described make some contribution to the appearance of these anxieties. As the stranger approaches an eight-month-old boy, he studies her face, retrieves his schemata for the familiar face he knows, and compares the two ideas in active memory, trying to relate them or resolve their inconsistency. If he cannot understand the new face, despite an attempt to do so, and has no behavior he can issue to deal with the resultant state of uncertainty, the child may cry. At the least the child will turn away from the stranger and stop playing.

A similar analysis is appropriate for separation anxiety. Following departure of the mother, the 12-month-old girl generates from memory the schema of the mother's former presence and compares that knowledge with the present situation in active memory. If the child cannot resolve the inconsistency inherent in the comparison, she becomes uncertain and may cry. However, because some children begin to cry as their mother goes toward the door, it is necessary to assume that other factors are involved. One possibility is that the enhanced retrieval and comparison capacity is accompanied by the ability to generate anticipations of the future—mental representations of events that might happen (What will happen now? Will mother return? What can I do?). If children cannot generate a prediction or issue some behavior that will resolve the uncertainty, they become vulnerable to distress. However, if children can generate a prediction, they may laugh; laughter in anticipation of a novel event increases considerably after eight months of age.

This interpretation of separation anxiety differs from the traditional one which assumes that the child cried after the mother departed because the infant anticipated pain or danger following the absence. Although this explanation seems reasonable, on the surface, one must ask why it is that one-year-olds world over, even blind infants and those who are with their mothers for most of the day, suddenly develop an expectation that an unpleasant event will occur when the mother leaves them. Moreover, children whose mothers leave them each morning in a day-care center do not show separation distress earlier or with more intensity than those who are with their mothers continually.

A second, more popular interpretation of separation anxiety is that it reflects the intensity of the child's emotional relationship—called attachment—to the mother or the primary caretaker. The child is presumed to cry because distress is a natural reaction of infants of many species when they are at a distance from their caretaker. The cry is the infant's way of bringing the object of attachment back to them. This explanation implies that infants who are separated daily from their mothers should be less closely attached than those who are with their mothers more or less continually throughout each day. The former should show a different pattern of separation anxiety. But as indicated above, the growth function for separation anxiety is similar for children growing up in nuclear families in the United States, children being raised on kibbutzim in Israel, children from !Kung San bands in Africa, and American children attending day-care centers. Although the variation in time with the mother across these settings is extraordinary, the developmental function for separation anxiety is remarkably similar. For this reason I favor the view that separation distress involves a cognitive component. However, it is possible—even likely—that the intensity of distress displayed by a child during the period 8 to 24 months may be related to the quality of the relationship with the caretaker.

We are left with one final puzzle. Why does the presence of a familiar person, like the father, or a familiar setting, like the home lower the probability of crying and distress to maternal departure as well as to strangers? I believe the presence of a familiar person or setting provides the child with an opportunity to make some response when a state of uncertainty is generated. Action often dispels anxiety in infants as well as adults. It seems that mere recognition of the fact that the child has the opportunity to behave can also buffer uncertainty. When the mother leaves but the father remains in the room, the father's presence provides the child with a potential target for behaviors—the child can approach the father or vocalize to him if she wishes. That knowledge mutes uncertainty and keeps it under control.

Separation distress, as well as other fears of this period, recede after 2 or 2½ years of age because the older child is able to understand the event, to predict future consequences (for example, the return of the mother), or express an instrumental reaction. The children's experiences during the second year have created knowledge which permitted them to solve the puzzle that caused the anxiety in the first place.

I do not suggest that all the fears of childhood involve the processes invoked to explain separation distress. But some may result from the failure to resolve the inconsistency between two schemata or the inability to generate a future possibility in a situation in which the child has no opportunity to make a coping response.

These new processes are likely to be consequences of maturational changes in the central nervous system, perhaps involving the ascendance of forebrain mechanisms. It may not be a coincidence that the proportion of quiet sleep, which is relatively constant from three to nine months, shows an increase at nine to ten months, which is the age when memory is enhanced. Since many physiologists believe that the neural control of sleep shifts from brain stem to forebrain mechanisms during the first year, it is possible that the behavioral changes that rather uniformly appear toward the end of the first year may be released by structural and/or biochemical events that are essential components of ontogenesis. It appears that Freud was approaching a similar insight toward the end of his career. In a prophetic paragraph in one of his last essays, he questioned the formative power he had assigned earlier to variation in infant experience with the caretaker and suggested that maturational forces would guarantee that all infants would display some common developmental profile: "The phylogenetic foundation has so much the upper hand over personal accidental experience that it makes no difference whether a child has really sucked at the breast or has been brought up on the bottle—and never enjoyed the tenderness of a mother's care. In both cases child development takes the same path."

FOUR

ThE EffEcTs of iNfANT dAy CARE ON psychologicAl dEvElopMENT

JEROME KAGAN   RICHARD B. KEARSLEY   PHILIP R. ZELAZO

THE QUESTION that provoked the work to be summarized here can be put in deceptively simple form. Do infants attending a well-run, nurturant, responsible, group-care center five days a week for a little more than 100 weeks display different patterns of psychological development during or at the end of that period compared with children of the same sex and family background who are being reared in a typical nuclear family context in the northeastern United States?

Why would two child psychologists and a pediatrician initiate such an investigation, and why would federal and private funding agencies be willing to allocate a considerable amount of money to obtain information on this issue? An answer to that question requires an examination of some of the unstated premises—"absolute presuppositions" in Collingwood's terms—that provoked the work.

Adapted from The effects of infant day care on psychological development, by Jerome Kagan, Richard B. Kearsley, and Philip R. Zelazo, *Evaluation Quarterly* 1 (1977): 109–42. Reprinted by permission of the publisher, Sage Publications, Inc.

An earlier version of this paper was presented at a symposium on "The Effect of Early Experience on Child Development," American Association for the Advancement of Science, Boston, February 19, 1976. This research was supported by Grant HD4299 from the NICHD, Office of Child Development, the Spencer Foundation, and the Carnegie Corporation of New York.

Rationale

THE DETERMINING ROLE OF ENVIRONMENT

Unquestionably the fundamental premises behind the research were that experience exerts a primary force on the young child's development, and the earlier the experience, the more profound the effect. The basis for this assumption lies everywhere, in our history as well as our contemporary literature. Two hundred years ago post-Revolutionary journalists regularly affirmed the critical importance of the early years. They urged mothers to stay home with their infants and young children and to treat them tenderly, while political leaders worked for the establishment of public schools to insure that the young child was exposed as early as possible to consistently responsible models who would guarantee the proper development of the child's character.

There are at least four relatively independent bases for the supposition that variation in early encounters contributes to variation in later childhood. One of the first is John Locke's metaphor of the *tabula rasa* and the desire of so many seventeenth-century intellectuals to make experience primary in the shaping of man's mind.

On the surface, Locke's catching metaphor was used as a weapon against Spinoza, Leibniz, and the continental rationalists who preferred to award the mind innate ideas that were not the product of encounter with life. Although the debate between Locke and the continental rationalists seemed to be a philosophical disagreement over the likelihood of innate ideas and the differential beauty of mathematical versus empirical truths, there was a hidden agenda, as there are in most intellectual controversies. In this case two more profound issues fueled the debate. One was the continuing attempt by the liberal intellectual class to weaken the secular power and dogmatism of organized European Christianity. An attack on innate ideas was equivalent to an attack on organized religion—a little like the *People's Daily* attacking Chou En-lai by criticizing Confucius. In addition to the desire to weaken the church's powerful hold on the citizenry, there was a deep belief in egalitarianism. The church held as a basic tenet that some were born superior to others because they were born in wedlock to Christian parents. Hence, from the beginning, their minds were stocked with superior ideas and sentiments, and nothing the non-Christian could do would make it possible for him to attain spiritual equality. To Locke and those like him who believed in political egalitarianism, the doctrine of innate ideas was an intellectual obstacle to the attainment of political equality. The only way to insure that society would attain this ideal among all of its citizens was to hold an epistemology that made all infants equally skilled or unskilled at birth and to place experience in the role of unbiased tutor to all. Under these conditions the society could, if it wanted, arrange for the experiences of all of its children to be equivalent and by that action guarantee that their minds would be equally pure and alert. For Locke believed that men were by nature, "all free, equal and independent," a statement that reflects the close relation between Locke's politics and his epistemology. Citizens who preferred an egalitarian society would be attracted to a psychological theory that insisted that experience was the primary determinant of psychological differences among humans.

THE INFLUENCE OF THE PROTESTANT ETHIC

A second historical force that promoted the primacy of early experience comes, oddly enough, from the church in the form of a maxim that one must prepare for the future. Good deeds are tallied and influence one's state of virtue. As with the Hindu view of karma, they constitute a kind of toteboard that summarizes each person's present moral posture. If a person's next life is determined by the virtue displayed in the present, then the future is, to some degree, knowable. Protestantism announces that the child can attain salvation by virtuous behavior, and parents are responsible for providing the socialization that makes virtue possible. The hope that the future might be made more certain by guaranteeing that the present be managed properly became a scientific creed for parents and social scientists. Parents implemented that credo by conscientious care of the young child.

THE PHYSIOLOGICAL BASES OF PSYCHOLOGY

The remarkable discoveries of the neurosciences of the last decade have reinforced an old view that it is potentially possible to translate psychological experience into sentences with purely physiological content. This attitude has extraordinary consequences for one's theory regarding the sequellae of experience. Although an introspective view of psychological experience is characterized by transience and change ("I am hungry now but was not moments ago"), popular descriptions of the brain are less dynamic. Many of the connections between receptor cells, ganglia, and cortical areas are presumably fixed at birth. If we add the recent discoveries suggesting that experience affects the weight of the brain and early stimulation can add dendritic spines to cells or alter the sensitivity of the visual cortex to vertical or horizontal lines, one is tempted to view the central nervous system as a version of Locke's tablet—a surface that accepts material marks that are difficult to erase.

It seems that we have lived with a paradox: a psychological characterization of human functioning that is marked by reversibility but a neurophysiological view that implies irreversibility. Since certainty is the primary criterion the West uses in evaluating knowledge, the neurobiological view of experience, which is materialistic, is more attractive. Hence, most citizens are friendly to the notion that experience is translated into material changes in the neurons—like marks on a tablet—that are fixed rather than transient. Marks on blackboards do not change spontaneously.

This view of the relation of brain to psychological experience evokes the metaphor of a tape and a tape recorder. The iron filings on the tape are permanently altered by a sonata and, if no one erases the tape, it will preserve that melody with fidelity for an indefinite period of time.

OUR RANK-ORDER SOCIETY

A fourth reason for maintaining the belief in the power of early experience is a derivative of entrenched social practices in our society, particularly the tendency to evaluate children on valued traits. This practice sensitizes every parent of a preschool child to the fact that rankings made at the end of the kindergarten year will influence the quality of education the child will receive through elementary and high school, the probability of gaining entrance into a good college and, it is assumed, the child's future vocational success.

From the perspective of parent and child, the goal is to be as high in the rank order as possible when the race begins, usually by six years of age. Most people believe, validly we think, that a six-year-old who is relatively high in the rank order on academic skills, IQ, or control of asocial behavior is more likely to remain high than to plummet. Hence the child who gets off to a good start in the development of culturally valued attributes is likely, other things equal, to remain ahead. Americans see a life span as a long race course with most runners of roughly equivalent ability, speed, and endurance. But some start the race a few days before others. Once the late starters begin to run, they make progress but many never catch those who started a little earlier. That view, which is partially compatible with the facts, would lead parents who want their children to gain positions of status, challenge, dignity, and wealth to assume that the differences at age five, which are so obvious, were the result of what happened before that time. Hence, they want to guarantee that their children have the best possible set of early experiences. These premises, some metaphysical and some rooted in social reality, contributed to the intellectual foundations of this study.

Background

Recent studies of the effect of the arrangements of rearing, other than the nuclear family, on the child's growth reveal that group care for young children does not seem to have much of an effect, either facilitating or debilitating, on the cognitive, social, or affective development of most children. The one exception to that statement seems to hold for children from poorly educated and less-privileged families. If these children attend special, well-run centers, they tend to perform a little better on the standard tests of cognitive development during the first few years of life than if they had been raised totally at home.*

In general, the presence of multiple caretakers and peers and their potential for providing different patterns of encounter during the early years do not appear to be of significant import for the cognitive and social criteria assessed in these studies. Either these criteria measures are too crude to detect real differences among the groups—a real possibility—the wrong variables are being assessed or, indeed, there are minimal or even trivial differences between children who have experienced good group care and those reared at home.

Before we turn to the methods used in this study, the results of which do not contradict those of earlier investigations, the reader should be acutely conscious of the hidden premises behind the variables we chose to assess. In some cases, the variables chosen and the evaluation of the "better score" reflect middle-class American values.

Students of human development find it almost impossible to avoid taking sides with respect to the criteria of adaptation, and the history of psychology is littered with their choices—sensory acuity, tapping speed, libido, low anxiety, formal operational thinking, grades in school, IQ, and income are just a few.

We can divide this list into two major classes: those that appear in all—or in almost all—humans as a result of experience in any normal environment, and those that are culturally specific. The latter can be further subdivided into those that are orthogonal to local "adaptation" and those that either facilitate or obstruct it.

* See Caldwell et al. 1970, Doyle 1975a, Kohen-Raz 1968, Leiderman and Leiderman 1974, Lippman and Grote 1974, Raph et al. 1968, Robinson and Robinson 1971, Schwartz et al. 1974, Tizard et al. 1972, and Winnett et al. 1975.

Adaptation in our society requires possession of a competence that is valued by a segment of the community, a capacity for autonomous decisions, and finally the belief that one is not basically inferior in value; that is, one has the opportunity to attain status and dignity. If those criteria are adopted, it is easy for the child psychologist to choose milestones which will preview the likelihood that a particular child will attain those prizes in adulthood. In our society verbal competence, problem-solving skill, burgeoning independence, sociability, and control of anxiety at age ten seem to predict the adult criteria. We selected criteria in the light of these considerations. But given another society, different criteria might have been chosen.

The informal theory that provided early nineteenth-century New England parents with guides as to how to insure that their children would be well-adapted insisted upon promoting obedience to the family, punishment of all signs of aggression and sexuality, and insulation from other children, especially children from less religious and less affluent homes. Such children, it was believed, could corrupt the child and lead him away from virtue. Indeed, Jacob Abbott—the Dr. Spock of his day—warned parents that if they did not keep their children at home, away from peers, they would invite trouble. It is likely we would have created test situations in 1825 that assessed the child's ability to resist influence from peers, rather than his tendency to initiate contact with peers.

This relativism in choice of criteria is especially relevant to the current project because half of our sample was Chinese, and some of our parents held traditional Chinese values. One of these values is that children should be quiet, not talkative. The battery we devised, responding to the value biases of middle-class American society, assessed the infant's tendency to vocalize and the 2.5-year-old's talkativeness and richness of vocabulary. Had we constructed the battery from the perspective of our working-class Chinese sample, we might have created an assessment situation in which a child sat opposite an adult, and hidden observers coded how long the child remained quiet before speaking. The longer that delay, the more mature the child. Such a decision would puzzle most American psychologists and administrators of grant-awarding agencies. Since "remaining quiet" is maladaptive in our society, we did not create such an assessment situation; but not because talkativeness is universally more mature or desirable, but only because this study occurred in this culture, and it was appropriate to accommodate to the community in which these children will have to function.

We are aware of the fact that some of the variables we chose to evaluate reflect local values and are not to be regarded as universal referents for growth. On the other hand, other dimensions—attentiveness, reaction to discrepancy, ability to adopt a problem-solving set—are more likely to be universally adaptive and to display a growth pattern over the first three years that may be representative of children in all locales.

Methods

SAMPLE

The subjects in this study were Chinese and Caucasian children from both working- and middle-class homes living in the Boston area. The original design called for three groups of children. Group 1, the experimental group, attended our research-administered day-care center. Group 2, the home control group, consisted of infants from the same ethnic and social class groups who lived at home. Group 3 consisted of infants who attended other forms of group care outside the home, either a day-care center or custodial care. But the sample size in this third group was small and will not be discussed in detail.

Generally, we performed two related analyses of the effects of group care. One analysis was a matched-pairs analysis in which pairs of children were matched on sex, ethnicity, and education of both parents, but one of the children attended our day-care center from 3.5 or 5.5 through 30 months of age, while the control member of the pair was reared at home. A second analysis included all the children in the experimental day-care and home control samples. This sample included children from the matched-pairs analysis. This analysis allowed us to inquire about the effects of ethnicity, class, and sex, as well as form of rearing. Maximal sample size for the matched-pairs analysis was 32 pairs of children. At some ages the number was a little smaller, but the minimal number was 23 pairs and occurred at 29 months. The maximal sample size of day-care and home control children was 99 children. When all the children are included—day care, home control, and mixed groups—the sample size for the older ages was 116. Table 4.1 lists the size of the sample by care, ethnicity, class, and sex.

The children in all groups were enrolled in the experiment when they were 3.5 to 5.5 months of age. The children in group 1 were usually in resi-

Table 4 · 1   Distribution of Children in Each Group by Care, Sex, Ethnicity, and Social Class

	Day Care		Home Control		Mixed	
	B	G	B	G	B	G
Chinese						
Working-class	4	5	9	6	0	0
Middle-class	3	4	6	9	5	2
Caucasion						
Working-class	5	2	5	14	1	0
Middle-class	5	5	6	12	5	3

dence at the day-care center five days a week from 8:30 in the morning until about 4:00 in the afternoon. Each infant was assigned to a primary caretaker, and in most cases the caretaker was of the same ethnicity as the child. A manual of procedures for interaction with the infant and toddler formed the basis for play between caretaker and infant. These prescribed interactions were administered when the infant was alert, biologically satisfied, and not playing alone happily. Typically, an infant experienced between one and two hours of this interaction each day.

The curriculum had a middle-class American bias: it encouraged cognitive development, one-to-one affective interactions between adult caretaker and child, and tried to maximize the opportunity that each child would have many successful mastery experiences.

The low child-to-adult ratio, together with the caretaker's assumption that she was, in part, an educator, made this an unusual day-care setting and not representative of typical infant day care in the United States.

The Assessments

Each child was assessed by a research staff member who was not involved in any aspect of caretaking. Moreover, the offices of the research staff were in William James Hall in Cambridge, Massachusetts, several miles from the day-care center. Infants were assessed at 3.5, 5.5, 7.5, 9.5, 11.5, 13.5, 20, and 29 months of age. The assessments from 3.5 to 13.5 months occurred in a special laboratory at the day-care center separate from the area where care was administered. The assessments at 20 and 29 months occurred in William James Hall.

We shall only be concerned in this report with some of the data gathered at 20 and 29 months and, therefore, shall only report the procedures for those relevant episodes.

BATTERY AT 20 MONTHS: SESSION I

1. *Attachment* • Child is observed for 45 minutes in a room containing his mother, an unfamiliar woman, and primary caretaker from day-care center (if he is a day-care subject) or a familiar friend of family (for home control child). *Variables coded:* duration proximity to each of the three adults, duration touching each of them, duration looking at each, number of times child brings toy to each, number of times child smiles at each, duration of vocalizing, and duration fretting or crying.

2. *Vocabulary Recognition* • Child is shown sets of pictures of objects and asked to point to the object that the examiner names. The sets are:

1. *fork*　　spoon　　knife
2. banana　　*apple*　　orange
3. chair　　sofa　　*table*
4. *carrot*　　lettuce　　tomato
5. shirt　　skirt　　*pants*
6. horse　　*chicken*　　cow
7. scissors　　*pot*　　shoes
8. *tree*　　cup　　flower
9. girl standing　　*girl sitting*　　policeman standing
10. *toothbrush*　　row boat　　duck
11. sink　　refrigerator　　*stove*
12. hat　　*comb*　　watch
13. moon　　necklace　　*star*
14. *clock*　　baby bottle　　bookcase
15. *pig*　　dog　　cat

Variables coded • Item in italics is one requested by examiner; score-correct number recognized.

BATTERY AT 20 MONTHS: SESSION II

1. Solo Free Play • Child is in room with his mother and a set of age-appropriate toys for 21 minutes. *Variables coded:* duration of attentional involvement with each toy, duration of time child relates to two or more toys, duration looking at mother, duration proximal to mother, duration each smile, duration vocalization, and duration fretting or crying.

2. Peer Play • An unfamiliar peer of the same age and sex as the child and the strange peer's mother enter the room, and a new set of toys is brought in. The child's behavior is observed for an additional 21 minutes. *Variables coded:* duration of involvement with each toy, duration of time child relates to two or more toys, number of times child initiates aggressive play with peer, number of times child initiates cooperative play with peer, number of times child stays when he is approached by peer, number of times child withdraws when approached by peer, number of times child resists coercion or aggression by peer, duration proximal to mother, duration looking at strange peer, duration looking at his mother, duration vocalization, and duration fretting or crying.

3. Bayley Scale • Age-appropriate items are administered.

4. Separation Episode • Mother leaves child alone while child is playing. *Variables coded:* occurrence of fretting or crying, and latency to the first fret or cry.

BATTERY AT 29 MONTHS: SESSION I

1. *Solo Play* • Child is in room with mother and set of age-appropriate toys for 21 minutes. *Variables coded:* same as at 20 months.

2. *Peer Play* • Same as at 20 months, but behavior was observed for 28 minutes. *Variables coded:* same as at 20 months, plus the addition of a variable called "imitation of peer."

3. *Concept Formation Index* • We modified slightly a test developed by Francis Palmer of the State University of New York at Stony Brook to assess the child's understanding of 31 concepts. The child is seated opposite the tester at a small table and is asked to play a game. For example, the tester presents two small toy dogs and asks the child to "put the dog *in* the box." Two boxes are available, one is "bottom up," the other open and empty. The child's response is recorded by a coder in the observational room. The concepts are: in, big, littlest of three, out of, little, biggest of three, up, white, moving, not moving, black, down, on, under, around, in front of, behind, over, close, open, more, full, long, plate *on* cloth, hard, empty, soft, short, cloth *on* plate, top, bottom.

4. *Separation Protest* • As at each previous age, a brief two-minute separation from the mother occurred. When the child was comfortably playing with toys in the center of the room, the mother rose, waved, said good-bye, and left the room. The child's latency to crying, his duration of crying, looking to the door, and latency to termination of the trial were recorded.

BATTERY AT 29 MONTHS: SESSION II

1. *Visit to Unfamiliar Day-Care Center* • Session II was held a minimum of seven days after session I. First, the target child visited an unfamiliar day-care center near William James Hall to determine his reactions to a group of completely unfamiliar peers in a novel situation. The mother, child, and examiner enter a room of about 10 to 15 children of approximately the same age who, along with their teacher, continued their activities. The examiner and mother were seated; coding began immediately and lasted until 30 minutes of behavior were recorded. When the child appeared comfortable, the mother encouraged him to join the other children. The mother was instructed to remain in her seat throughout the session, although the coder, of course, followed the child.

Eight variables were coded on a prepared form in ten-second blocks for three ten-minute epochs. Each ten-minute epoch was followed by a two-minute rest period until thirty minutes of coding had been completed. The following behaviors were observed: proximity to mother; fretting; the child's looking at another child or group of children; the child's reciprocal play with another child involving contingent cooperative interaction; the child's initiation of cooperative play to another child and the child's initiation of an aggressive act directed toward another child; the child remains when approached by another child; the child withdraws when approached by another child; and the child plays with an object, such as a toy, rather than a person.

2. *Embedded Figures Task* • Upon returning to William James Hall, the child was seated at a table opposite the examiner and presented the embedded figures task. This task assessed the child's impulsive and reflective tendencies in a visual search situation. The test consisted of practice items in which the child was to find a picture that was identical with the model, where the foils were similar to the model in form. The child was shown a standard picture—a bird, for example—and asked to point to the bird in the illustration that was exactly like the bird on the standard card. The standard always remained present above the illustration. The child was trained to point unambiguously before he began. In the critical test items, the standard to be located was embedded in a series of distracting lines. There were nine critical test items—three for a cat, three for a car, and three for a flower. The examiner recorded the latency to the child's response from the moment search began and whether the child's response was correct or incorrect. If incorrect, the child was asked again to find the standard.

3. *Memory for Locations Task* • The child's short-term memory capacity for locations was assessed following the embedded figures task. This task required the child to recall the location of a familiar object after it was hidden under one of five distinctive containers. For example, the experimenter hid a toy shoe under a brightly colored, pyramid-shaped container. A barrier was placed in front of the containers for five seconds. The barrier was removed, and the child asked to find the shoe. Number of containers and number of objects hidden were increased from one object under one container to a maximum of five containers and five objects. During the first five trials, only one object was hidden under one, two, three, four, or five containers. These were used as training trials. In the four critical test trials, two, three, four, or five objects were hidden under one of five containers. The child was asked to find one of the objects. If successful, he was also asked to find a second object.

Results

We shall consider first the five tests of cognitive development: memory for locations, concept formation index, and embedded figures at 29 months, and the vocabulary and Bayley test items administered at 20 months.

MEMORY FOR LOCATIONS AT 29 MONTHS

The analyses are presented for two classes of comparisons. The first is for the closely matched pairs of children; the second involved the entire population tested at 29 months. In all the analyses using the entire population, the statistical procedures take into account the cell-size differences between the experimental and control groups. Both social class and ethnicity are introduced in these analyses. Since their intercorrelation is not statistically significant ($r = .12$), they are treated as orthogonal variables in the analyses of variance undertaken.

Matched Pairs • The matched pairs performed similarly. On easy items where only two objects were hidden, most children (27 of 36) passed the item. On the difficult item in which five objects were hidden, only four children were correct. On the two items of intermediate difficulty, there was a slight but not significant tendency for more day-care children to pass these items, but the difference was not reliable.

Larger Sample • There was no difference among the children in the three types of care within each of the ethnic groups and, of course, no difference between day-care and home control children when the ethnicity and social class subgroups were collapsed. Table 4.2 contains the proportion of subjects in the day care ($n = 21$) and home control groups ($n = 44$) who passed each of the four items, separated by ethnic group.

Table 4·2 Percentage of Children in Each Subgroup Passing Each of the Test Items ($N = 65$)

	Two Objects Hidden	Three Objects Hidden	Four Objects Hidden	Five Objects Hidden
Chinese day care	57	36	50	14
Caucasian day care	100	29	43	29
Chinese home control	70	35	35	15
Caucasian home control	83	29	42	46

CONCEPT FORMATION INDEX AT 29 MONTHS

Matched Pairs • The matched-pairs analysis revealed no difference between the day-care or home control pairs (mean of 16.2 and 15.4). An item analysis revealed that on only four items did a significant day care versus home control difference appear.

Larger Sample • Table 4.3 contains the mean scores for the eight major subgroups. There was no simple effect of form of rearing but a strong class effect, with the middle-class children attaining higher scores ($F = 7.65$, 1/61, p < .01). The effect of educational level of the family on the child's language development, which is a consistent result in many other studies, appeared once again.

Table 4·3 Average Number Correct on the Concept Formation Index

	Day Care	Home Control
Chinese working-class	13.4	10.7
Chinese middle-class	17.5	18.0
Caucasian working-class	15.0	18.3
Caucasian middle-class	19.4	22.0

Significant effects: class—$F = 7.65, 1/61$, $p < .01$; care by ethnicity—$F = 3.51, 1/61$, $p < .06$.

The working-class Chinese children in day care performed better than the working-class Chinese children reared at home. But this difference was absent for the Caucasian or middle-class Chinese children. This fact is reflected in the interaction of care by ethnicity ($F = 3.51$, $1/61$, p. $< .05$).

But among the Caucasian children, the home environment was more facilitating, for among both working- and middle-class Caucasian children the home-reared children attained higher scores than those attending the day-care center. Hence the facilitating effect of day care on language development was dependent on the child's home environment.

EMBEDDED FIGURES TEST AT 29 MONTHS

Matched Pairs • The matched-pairs analysis revealed no difference between the day-care and home control groups on response time or accuracy to the nine critical test items.

Larger Sample • All children showed longer response times to the most difficult items in each series, and there was no significant day care-home control difference in latency or accuracy of performance. Day-care children had a mean of 7.1 out of 9 correct for the critical items; home control subjects had a mean of 6.9. All children were competent at this task, and there was no significant advantage associated with form of rearing, ethnicity, or class.

RECOGNITION VOCABULARY AT 20 MONTHS

For the matched pairs, there was no difference between the day-care and home control groups in the number of items correctly recognized. For the larger sample, Table 4.4 presents the mean score for day-care versus home control groups within each ethnic and class subgroup. There was no effect of rearing within any of the class-ethnicity subgroups and no interaction. But the Chinese children in both day-care and home control groups had lower scores than the Caucasians ($F = 4.96$, $1/71$, $p < .01$).

Table 4 · 4   Mean Number Correct on Vocabulary Recognition Test at 20 Months

	Chinese		Caucasian	
	Working-Class	Middle-Class	Working-Class	Middle-Class
Day care	5.6	6.7	9.0	7.3
Home control	4.7	6.7	7.7	7.9

We interpret the difference to reflect the differential exposure to and encouragement of language in Chinese and Caucasian homes in Boston. Informants have suggested to us that Chinese parents are less concerned than Caucasians with early language development.

THE BAYLEY SCALE ITEMS AT 20 MONTHS

The Bayley items at 20 months were divided into two scales: a language scale of 15 items and a nonlanguage scale of 13 items—6 of which involved imitation of the examiner and 7 of which involved putting forms in a form board (see Table 4.5).

Table 4 · 5   Average Score on the Bayley Items at 20 Months

	Day Care		Home Control	
	Middle-Class	Working-Class	Middle-Class	Working Class
Language items[a]				
Chinese	8.0	6.1	9.0	5.0
Caucasian	10.0	9.0	9.4	9.8
Nonlanguage items[b]				
Chinese	8.6	6.7	8.6	5.3
Caucasian	8.1	7.6	6.6	5.4

	Matched Pairs	
	Day Care	Home Control
Language	8.3	7.8
Nonlanguage	7.8	6.4

[a] Significant effects: ethnicity—$F = 7.92$, 1/70, $p < .01$; class—$F = 3.30$, 1/70, $p < .07$.
[b] Significant effects: care—$F = 5.65$, 1/70, $p < .05$; class—$F = 10.58$, 1/70, $p < .01$.

The language scale failed to reveal any effect of care or any interaction with care for the matched pairs or the larger sample. But both social class and ethnicity influenced the language scores. The Caucasian children had higher language scores than the Chinese ($F = 7.92$, 1/70, $p < .01$), and children from middle-class families had higher language scores than those from the working-class families ($F = 3.30$, 1/70, p. $= .07$).

Performance on the nonlanguage items yielded one of the rare instances in which the day-care experience had a clear and simple effect. For three of the four groups (Chinese working class and both Caucasian groups), the day-care children obtained higher scores than the corresponding groups being reared at home ($F = 5.65$, 1/70, $p < .05$). For 11 of the 13 items on the nonlanguage scale, the proportion passing was higher for day care than for home controls. This difference in performance on the nonlanguage items also held for the matched pairs (t = 2.51, 28 df, p < .05).

Although unanticipated, the higher scores on the nonlanguage items for the day-care children is not unreasonable. The day-care teachers spend much time with the infants encouraging them to imitate acts that they have first demonstrated. Hence, the day-care child has considerable experience imitating adults in the center, perhaps more than a child living at home. Moreover, the day-care child has many form boards in the center and, therefore, the day-care child has the potential for greater opportunity to practice the tasks that resemble those on the nonlanguage scale.

ATTACHMENT SESSION AT 20 MONTHS

The attachment session, which was the first of the assessment episodes at 20 months, occurred in a large room in William James Hall decorated as a living room. The actors were the child, the child's mother, an unfamiliar woman, and, for the day-care children, the primary caretaker from the center, while for the home controls the familiar person was a female friend with whom the child had previous contact. The child was given only a few toys because we wished to promote mild boredom in order to see to whom the child went for comfort, if and when he became satiated with the toys. Additionally, in order to create mild apprehension, at two points in the session, at 15 and again at 30 minutes, each of the three adults suddenly changed their positions and took different seats. This event, apparently unprovoked from the child's point of view, alerted most children. We coded to whom the child oriented after the change and whether he altered his proximity to any of the adults. The main question asked was whether the day-care experience altered the child's tendency to seek his mother when he was bored or mildly apprehensive.

Matched Pairs • There was no significant difference between the day-care and home control groups for any of the variables across the 45-minute session. For the critical variable of proximity to mother, the data did not reveal a difference between day-care and home control children.

Larger Sample • There were no differences associated with rearing for any of the variables except smiling. The home control children smiled a little more than the day-care group (F = 4.98, 2/75, p < .01). We have no easy interpretation of that difference.

The most important observation from this session was the overwhelming preference that all children showed for their mothers when they were bored or distressed. Table 4.6 shows the average duration (in seconds) the

Table 4 · 6   Proximity to Mother, Familiar Adult, and Strange Adult for Attachment Session (mean value in seconds)

	Chinese			Caucasian		
	DC	HC	Mixed	DC	HC	Mixed
Mother	117	85	80	62	59	55
Familiar adult	4	17	6	11	19	9
Stranger	0.4	0.6	1.4	0.7	2.0	1.6

child was proximal to each of the three adults across the entire session. All children, day care and home control, as well as Chinese and Caucasian, selected their mother as the primary target. The ratio of time proximal to mother versus the familiar adult was about 7 to 1, and the day-care children were as likely to choose their mother over the familiar adult as were the home controls. If approaching the mother when bored or uncertain is regarded as a moderately sensitive index of attachment of child to mother, it appears that the day-care children were no less strongly attached to their mothers than the home controls. However, the Chinese children spent more time proximal to their mother than the Caucasians ($F = 6.48$, $1/75$, $p < .01$).

Behavior at Time of Adult Movement • We coded each child's behavior for the 30 seconds prior to the adult's move and compared it with the child's behavior during the 30 seconds after the move. Since some children were proximal to their mother at the time of the movement, a simple change score might have given a distorted picture of the effect of the intervention. We constructed a scale from 1 to 5 which reflected the child's tendency to approach the mother at the time of the adult movement. There was no difference between the day-care and home-reared children for average scale score across both rotations. However, the Chinese children showed higher average scale scores ($F = 7.95$, $1/83$, $p < .01$). At the time of the first movement, the Chinese children were more likely than the Caucasians to be near their mother during the 30 seconds prior to the rotation and to remain near her for the next half-minute ($F = 11.1$, $1/69$, $p < .01$).

At the time of the second rotation, 15 minutes later, the middle-class Chinese children had extinguished some of their apprehension. There was no overall ethnicity difference at the second movement, although the working-class Chinese children were most likely to be near their mother at the time of rotation and to remain near her for the next half-minute.

These data imply that home experience and temperament are more important determinants of apprehension than attendance at a day-care center. In this context, the day-care experience did not appear to change the child's tendency to seek his mother as a target when he was distressed or bored. The day-care child did not vacillate between choosing his mother or day-care teacher, and he chose the former with the same frequency as the home control child.

SEPARATION PROTEST

A second measure which many investigators regard as indicative of the child's attachment to his mother is the degree of protest the child displays to maternal departure. At the end of each assessment session from 3.5 through 29 months, we evaluated the child's tendency to cry or fret following departure of his mother, leaving the child alone in a room where he had been happily playing. The procedure was identical at all sessions. When the child was happily playing, the mother said, "Good-bye," and left the room, and we noted the occurrence and duration of any protest, fretting, and crying for a two-minute period. Figure 4.1 shows the proportion of children who fretted or cried during the two minutes of departure. There was no difference between the day-care and home-reared children at any age. More important, there was a clear growth function for separation distress. The tendency to become upset was low for all children prior to 9.5 months, rose from 9.5 to 20 months, and then declined. This growth function for distress to separation has been replicated in similar infant studies for American and non-American

Figure 4 · 1

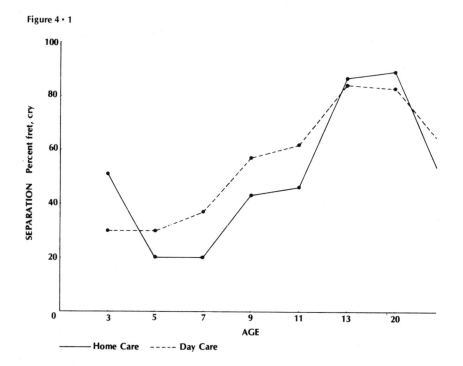

cultures. These studies in different cultures all report an inverted U-function relating separation anxiety to age. This fact suggests that the occurrence of separation distress during the first 2.5 years of life is monitored closely by the child's level of cognitive development.

PLAY AND SOCIAL BEHAVIOR

This section summarizes the data gathered on the solo and peer play sessions administered at 20 and 29 months of age. It will be recalled that at 20 and 29 months the children were observed in a pair of play sessions at William James Hall. Initially, the child played alone with his mother and an interesting set of toys. After a short recess, an unfamiliar child and that child's mother were brought into the room along with a new set of toys, and we observed the child in this new context. We are primarily interested in the change in the child's play and relationship to his mother from the solo to the peer sessions.

The 20-month Session: Matched Pairs • There were very few differences between the day-care and home control children during the solo play session at 20 months. The day-care and home control children were equally at ease (or equally apprehensive) during the period when they were playing alone with their mothers in the room.

During the subsequent session with the unfamiliar peer and mother, the home control children played less than those in day care. Table 4.7 contains the 20-month values for play, proximity to mother, and looking at the unfamiliar peer for the solo and peer sessions for the first 15 minutes of the session and for the entire session. Both day-care and home control children showed significant inhibition to the introduction of the peer, for both groups

Table 4 · 7   **Play Behavior at 20 Months for Matched Pairs (N = 29 pairs; mean values in seconds per minute)**

| | Day Care | | Home Control | |
	Solo Play	Peer Play	Solo Play	Peer Play
Proximity to mother				
Mins. 1 to 15	12.3	16.9	10.3	23.7
Entire session	14.1	16.7	11.9	23.3
Average time playing				
Mins. 1 to 15	45.6	33.9	48.5	21.9
Entire session	44.1	34.6	45.8	22.4
Duration look at peer				
Mins. 1 to 15	—	15.0	—	22.0
Entire session	—	13.9	—	21.1
Looking at peer while proximal to mother				
Mins. 1 to 15	—	7.0	—	12.8
Entire session	—	6.3	—	12.0

showed increased proximity to the mother and decreased play—both absolute amount of time playing as well as the average length of a typical play epoch. But the decrease in play was greater for the home control children. A comparison of the data from the peer play session revealed that the average amount of play per minute was larger for the day-care than for the home control children ($t = 3.78$, $p < .01$).

Although most children were made uncertain by the introduction of the unfamiliar peer and mother, the home controls apparently were made more apprehensive by this event, even though both day-care and home control children were with their mothers. The greater deterioration in play among the home controls implies that they were more uncertain with the unfamiliar peer. Most children during the second year of life display mild apprehension to an unfamiliar child, owing perhaps to the child's new ability to generate anticipations of possible actions of others but the temporary inability to resolve the questions inherent in those anticipations. Prior experience with unfamiliar peers—which was greater for the day-care children—apparently buffers that uncertainty at this age. As we shall see, this difference between day-care and home control children disappears at 29 months. When the child has matured to a point where he is better able to resolve the uncertainty generated by the unfamiliar child, the difference between day-care and home-reared children vanishes.

The 20-Month Session: Large Sample • All the indexes of inhibition and apprehension increased following the introduction of the unfamiliar peer. The majority of the children stayed closer to their mother for a longer time ($F = 7.04$, $1/68$, $p < .01$), vocalized less to the mother ($F = 15.68$, $1/68$, $p < .01$), and displayed fewer undirected vocalizations ($F = 45.91$, $1/68$, $p < .001$). The children also played less ($F = 52.09$, $1/68$, $p < .001$) and had shorter average play epochs ($F = 32.41$, $1/52$, $p < .001$) during the peer than during the solo session.

As with the matched pairs, the home control children showed a greater inhibition of play following the introduction of the unfamiliar peer, although both groups played less during the peer session (care by session $F = 6.26$, $1/68$, $p < .05$ for average time playing). The day-care children also looked less than the home controls at the unfamiliar peer ($F = 7.76$, $1/68$, $p < .01$), suggesting that the peer was less of a discrepant event to the day-care child.

The Chinese children stayed closer to their mother during both solo and peer sessions, vocalized less during both sessions, and played less than the Caucasians.

The 29-Month Session: Matched Pairs • As at 20 months, there was no difference between day-care and home control children for any of the variables—play, vocalization, or proximity—during the solo session (see Table 4.8). Hence, we assume the children were in an equivalent state prior to the introduction of the peer. Unlike the 20-month data, there were no significant differences in duration of play between home control and day-care children during the peer session. Moreover, at 20 months the duration of an average play epoch decreased from solo to peer; but at 29 months these values increased from the solo to the peer session, suggesting that the unfamiliar peer was a less serious source of uncertainty and apprehension to the older child.

With maturity, the children seemed to become less apprehensive with the unfamiliar peer and the difference between the rearing groups disappeared. Psychological investigations which provide only one assessment at one point in time tempt investigators to assume that any difference noted at one age is likely to persist in the future or become amplified. These results demonstrate the danger of that inference.

The rate of cooperative, aggressive, or reciprocal play was very low, and there were minimal differences between the rearing groups. There was no support for the notion that day-care children are either more aggressive or more cooperative than children reared at home.

The 29-Month Session: Larger Sample • As in the matched-pairs analysis, there were no differences between day-care and home control children in time playing, amount of inhibition of play from solo to peer session, or proximity to mother. Only two variables produced a simple effect for care. One was the percentage of total time playing in which the child was involved in relational play. The day-care children had a larger ratio (F = 4.70, 1/60, p < .05). The other variable was duration looking at the unfamiliar peer. As

Table 4 · 8   Play Behavior at 29 Months for Matched Pairs (N = 20 pairs; mean values in seconds per minute)

	Day Care		Home Control	
	Solo Play	Peer Play	Solo Play	Peer Play
Proximity to mother				
Mins. 1 to 15	11.8	22.9	6.1	24.3
Entire session	12.0	21.6	7.0	24.7
Average amount of play				
Mins. 1 to 15	48.2	38.2	51.0	32.0
Entire session	47.5	37.4	50.6	31.3
Duration look at peer				
Mins. 1 to 15	—	11.2	—	15.5
Entire session	—	11.4	—	14.6
Duration proximity to mother while looking at peer				
Mins. 1 to 15	—	6.3	—	9.1
Entire session	—	5.3	—	8.3

at 20 months, the home controls stared longer at the peer than the day-care children ($F = 3.20$, $1/60$, $p = .08$) and also stared at the peer more frequently ($F = 4.56$, $1/60$, $p < .05$).

Chinese children remained more uncertain than Caucasians. The Chinese stayed closer to their mother ($F = 11.86$, $1/60$, $p < .01$), vocalized less ($F = 9.77$, $1/60$, $p < .01$), played less ($F = 4.98$, $1/60$, $p < .05$), stared at the unfamiliar adult more ($F = 7.60$, $1/60$, $p < .01$), and looked at the unfamiliar peer while proximal to their mother more often than Caucasians ($F = 3.98$, $1/60$, $p < .05$).

Although the effects of day care on play—both alone and with the unfamiliar peer—were small, they were less dramatic at 29 than at 20 months. A simplistic view of the relation between experience with other children and behavior with an unfamiliar child would have predicted a greater difference at the older age, since the day-care children had nine additional months to interact with other children their own age. But if one views the inhibition at 20 months as a temporary phenomenon due to the child's inability to assimilate the discrepant experience of the unfamiliar peer, one would be more prepared to expect the data presented here.

Discrete social behaviors which included an interaction with the unfamiliar peer were infrequent at both 20 and 29 months, although a little more social behavior occurred at the later than at the earlier age. We performed a frequency analysis on the data at both ages. Table 4.9 contains the proportion of children of each group showing any occurrence of the variables in question (one or more occurrences). There is only slightly more social interaction at 29 than at 20 months, and at the later ages the home control and Caucasian children are more interactive. They initiate more cooperative as well as more aggressive responses and are involved in more social interactions. It is not valid to view the home control or Caucasian child as either more cooperative or more aggressive, but rather as simply more interactive. The day-care Chinese children were the least interactive, while the home control Caucasians were the most. For the two variables that required initiation by the child, more Caucasians—both day care and home control— displayed social overtures. Since the home control children are a little more social than the day-care children at 29 months, it is clear that daily encounter with other children does not automatically lead the child to be socially more responsive with an unfamiliar child.

VISIT TO UNFAMILIAR DAY-CARE CENTER

Matched-Pairs Analysis • Table 4.10 contains the mean scores for proximity to mother, looking at peer, and playing with objects for the three suc-

Table 4 · 9   Selected Social Behaviors in Peer Play

A. Proportion of the Group Displaying the Variable in Question (≥1)

	Initiates Cooperatively	Initiates Aggressively	Stays	Resists	Withdraws
Day care Chinese					
20 months	50	56	75	38	44
29 months	46	46	77	30	30
Home control Chinese					
20 months	50	44	78	61	39
29 months	57	33	77	24	28
Day care Caucasian					
20 months	71	71	64	43	50
29 months	77	55	55	22	22
Home control Caucasian					
20 months	68	54	71	46	39
29 months	84	80	84	52	48

B. Proportion of Children Displaying Reciprocal Play or Imitative Behavior at 29 Months

	Reciprocal Play	Imitates Peer
Day-care Chinese	0	23
Home control Chinese	24	48
Day-care Caucasian	22	55
Home control Caucasian	56	64

cessive 10-minute periods for 20 matched pairs of children. There were no rearing differences for proximity to mother or staring at peer, but the day-care children played with objects longer than the home controls during the entire half-hour episode (t = 2.1, df = 19, p = .05). Since play is a moderately sensitive index of the degree of uncertainty in an unfamiliar situation, the data imply that the day-care children were a little less apprehensive than the home controls.

Table 4 · 10   Behavior in Unfamiliar Day-Care Center for Matched Pairs at 29 Months[a]

	Day Care	Home Control
Proximity to mother		
Min. 1–10	3.6	3.1
11–20	2.7	3.1
21–30	2.6	2.6
Look at other child		
Min. 1–10	3.4	4.0
11–20	2.7	3.0
21–30	2.2	2.7
Play with objects		
Min. 1–10	2.6	1.7
11–20[b]	3.9	2.3
21–30	4.0	2.8

[a] Values are rate measures: mean number o. 10-second epochs per minute during which a given behavior occurred.
[b] Difference: t = 2.59; df = 19, p < .01.

The Larger Sample • The day-care children played more during each of the ten-minute periods (F for all 30 minutes = 4.48, 1/61, p < .05). Indeed, except for the Caucasian middle-class boys, for every other ethnicity–sex–social class subgroup, the day-care children were less apprehensive in this setting. This is supported by the fact that the day-care children stared less at the unfamiliar children than did the home controls (F = 6.45, 1/61, p < .01).

As in the matched-pairs analysis, there was the expected ethnicity difference for both play and proximity to mother, with Chinese children playing less than the Caucasians (F = 7.87, 1/61, p < .01) and remaining close to their mothers for a longer period of time (F = 7.15, 1/61, p < .01). The home control Chinese had the lowest play scores of all four groups (1.9 for the home control Chinese versus 3.5, 3.7, and 3.2 for the other three groups). As with the cognitive measures, the day-care experience seemed to alleviate the apprehension and inhibition characteristic of the home-reared Chinese. Only 40 of the 69 children made any social overture toward another child. There was no effect of rearing on this variable.

The effect of the day-care experience, although not extreme, was in the expected direction. One would anticipate the day-care children to be a little less apprehensive in this unfamiliar group-care setting than children reared at home. The lack of any difference between the two groups on proximity to mother, together with the parallel increases in play and decreases in proximity to mother across the half-hour, imply that both groups were equally apprehensive initially and extinguished that initial apprehension at a similar rate. Once again, the similarities between the day-care and home control children are as, or more, salient than the differences.

Discussion

The central question that provoked the investigation can be answered with some assurance. Attendance at a day-care center staffed by conscientious and nurturant adults during the first 2.5 years does not seem to sculpt a psychological profile very much different from the one created by total home rearing. This conclusion is based not only on our formal assessments but also on our informal observations of the children over the 2.5-year period. These data did not confirm several popular notions about early group care. Although it is reasonable to assume that daily encounter with other children during the first two years might speed up the maturation of the social interaction sequences usually seen in three- and four-year-olds, our data did not provide dramatic support for that prediction. The 20- and 29-month-olds were simply not very social and did not often initiate play with other children. Both cooperative and aggressive play occurred infrequently among both groups. There were as many shy children among the day-care groups as there were among the home controls. Indeed, on one occasion we satisfied our curiosity about a particular girl who was inordinately shy with a strange peer in our 20-month assessment by bringing an unfamiliar peer to the day-care center. The girl retreated at once to her day-care teacher, even though she was in her territory. The day-care children were neither more coopera-tive nor more aggressive than home controls.

Some have argued that day-care experience promotes an insecurity in children which makes them more prone to seek their mother when fright-ened or bored. All the children were disposed to approach their mother when they became uncertain in the presence of the unfamiliar peer or as a result of the unprovoked movements of the adults during the 20-month at-tachment session. The separation anxiety situation revealed a remarkably similar growth function for both day-care and home controls, verifying data from other studies.

Some investigators have suggested that multiple caretaking by adults other than the mother weakens or dilutes the child's emotional bond to his mother. The day-care child had two primary caretakers in addition to the mother—one caretaker from 3.5 to 13 months and a second caretaker from 13 to 29 months. In addition, all were exposed to other adults who adminis-tered occasional care at the center. Nonetheless, day-care and home control children were equally likely to choose the mother as the target for solace and attentive nurturance when they were bored, tired, or afraid. The day-care child was no more likely to approach his or her primary caretaker from the center than was the home control child to approach a friend of the family during the 20-month attachment session.

The entire corpus of data supports the view that day care, when respon-sibly and conscientiously implemented, does not seem to have hidden psy-chological dangers. Since this conclusion flies in the face of much popular belief—including a prior prejudice of one of the principal investigators—it is both useful and natural to maintain a skeptical attitude toward this general-ization. One objection is to question the sensitivity of our methods of assess-ment. It is always a possibility that a scientist's methods are insufficiently valid indexes of his constructs. The history of psychology is littered with Type II errors. Many investigators who found no class differences on the Bayley Scale under one year concluded that class had no effect on cognitive development during the first year of life. But when different methods were employed—for example, fixation time to discrepant events or vocalization to samples of speech—clear class differences emerged. The Bayley was not sen-sitive enough to detect them. It is, of course, impossible to assert that the day-care and home control children are not psychologically different. It is the responsibility of the investigators who believe that early group care makes a difference to invent more sensitive methods to demonstrate the validity of that hypothesis. We will be among the first to accept that finding if the data so indicate.

But let us suppose that our methods are relatively sensitive—and, indeed, there are trivial and nonenduring differences in cognitive, social, and affective development between our two main groups. How is that possible, considering the fact that the day-care children spent as much time in the center as they did at home? An initial attempt at interpretation assumes that the psychological experiences at home have a priority: they are more salient and more affectively charged than the experiences at the center. Let us consider some speculative arguments that might account for the differential salience of caretaking experience at home versus the center. If we assume that the biological mother has been the primary caretaker at home for most of the children (our informal observations are in accord with that assumption), the question reduces to: why does the mother's psychological impact on her child seem to be greater than that of the female caretaker in the day-care environment? Part of the answer to that question may lie with the greater unpredictability of the mother that leads her to become a more salient object in the infant's world.

A conscientious and nurturant caretaker in a group setting is keenly aware of the psychological diversity among the children in the setting as well as the differences in the values between each parent and herself. As a result, she is unlikely to hold rigid standards of behavior for each child regarding talkativeness, cooperativeness, cleanliness, aggression, quality of play, or the age when particular developmental milestones should appear. She is likely to be more relaxed about these standards than the parents because she is less profoundly identified with the children in her care. It is neither a source of deep pleasure if one of her children is slightly precocious in learning to drink from a cup nor a source of anxiety if a motorically retarded child spills his milk every day. This tolerant attitude toward diversity in growth patterns leads the caretaker to give each child considerable license to behave in accord with his temperamental disposition and relative level of maturity. As a result, with the exception of extremely destructive or regressed children, the caretaker does not impose constraints on the children when they seem occupied and happy. As a result the average child does not generate serious uncertainties about the caretaker's actions when he is exploring his environment.

By contrast, the typical mother is identified and emotionally involved with her young child. She has a set of discrete standards for his behavior, and she vigilantly watches for deviations from those standards. One mother may believe that any defiance of her requests is a sign of future rebelliousness, and she quickly and firmly reacts to it with disapproval or punishment. Most mothers hold standards for cleanliness, potentially dangerous acts, aggression, talkativeness, time of walking, talking, and other developmental milestones. The mother diagnoses deviations between her child's developing profile and her idealized standards, and when those deviations are too large, she intrudes into the child's life space and attempts to shape his behavior so that it is in closer conformity with her understanding of the appropriate growth curve. Each intrusion—be it punishment, praise, or command—punctuates the child's ongoing behavior and consciousness and creates a temporary node of uncertainty which alerts the child to the mother and to the action just issued.

This speculative line of argument implies that the typical mother in our sample was a more distinctive source of uncertainty for the child than the surrogate caretakers in the center. The mother was less predictable than the caretaker; she was more difficult to understand. In the language of classic psychoanalytic theory, the mother was more highly "cathected" than the caretaker. In the more modern language of information-processing theory, the mother was a more salient "event." In a special sense, a parent's behavior poses a more difficult discrimination problem for the child than does that of the caretaker. As a result, the parent is a more affectively charged object. Of course, if a caretaker behaved like our caricature of a mother (that is, she held fixed standards for the behavior of the child and intruded when the child deviated), the caretaker would also become highly salient and affectively charged. But in a typical day-care center—and certainly in our center—most caretakers did not behave in this manner.

It is interesting to note that a recent study of kibbutz-reared children, who spent over 20 hours of each day in an infant house with a metapelet, also revealed the salience of the mother over surrogate mother. The 12- to 15-month-old children were more likely to approach their mother than their metapelet when a female stranger was in the room with both caretakers, and they were less apprehensive when they were with their mother and a stranger than when they were with a metapelet and the same stranger. It is unlikely that the amount of time a child spends with a caretaker is a critical variable. Rather, the nature of the psychological interaction is essential.

We do not know if these speculations have any validity. But these data, as well as those of studies reviewed earlier, suggest that children from intact and psychologically supporting families who experience surrogate care during infancy and early childhood resemble home-reared children from their own social and ethnic group to a greater degree than they do children of other ethnic and class backgrounds who are in the same extrafamilial environment. The effects of the home appear to have a salience that is not easily altered by the group-care context. The family has a mysterious power, which is perhaps one reason why it has been the basic and most stable social unit in this and other societies for so long a time.

FIVE

A CONCEPTION of EARly adolescence

THE WESTERN mind is friendly toward the construction of discrete, abstract categories, each with its special set of defining characteristics, a prejudice best appreciated by comparing the perspective of the West with that of the classical Chinese. The latter preferred to view nature and experience as a contained and continuous whole. Day and night, to the Western eye, are two discrete entities separated by a transitional stage; to the Chinese they are part of one process, each being a diminution of the other. This conceptual posture had profound effects on the early development of physical science in each community. Western science, by celebrating atomism, made extraordinary advances in the physical theory of matter; early Chinese physics, by adhering to a philosophy of wholeness, focused on wavelike phenomena and made discoveries in fluid mechanics and sound that were in advance of the Europeans.

The particularism of the contemporary Western psychologist, perhaps an heir of atomism, leaps naturally to a view of human development as a sequence of discrete stages, each with its own unique attributes, catalyzed into manifest form by a delicate marriage of biological maturation and experience. "Now you see it, now you don't" is the metaphor for growth, and Western psychologists have provided us with a sequence of nodes called infancy, childhood, adolescence, and adulthood. Freud and Piaget invented four more exotic names to mark this journey, while Erikson expanded the list to seven by focusing on the changing profile of psychological conflicts,

From 12 to 16: Early adolescence, *Daedalus*, Fall 1971, pp. 997–1012.

Preparation of this paper was supported in part by grant HD4299, National Institute of Child Health and Human Development, U. S. Public Health Service, and a grant from the Carnegie Corporation of New York.

rather than the biological bases of sensuality or complexity of thought. Stage theorists have been enormously attractive to Western intellectuals, and Freud, Erikson, and Piaget owe their justly earned popularity to the fact that they chose to describe development in a form that the larger community was prepared, indeed, wanted to believe.

These introductory comments are not intended to negate the simple observation that behavior changes with growth, or the less obvious fact that the rapidity of many of these changes is correlated with particular periods of time. A child's stature increases most rapidly during the first three years and again at puberty, and this knowledge is a sufficient reason to call these time epochs by some name that implies stages of physical development. It is reasonable, therefore, to ask if the period between ten and fifteen years of age should be regarded as a stage of psychological development. Are the changes that occur during this five-year epoch psychologically more coherent than those that occur during the five years that precede or succeed that time? We cannot answer this question easily, for dramatically different environmental pressures operate during the successive five-year eras from kindergarten through college. We can tame the equivocation by noting that puberty, which occurs in the middle of this period for the vast majority of children all over the world, supplies a firm platform for further inquiry. This essay poses a simple question—Do the changes that occur around puberty justify the positing of a psychological stage called early adolescence?—and answers that question affirmatively.

The soundest basis for postulating a stage in psychological development occurs when biology has prepared the child for a change in cognitive structure, motive, affect, or behavior, with experience playing the role of inducer. Exquisite, time-locked mechanisms alter the individual's psychic competence so that he is able to react to events in a new way. An embryological analogy may be helpful. The concept of critical period, which was born in experimental embryology and nurtured in comparative psychology, is appropriately applied whenever there is a delimited period of time when certain events—internal or external—have formative effects on a developing physiological system, organ, or tissue. The biologists conceptualize this process in terms of an inherent biological competence potentiated by external forces. To illustrate, at a particular time in development certain ectodermal cells in the salamander acquire the potentiality to become the lens of the eye, if and only if certain inductive endodermal tissue is present in the vicinity to alter surface properties of cells and allow that competence to become manifest.[1] The lens will not develop if the inducing tissues and their appropriate chemical substances are introduced before the competence is acquired or after it has been lost. It is possible that biological developments of which we are unaware prepare the child for major psychological changes in early adolescence, if and only if the proper inducing experiences occur. If they occur too early or too late, the psychological structures may be aberrant.

How shall this new psychological competence be characterized? Although man has been described as a sensory surface, a collection of responses, a reservoir of affect, or a structure of beliefs, we shall focus on the latter characterization because cognitive functions seem to be central to the changes that occur at puberty.

The essence of the argument is that the 12-year-old has acquired a new cognitive competence—the disposition to examine the logic and consistency of his existing beliefs. The emergence of this competence, which may be dependent on biological changes in the central nervous system, is catalyzed by experiences that confront the adolescent with phenomena and attitudes that are not easily interpreted with his existing ideology. These intrusions nudge the preadolescent to begin an analytic reexamination of his knowledge.

Biological puberty is the only universal source of conflict-inducing information, and it should be appreciated that cultures differ in how many additional inductive catalysts they provide. Since we have insufficient information about the detailed conflicts posed by other cultures, I shall restrict most of the discussion to the American community and consider those experiences that might induce cognitive conflict in American 14-year-olds. It seems reasonable to suggest that these experiences are intimately yoked to family, school, religion, and sexuality.

The Nature of the New Cognitive Competence

During the few years prior to puberty the child is gradually acquiring several new and profound intellective capacities. First, he gains an ease in dealing with hypothetical premises that may violate reality. The 12-year-old will accept and think about the following problem: "All three-legged snakes are purple, I am hiding a three-legged snake, guess its color?"

The seven-year-old is confused by the fact that the initial premises violate his notion of what is real, and he will not cooperate. The younger child, unlike the adolescent, does not appreciate the discontinuity between the self-contained information in a hypothetical problem and the egocentric information he carries with him for more practical challenges. Hence if an adolescent is asked, "There are three schools, Roosevelt, Kennedy, and Lincoln schools, and three girls, Mary, Sue, and Jane, who go to different schools:

Mary goes to the Roosevelt school, Jane to the Kennedy school, where does Sue go?" he quickly answers, "Lincoln." The seven-year-old may excitedly reply, "Sue goes to the Roosevelt school because my sister has a friend called Sue and that's the school she goes to."

To appreciate that problems can be self-contained entities solved by special rules is a magnificent accomplishment that is not usually attained until early adolescence.

The adolescent is more consistently able to induce rules from events with multiple attributes. Specifically, he is capable of inferring conjunctive and disjunctive concepts from appropriate data. An aunt is both a female and a blood relative; a mammal is an animal who nurses its young. A game is an activity that can be played either alone or with others; a strike is either swinging at a ball and missing it, or failing to swing at a ball thrown in the appropriate area. The adolescent can deal with multiple attributes simultaneously and is not limited to a one-at-a-time analysis. This ability allows the adolescent to think about events as arrangements of multiple dimensions, and to appreciate that an experience is often dependent on events not in the immediate field. He knows that his mother's anger can be provoked by any one of several violations, and realizes that her anger at dinner might be a product of yesterday's report card.

The adolescent can assume a relativistic view and is not troubled by the fact that the acceptability of a lie depends on both the situation and the intentions of the actor. He can excuse a hostile greeting from a friend if he believes the original incentive for the coolness occurred hours earlier in another context. The younger child is more absolute and mechanistic in his inferences. A lie is always bad; a hostile attack is seen as a direct and immediate result of the child's action or existence.

Of special relevance for this essay is the fact that the adolescent is disposed to examine his beliefs in sets, and to search for inconsistencies among them and between the beliefs and related actions. This inclination depends partly on the previous abilities, because critical examination of the logic of a set of related beliefs requires the capacity to consider multiple rules simultaneously. Thus, the 14-year-old broods about the inconsistency among the following three propositions:

1. God loves man.
2. The world contains many unhappy people.
3. If God loved man, he would not make so many people unhappy.

The adolescent is troubled by the incompatibility that is immediately sensed when he examines these statements together. He notes the contradiction and has at least four choices. He can deny the second premise that man is ever unhappy; this is unlikely for its factual basis is too overwhelming. He can deny that God loves man; this is avoided for love of man is one of the definitional qualities of God. He can assume that the unhappiness serves an ulterior purpose God has for man; this possibility is sometimes chosen. Finally, he can deny the hypothesis of God.

The last alternative, which has become the popular form of the resolution in Western society, has profound consequences. This conclusion is a denial of a belief that has been regarded as true for many years and invites the implication that if this statement is not tenable, then all other beliefs held at the moment are also in jeopardy. Suddenly, what was regarded as permanently valid has become tentative.

A 14-year-old girl who was asked how her present beliefs differed from those she held several years ago replied, "I had a whole philosophy of how the world worked. I was very religious and I believed that there was unity and harmony and everything had its proper place. I used to imagine rocks in the right places on the right beaches. It was all very neat and God ordained it all, and I made up my own religion, but now it seems absolutely ridiculous."

Consider another inconsistency many adolescents discover and try to resolve.

1. Parents are omnipotent and omniscient.

2. My parent has lost a job, or failed to understand me, or behaved irrationally—or any other liability the reader cares to select.

3. If my parents were omniscient, they would not be tainted with failure and vulnerability.

The statements are examined together and the inconsistency noted. As with the first example, the adolescent can deny the truth of the second premise, but it demands too severe a straining of objectivity and is not usually implemented. The adolescent can invent a statement about parental motivation and excuse the show of incompetence on the basis of willingness, rather than capacity. This alternative is infrequently chosen because its acceptance elicits another troubling notion, for it implies that the parent does not care about the emotional consequences of his motivation for the affect life of the family. Hence, the child is tempted to deny the original hypothesis of parental omniscience. As with the denial of God, the fall of this belief weakens all the others.

A third set of propositions placed under analytic scrutiny involves sexuality:

1. Sexual activity—self-administered or heterosexually experienced—is bad.

2. Sexuality provides pleasure.

3. If sex is pleasant, it should not be bad.

We shall forgo the obvious analysis of these propositions and simply note that again the most likely conclusion is that the first assumption is not tenable. The increased masturbation at puberty forces the child to deal with the fact that he is violating, in private, a strong social prohibition. However, the consistent sensory pleasure cannot be denied, and this silent violation has to be rationalized. As that rationalization is accomplished, the child is tempted to question a great many other standards, and he begins to examine all prohibitions with the same skepticism.

Although the known physiological changes at puberty are not necessary antecedents to the increased sexuality, it is likely that they contribute to the ascendancy of sexual thoughts, feelings, and actions. The adolescent must deal with the temptations of masturbation, petting, intercourse, and homosexuality. The statistics unambiguously indicate that the frequent sexual behavior of the 17-year-old is not yet manifest in the 11-year-old, who may be informed but not yet active. One reason is that he is afraid; afraid of incompetence, parental discovery, and guilt. It is also likely that the sheer intensity of passion that is so urgent in the older adolescent is attenuated at this earlier age. The tension that is so overpowering in a 17-year-old is more like a tickle at 11 and, hence, more easily put aside. However, the 11-year-old knows that his time is coming and he must prepare for it.

These major ideological conflicts pivot on the fact that old assumptions are challenged by new perceptions, and the resulting incompatibility is resolved by delegitimizing the earlier assumption. The inducing perceptions include the acknowledgment of unhappy people, agnostic peers, and the pleasures of sexuality. The sequellae are a questioning of old beliefs and a search for a new set of premises. Each culture presents its children with a different set of beliefs to examine. In our society, standards surrounding family, religion, sexuality, drugs, and school are among the major ideological dragons to be tamed. Partial support for these ideas comes from interviews suggesting that American adolescents begin to wonder about the legitimacy of their belief systems, where, prior to this time, inconsistent propositions were not examined as a structure. Sometimes this analysis leaves the adolescent temporarily without a commitment to any belief. The author asked a 15-year-old about the beliefs she was most certain of: "None really. I just take in things and analyze them. Maybe it will change my opinion and maybe it won't. It depends, but I'm not really stuck to anything."

This open wondering produces a state of uncertainty and a need to resolve it. A fundamental principle of human psychological functioning states that child and adult are alerted by events and thoughts inconsistent with their prior understanding. These events provoke the mind to resolve the uncertainty, and, through that work, premises are changed. A 14-year-old said, "I think religious attitudes change if you go to Sunday school. At that time you just accept it, but when you become older and start thinking about it and try to analyze it, that is, whether there really is a God, then it depends on what your religious beliefs are. I've asked myself this over and over again. I just started thinking about it at that time and I just can't get it off my mind; whether there really is a God. I ask myself questions: Is there a God and I have arguments inside myself. How there might not be, how there might be."

Many of the traditional solutions used to deal with uncertainty have lost their potency because a large portion of the population, including the child's friends, have stopped believing in the effectiveness of these slogans. Young people are confronted with the discrepant experience of knowing large numbers of adults and adolescents to whom they feel similar, but with whom they do not share beliefs about the rituals that heal. This inconsistency weakens the effectiveness of any ideology. As a result, many high school students are caught in a strangling web of apathy. They are confronted with all the major sources of uncertainty—a future that cannot be predicted, bizarre headlines, and persistent doubting of the simple truths their parents made them recite. But they have no effective set of ideas or behaviors to deal with these puzzles.

As hinted earlier, puberty *qua* puberty makes an important contribution to this process. The child's body changes visibly, and there is an accompanying alteration in perceived feeling-tone. The psychological acccompaniments to this change include the rush of new thoughts, their evaluation, and their arrangement in a fresh structure. The adolescent dimly recognizes that he is capable of fertility and must decide how to handle this power, but many are unclear as to how conception occurs. One 13-year-old said, "Up until I was about ten years of age I was told that a seed produced the baby. So we go to this Chinese restaurant and they serve a little piece of candy with seeds all over it, so I said 'Hey, mom, I'm not going to eat this cause I don't want to have a baby.' "

Puberty is also interpreted as a signal that childhood is over, and a reminder that regressive actions and beliefs should be replaced, transformed, or eliminated. This character renovation requires the adolescent to generate a cognitive structure as sturdy as the one being replaced.

A 15-year-old girl was asked to recall her thoughts following her first menstrual period: "It was like growing up overnight. I felt that I was not a little kid anymore. I couldn't ride my bicycle anymore; really, I'm not kidding you."

INTERVIEWER: "Were you happy?"
GIRL: "No, but I just thought I was above riding a bicycle or playing with dolls. I thought I was cool."
INTERVIEWER: "Did you feel that you had to act more grown-up?"
GIRL: "Yes, that's why I wouldn't ride a bicycle or play with dolls."

A second 15-year-old girl noted, "Friends became more important than toys. You had to have a lot of friends, that was more important than anything. And toys were a thing of the past. My mother would say, 'Are you going out to play now?' and I'd say, 'No, I don't play.' I went around to a lot of women and I asked them what it was like to have children. I didn't want to grow up."

INTERVIEWER: "Was there something apprehensive about it, something you didn't like about this new role?"
GIRL: "I didn't like it. I remember thinking I'd really hate to be an adult and I started staying in on Saturdays with my mother instead of going out. I didn't want to have to think for myself."

A third 15-year-old agreed. "I started thinking that I couldn't ride my bike and couldn't do things that made me look like a baby. I used to think, when are you going to start getting more attention from people. After a few years, I felt that people were treating me like I was older and in a different way from when I was younger. When I went to my grandmother's when I was little, I used to get a glass of milk or tonic, you know, but after I was a certain age I started getting a cup of tea or coffee."

The adolescent knows he must make his own decisions but must feel free enough to ask adults for advice. He orients toward extrafamilial adults and tries on, with more seriousness than earlier, the beliefs and posturing of teachers and cultural heroes. Closer examination of adult characteristics leads to new insights that have to be assimilated. He notes defect and taint in adults, and he must find a rule that permits him to accept this disappointment, while not turning complete skeptic. He initiates heterosexual relationships and must rationalize both his exploitative urges toward others, as well as potential or actual rejection by the beloved other. He must preserve the self's integrity in the face of massive, cognitive taunts.

There are also special institutional changes that occur during early adolescence, especially in Western culture, that are influential. In most communities in the United States the child between 12 and 15 enters junior high or high school. There are two significant consequences of this structural change. First, unlike the elementary school, the junior high and high school contain many individuals who hold different beliefs. The beliefs concern drugs, sex, authority, the value of study, and attitudes toward parents. Each ideological position has many advocates. The sources of these new views cannot easily be discredited, and the adolescent must deal with the dissonance.

Second, many schools begin tracking at this age. This hard event forces each student to scrutinize his intellectual profile in some detail. Tracking often frightens those in the top track, many of whom do not believe they are talented enough to warrant the challenging assignment. It saddens and angers those in the lower track, who resent the invidious categorization and are forced to invent a rationalization against the importance of academic accomplishment. Once that rationalization crystallizes, it becomes incredibly resistant to change.

American adolescents must create a rationale for school attendance and, what is more difficult, continued effort. Earlier generations were given some incentives to promote involvement in the mission of the school. They were told that education prepared them for a vocation, status, and financial security. But as disbelief with this simple summary of life became public, the power of these incentives became eroded, and the adolescent found it increasingly difficult to accept the dissonance created by the school's arbitrary, monotonous, and often unworkable assignments. There is no reason for a student to work for A's in his courses if he has decided to ignore college and anticipates feeling no pain upon a rejected application. If prestige is empty and elitism wicked, it is easy to forget about grades, for students of every age view the grade as a good-conduct medal to be used in parades or to gain entry into hallowed halls, rather than as a confidential report on the state of their expertise. During the late 1960's many youth found it difficult to rationalize working for grades. The adult community sensed the danger and reacted with an impulsive diagnosis that the school organization was defective and faculty incompetent. "Change the schools" was the cry, and parents and teachers rushed around in a frenzy, opening up classrooms, knocking down walls, organizing different kinds of outings, or creating nonschools under a variety of exotic names. The conflict is neatly set down:

1. The child must be happy while he is learning the intellectual foundation of his culture.

2. Children are not happy in school.

3. Therefore, the school must be doing something wrong.

Rather than examine the first permise, we focus on the conclusion. The

12-year-old is willing to believe that learning is valuable and that certain skills which seem irrelevant now are probably necessary for his role as adult. He needs a more persuasive adult community that believes what it professes, not a different place to learn.

The adolescent needs a firmer set of motivational supports that will allow him to work at school requirements while he is trying to fit the catechism of academic competence into the larger structure we call the self. Insufficient motivation has always been, and will always be, the primary problem in junior high and high school, and the reasons are not complicated. Man's major motives exist in a hierarchical structure, much like the dominance hierarchy of a group of baboons. One baboon, or a small group, is temporarily dominant until displaced. So too with motives. Although resolution of uncertainty, hostility, sexuality, and mastery are always potentially capable of seizing the motivational reins for a part of the day, the more specific goals that serve these general intentions change dramatically with development. The two-year-old is uncertain about the actions that will be punished or praised by his parents, and he "tests the limits" to gain this information. The 13-year-old has solved that problem, but is unsure about his or her sexual attractiveness and, like the two-year-old, ferrets out those situations that will provide answers to the question of sexual adequacy.

The preoccupying motives for most American adolescents revolve around resolving uncertainty over sexual adequacy, interpersonal power, autonomy of belief and action, and acceptability to peers. The urgency of these questions dominates the weaker desire to acquire competence at mathematics, history, or English composition. Hence the school halls exude combinations of apathy and hostility. This mood is not a recent phenomenon. It has always been that way and will continue to be until we are able to help the 13-year-old find solutions to the four more pressing desires. There are some students, about 10 to 20 percent of a typical classroom, who appear motivated, and the constancy of that proportion seduces many citizens into believing, "If some, why not all?" There is some basis for this optimistic mood of reform. A small group of children in every classroom has unusually strong affective relations with their parents, relations that combine the desire to please them with an intense identification with their values and roles. If these children happen to have parents whose lives and pattern of encouragement center on academic competence, motivation for mastery of school content is capable of competing with the motives listed earlier. But this contest among motives will not be acutalized if the child has not established a belief in eventual success. It is this issue that weakens the power of the position that argues that all children can love school.

Man has two kinds of characteristics—a small set that are defined absolutely (hair and skin color, angle of teeth, and presence and thickness of bodily hair), and a much larger set of evaluative attributes that can only be defined in relation to a reference group. This set includes adjectives like intelligent, wise, athletic, brave, pretty, confident, independent, responsible, and sociable. Assignment to positions on these dimensions, by adult or child, requires the slippery judgment of comparison. Regardless of the absolute ability of the top six students in any classroom, the child in rank six who perceives that there are five who are more talented than he will begin to doubt his ability either to perform with excellence or to challenge the expertise of the first five. As a result his motivation for geometry may descend in the hierarchy. It is likely that the adolescent only uses five categories to name levels of talent—the smartest, the very bright ones, those above average, those below average, and the dumb ones. Hence the top 25 to 30 percent of any classroom has the easiest time maintaining motivation over the course of the school year, for they and their friends have come to an agreement about who has a better than average probability of success. The less fortunate two-thirds withdraw effort in proportion to their anticipation of less than average performance. As long as educators and children are forced to evaluate talent relativistically, most adolescents will require prompting to complete their assignments. The rank-order structure of the school demands this psychodynamic result. There are mild antidotes to apply. The school can try to generate absolute standards of performance and ability. More realistically, it can promote more pluralism in the talents it rewards and celebrate self-improvement as enthusiastically as it credits rises in the rank order. Teachers should defuse the salience of interstudent comparisons and acknowledge the significance of intrapersonal change. We should not be pollyannaish about the difficulty of averting the youth's gaze from his neighbor, but the school can do more to underplay the comparative philosophy of pupil evaluation which must, of necessity, leave two-thirds of the class with a barrier to serious involvement in the mission of the school.

There are a few special motivational conflicts, aside from expectancy of success, that affect some students. A few have decided that any semblance of power or status among their peers is corrupting of character. Since excellence in school often brings prestige, these adolescents avoid these tainted roles by restraining effort. Still others view passive acquiescence to adult authority as defiling, and view the teacher's assignments as commands rather than as suggestions for self-actualization. The third group views selected school subjects as inconsistent with sex-role integrity. The 12-year-old boy who is trying to quiet doubts over the solidity of his maleness may view

French as feminizing. The plain girl who questions her attractiveness to boys may view the masculine halo of geometry as too much of a threat to the primary goal she is seeking.

In all three cases the obstacle to school motivation derives from a personal interpretation of the academic assignment that in turn is inconsistent with a motive that, at the time, dominates the hierarchy.

Although America's natural preference for idealistic solutions nudges us to assume that apathy is not a necessary ingredient in junior high school, history dictates a more skeptical conclusion. In 1970 most of the academically apathetic children in Boston were black; a century earlier they were Irish Catholic. The reasons are the same in both cases, although the actors have changed.

The schools have been given the impossible responsibility of proselytizing a faith that does not have intuitive validity for many adolescents. Since both parents and school faculty have been unsuccessful, they are throwing the responsibility of the persuasion back upon the child, hoping he will solve for himself the problem adults have never been able to resolve. We want the young adolescent to win the battle that we lost. The adult generation has lost faith in learning, but hopes that if the child can gain it, parents will have gained salvation for themselves. This dynamic is not unlike our vicarious identification with the youth's permissive attitude toward drugs, work, and sex. Some adults use youth for their salvation; that exploitation is selfish and dangerous.

If adolescents had another goal to replace school there would be less alarm, for there would be no apathy. But they do not; they are searching for a substitute. Several candidates are gaining popularity on high school campuses. The wish to test the depth and strength of one's emotional capacity has become one alternative. The availability of drugs has made this game exciting and easy to enter. Many adolescents ask themselves a question early generations never thought of: "How much pounding can my emotional self accept and assimilate?" The motive to master this challenge is likely to expend itself in a short while, for the total intensity and variety of experience is soon exhausted and the answer to the original question clear. The adolescent will have learned how tough or fragile his inner self really is. A second goal is the search for honesty and intimacy in human encounter. Any ritual that carries the flimsiest decoration of artificiality is shunned, for it prevents contact and dehumanizes by forcing unnatural roles on unwilling actors who do not like the game of pretend. This code is more viable, for it is more profoundly human. Since it is, in the extreme, unattainable, it is forever laced with some uncertainty and, therefore, satisfies the main requirement for permanence. It is, fortunately, a more healing catechism than the individualistic competitiveness that captured the energy of earlier adolescent generations. If our community can nurture this freshly born objective, our several million adolescents may be able to find a more comfortable and involving morality that will be toxic to the boredom and hostility being carried into and throughout our institutional structures.

The early adolescent wants many friends, for he needs peers to help him sculpt his beliefs, verify his new conclusions, test his new attitudes against an alien set in order to evaluate their hardiness, and obtain support for his new set of fragile assumptions. However, he still needs his family, for it has several important psychological functions, even though the helplessness of childhood is past. The family provides the child with a set of arbitrary standards that give structure to his motives and actions. They provide models for identification which, if exploited, help establish a self-concept. The family provides the first set of adults who communicate their estimation of the child's worth. And many preadolescents still require this evaluation, because youth continue to award the family a special wisdom and legitimacy. The family's respect for his beliefs, taste in music, dress, or talk is reassuring, for it persuades him that he is able to make reasonable decisions. One 15-year-old said succinctly, "I hardly ever see my mother because she has demanding jobs. She goes out at night. But I think that makes her even more important to me, for when she is there, it is a good thing; for she tells me I am right and that she's proud of me."

Adolescents of all societies must build a sense of self, and the ingredients used in this construction vary with time and community. Each group announces the rules by which the adolescent infers the rate at which he is progressing toward maturity. In many cultures, acceptance of the simple, traditional roles of wife, mother, father, and husband are the only requirements. Our own community has placed a special obstacle in the path of the adolescent, for it celebrates the primacy of an autonomous belief system— possession of a separate and distinct set of values—as a necessary prerequisite for a well-delineated identity. Since the ten-year-old realizes that his values are borrowed from his parents, he experiences a deep conflict between what he must attain and his current state. He strives to make alterations in his beliefs in order to persuade himself that the resulting arrangement is his creation, and not a "warmed-over" catechism taken from his family.

One 14-year-old girl said, "Before I didn't know what I was doing, and now I feel that what I am doing is my own." She continued, "I think many adolescents are uncertain about their beliefs. They are preoccupied because they don't have their own individualism and they don't have their own beliefs yet. Their minds, their thoughts, are not concrete, they are just a lot of different thoughts." A 13-year-old boy added, "You begin to question what your parents have been influencing you to believe. Up to a certain time you are strictly going by your parent's ideals and until you are influenced by something else that's what you've got to go by. That's why junior high school is so important because it helps to determine what's going to influence you."

The ideational rebellion that has become definitional of adolescence does not primarily serve hostility, but, rather, the more pressing need to persuade the self that its mosaic of wishes, values, and behaviors derives from a personally constructed ideology. If "what one believes" were less central to the identity of the American adult than it is at the present time, the clash of values between child and parent might not occur with such ferocity.

Summary

We have argued that maturational developments, in a still not completely understood way, prepare the mind of a 12-year-old to examine sets of propositions for logical consistency. This competence, when applied to his own premises, can produce new assumptions if it is catalyzed by encounter with experiences that jolt the mind into using this capacity. Puberty is one such inducing event in all cultures. Western society adds local phenomena surrounding school, drugs, sexuality, authority, and family, each of which generates uncertainty that the child must resolve. In so doing, he creates new beliefs. The specific form of the conflict and its resolution depend on the belief clash that initally generated the uncertainty, as well as the community in which the child lives. Contemporary, middle-class, American 15-year-olds are waging war against feelings of isolation, commitment to action and belief, loyalty to others, and capacity for love. Earlier generations grappled with the themes of social status, financial security, and petting. It is not clear what issues future generations will engage and subdue. It is usually the case that each era is marked by one or two social problems of enormous priority that give substantive direction to the brooding. Racial strife, density of population, and, most important, lack of a central transcendental ideology continue to loom as the potential catastrophes of the future. These themes will probably shape the form of the incompatible propositions that future adolescents will attempt to understand and comprise the heart of the essay on adolescence another psychologist will write in 1990.

SIX

psychology of
sex diffeRENCES

Introduction

$\mathbf{A}$N ANALYSIS of the psychology of sex differences proceeds from two simple facts. The first is that in every known society males and females differ, not only in genes, physiology, and growth patterns but also in profile of behaviors and organization of beliefs. The second, which is less well documented, is that boys and girls are treated differently from infancy through adulthood. This information suggests two questions.

The first of these can be disposed of quickly, for it asks whether biological differences between the sexes necessarily imply different roles in Western society. On the basis of current knowledge, there is no good reason for arguing that the anatomical and physiological differences between human males and females, which are summarized in other chapters, place serious constraints on the successful assumption of the total variety of vocational and social roles available in our society. Even if we acknowledge that a small proportion of vocations—probably less than 1 percent—are biologically better suited to one sex (a male hod carrier is more efficient because of his heavier musculature), most jobs in Western society probably can be filled satisfactorily by adults of either sex. Hence, the ideas presented in this chapter do not have strong sociopolitical implications. Instead, the following discussion is purely an intellectual adventure.

The second, and more profound, question inquires into the nature of

Adapted from The psychology of sex differences in *Human Sexuality in Four Perspectives*, ed. F. A. Beach (Baltimore: The Johns Hopkins University Press, 1976), pp. 87–14.

Preparation of this chapter was supported in part by research grant HD4299 from NICHD, United States Public Health Service, and a grant from the Carnegie Corporation of New York.

the interaction of biology and experience that will explain the differential psychology which has characterized men and women throughout history, and continues to do so across the contemporary cultures of the world. It is *interaction,* rather than the relative contribution of biology or experience, which is the primary issue. An analogy to the weather may be heuristic. Meteorologists want to understand how temperature and humidity interact to produce snow. They do not conceptualize their task as one in which they must determine the degree to which snow is produced by a cold temperature or high humidity. Analogously, psychological differences between the sexes are products of an intimate interaction of life events and physiology. This chapter summarizes current progress toward understanding that enigmatic process. As one tries to weave the pattern of facts into a coherent theme, it is important to remember that interpretation of the significance of a particular pattern of behavior or a belief in one sex is completely dependent on the corresponding value for the other sex. For example, American men, in general, are sexually more aggressive than American women. At the same time, American women are more aggresive sexually than Japanese or Mexican women. Thus, when we speak of sex differences in aggression, dominance, sexuality, passivity, or dependence, we are not talking about absolute values or intensities. We are referring to the differences in that dimension for males and females in a particular culture.

Psychological Differences between the Sexes

PATTERNS OF INTERPERSONAL BEHAVIOR

In most cultures of the world, boys and men are more aggressive, engage in more dominant and power-maintaining actions, are less nurturant, and are more active initiators of sexual contact than are girls and women in the same society. Of course, there are exceptions at the individual and societal levels, but in general it remains true that females are more cooperative, more passive, socially more responsible, and more conforming to the rules of the group than are males.

A recent study of children in six widely different societies illustrates the cross-cultural generality of these statements. Children between three and eleven years of age were observed in and around their homes in one of the following six settings: (1) a small village in northeastern Okinawa, (2) a village of 5,000 in northcentral India, (3) a town in Oaxaca, Mexico, (4) hamlets in northern Luzon in the Philippines, (5) villages on the rolling hills of the western provinces of Kenya, and (6) a small town in New England. In five of the six cultures, girls helped adults and other children more often than did boys, and in all six groups girls offered psychological support more frequently than did boys. By contrast, the boys, in the majority of cultural settings, more often sought attention from adults and attempted to dominate other children (Whiting and Whiting 1975).

Sex differences in cooperation and aggression are evident in very young children. In one study, two-year-olds who were strangers to each other were brought, in same sex pairs, to a room in an apartment located in the building complex where the children resided. After both children had become adapted to the setting an attractive toy was placed between them, and the observer withdrew to see what would happen. Girls were much more trusting of each other than boys. A girl without the toy would approach her temporary playmate, and the latter usually permitted the first child to play cooperatively. The first girl reacted as if she expected that the one who possessed the prize would be gracious.

Boys were more suspicious and sometimes more aggressive. Typically, one boy would pick up the toy, while the other would stare at his face and inspect his posture, as if trying to determine if he would be permitted cooperative access to the toy. If the second boy attempted to play with the object, a fight occasionally erupted (Shapiro 1969). Such mutual suspicion and easy disposition to aggression in the service of protecting possessions occurred less frequently among the girls.

Such differences among children of varied ages and varied residential settings resemble the behavior of nonhuman primates. Female baboons, chimpanzees, and langurs are more likely to groom other members of the species; males are more likely to challenge other males in attempts to gain a higher position in the dominance hierarchy (Crook 1970; Devore & Hall 1965; Poirier 1970). Even among some species of birds, the male is less tolerant of incursions into his behavioral space, for a male chaffinch will not tolerate another male to come within 25 centimeters of his location, while a female will tolerate an approach as close as 7 centimeters (Marler 1956).

DREAMS, BELIEFS, AND ATTITUDES

The dreams of males and females vary in ways that are consonant with the differences in behavior (Brenneis 1970). The dreams of American college women, as contrasted with those of men, contain more familiar settings and people, more parent figures, and are generally more pleasant. The dreams of men contain more action, are less realistic, often bordering on the improbable, and portray the hero as active rather than passive. The following dream of a college-educated, politically liberal woman who favors egalitarianism among the sexes is a good example of dreams of adult women in our society (Auchincloss 1971), for it captures the passive orientation still present in the psychological posture of women vis-à-vis men.

> I and several other people were taking a walk through a city which was in Europe. We passed a strange antique shop, a restaurant with sheep in the window. Finally, we started up a long passage in the rocks and near a wall by the sea which became vertical and narrow and had to be climbed by hauling oneself up small, metal rings. *The men were ahead—out of sight—when I got to the top there was a sheer drop into the sea around three-fourths of the exit. The men were there to help, but there was nothing too secure to hold on to in making the last move to safety. I am terrified of heights. I felt I couldn't do it. I forced myself to wake up.* [Italics supplied.]

Sex differences in dream themes are in accord with the stereotypes of Western men and women and strengthen the assumption that behavioral differences noted in the laboratory or in the natural environment are not a thin or misleading veneer but a reflection of profound psychological factors. The presence of more familiar people and scenes in women's dreams is usually interpreted to mean greater fear of the strange.

Female primates of some nonhuman species tend to be more fearful and less adventuresome than males. For example, in the langur of South India, females are more reluctant than males to leave familiar surroundings (Poirier 1970); and infant female rhesus monkeys are less likely to leave the safety of proximity to their mothers than males (Jensen, Bobbitt, and Gordon 1967).

There are more subtle sex differences among children that may be limited to only a few cultures. For example, both in the United States and among rural Guatemalan Indian children there is a higher positive correlation for girls than for boys between the family's social class and the child's IQ. Similarly, duration of attention to interesting pictures—which is an index of cognitive development among one- and two-year-old children—is more closely related to the family's social class for girls than for boys (Kagan 1971). Finally, quality or level of intellectual performance is more stable across time for girls than for boys. For example, if one-year-old boys and girls are given a test for measuring IQ in infants, the correlation with a second intelligence test given when the same children have reached school age will be much higher for girls than for boys. This finding is consonant with the girls' more impressive continuity for physical growth.

The Basis for Sex Differences

How can we explain these provocative observations? Most developmental and social psychologists assume that the behavioral differences between men and women are largely the result of different standards surrounding the socially approved psychological profile for their sex. A person's belief about the culturally appropriate response for his sex is called the *sex-role standard,* and it defines the physical attributes, overt behaviors, and attitudes most appropriate for each sex. The sex-role standards are conveyed to the child through a process called *sex typing.*

A standard is a cognitive belief about the appropriateness of a characteristic, whether it be an attitude, an emotion, or an overt action. Children and adults try to maintain continued congruence between what they do and think, and what they believe is correct. They renounce and avoid actions and attitudes incompatible with the standard for their sex and strive to adopt and maintain those that are compatible.

The discrimination of people into distinct conceptual categories based on sex is facilitated by the presence of a variety of clearly discriminable cues, including dress, genital anatomy, bodily form and proportion, distribution of hair, depth of voice, posture during urination, and interactive style with other people. Observation of other individuals, complemented by patterns of reward and punishment, give the child the information he requires to construct the symbolic dimensions that define the sex roles.

Among American children, boys regard height, large muscle mass, and facial and bodily hair as desirable physical characteristics, whereas girls wish to be less muscular, smaller, and pretty. Physical aggression and dominance over others have been, and continue to be, primary sex-typed behaviors. This standard requires inhibition of extreme forms of physical and verbal aggression among girls and women but grants boys and men license and, occasionally, encouragement to strike another when attacked, threatened, or dominated. The same standard influences the fantasies of children as well as the child's perception of adults.

Young boys and girls agree that the father is more aggressive, punitive, and dangerous than the mother; and this characterization of the parents is maintained, even when aggressive and nonaggressive animals are used symbolically to represent the sexes. If a six-year-old is shown pictures of a rabbit and a tiger, he will say that the tiger is more like his father, the rabbit more like his mother (Kagan, Hosken, and Watson 1961). Nurturance, dependency, conformity, and passivity are essential elements of the female sex-role standard in many societies, and females are allowed more freedom than boys and men to express these behaviors.

Mexican society is even more extreme than our own. Octavio Paz describes his conception of women in contemporary Mexico:

> The Mexican woman, quite simply, has no will of her own. Her body is asleep and only comes really alive when someone awakens her. She is an answer rather than

a question, a vibrant and easily worked material that is shaped by the imagination and sensuality of the male. In other countries, women are active, attempting to attract men through the agility of their minds or the seductivity of their bodies, but the Mexican woman has a sort of hieratic calm, a tranquillity made up of both hope and contempt. . . . Instincts themselves are not dangerous; the danger lies in any personal, individual expression of them. And this brings us back to the idea of passivity: woman is never herself, whether lying stretched out or standing up straight, whether naked or fully clothed. She is an undifferentiated manifestation of life, a channel for the universal appetite. In this sense she has no desires of her own. (p. 37)

As the foregoing quotation implies, attitudes and beliefs are part of the sex-role standard. The feminine standard in our culture announces that a woman should be able to elicit sexual arousal in the male and to gratify him. The desire to be a wife and mother, and the correlated desires to give nurturance to children, affection to a love object, and the capacity for emotions, have been more clearly feminine than masculine. Bardwick (1970) has described the difference in the following words: "Whereas masculinity is at least partially defined by success in marketplace achievements, femininity is largely defined by success in establishing and maintaining love relationships and by maternity. A woman's attractiveness is clearly instrumental in attracting men and her self-evaluation as a woman will largely depend on her sexual and maternal success (p. 3)."

Bardwick suggests that women perceive the world in interpersonal terms and regard themselves positively to the degree that they are esteemed by those they love. Hence, women seem, at present, to be more dependent than men upon the affectionate reaction of their lovers, husbands, and children.

The primary covert attributes in the sex-role standards for men include a pragmatic attitude, sexual prowess and capacity, and the ability to control expression of strong emotions that signify weakness, especially fear, sorrow, and loneliness. Whether it be ancient Mesopotamia and Sumeria (Kirk 1970), or contemporary Mexico, "manliness is judged according to one's invulnerability to enemy arms or the impacts of the outside world" (Paz 1961, p. 31).

GROUP DIFFERENCES IN POLARIZATION OF THE SEXES

Since male dominance and female passivity are central sex-role standards in many societies, it is reasonable to expect that these polarized attitudes might influence other psychological processes, besides preferred posture vis-à-vis other individuals. For example, a person who believed it was improper to be assertive, inquiring, or exploring might perform poorly on difficult intellectual tasks because of an ingrained passive attitude which could lead to inhibition of persistent effort and weakening of any tendency to search for novel solution strategies. Passivity breeds caution, inhibition, and defensiveness—attitudes that constrain creative intellectual work. Hence, we would expect that the magnitude of sex differences on tests requiring intelectual analysis should covary with the degree to which the culture imposes a sharp psychological distinction between the sexes.

The Temne of Sierra Leone rigidly promote a passive attitude among the females, and in that society boys and men perform better than girls and women on tests of spatial reasoning. Among the Eskimo, however, who do not enforce feminine passivity as severely as the Temne, there are no sex differences in performance on the same tests (Berry 1966).

Similarly, Mexican society stresses passivity as an essential feminine trait much more emphatically than American society, and sex differences in performance on tests of arithmetic and spatial ability are more striking in children living in Mexico City than in those living in Austin, Texas (Díaz-Guerrero 1967).

Comparable differences exist in our own culture. Children of working-class parents are exposed to more polarized attitudes toward sex-role standards than are middle-class children, and sex differences in behavior and intellectual performance are greater for working-class boys and girls than for those reared by middle-class parents. In general, the higher the educational level of a girl's family, the greater her involvement in what our culture regards as "masculine activities."

This liberation of the middle-class female from the dominant sex-role standard of the culture affects the quality of her sexuality, for it is claimed that the women who have attended graduate school "tend to be the most successful sexually—at least if one is willing to accept as a measure of success the relatively crude indicator of the proportion of sexual acts that culminate in orgasm. . . . In a society which still strongly encourages women to form primary allegiances to roles as wives and mothers the decision to go on to graduate school represents something of a deviant adaptation. This adaptation represents, in turn, a failure or alienation from modal female socialization pressures" (Simon and Gagnon 1969, p. 747).

Because the early acquisition and continued operation of sex-role standards are the primary mechanisms responsible for differences in the behavior and attitudes of men and women, it is important to understand *how* these standards become so strong and remain so resistant to change. We shall, therefore, examine three sets of explanatory factors that contribute to the psychological differences betwen the sexes. They include direct familial treatment of children, symbolic creation and assumption of sex roles, and biological factors that appear during infancy.

DIFFERENTIAL TREATMENT IN THE FAMILY

From the moment the infant is born, its biological sex influences how it will be treated by its parents. In Western culture mothers engage in more muscular rough-and-tumble play with their sons than with their daughters. The mother tickles them, throws them in the air, rubs their tummies, and stresses their musculature with greater vigor than she does her daughter's (Moss 1967). Mothers of daughters enter into more quiet play and engage in more face-to-face talking and imitation than mothers of sons. If a four-month girl smiles or babbles, the American mother is more likely to bend toward the infant and respond in the same mode than if her son should display the same action (Moss 1967). However, comparable observations of mother-infant interaction in poor, rural Indian villages in eastern Guatemala reveal that, unlike the situation in the United States, boys receive slightly more vocal interaction from mothers than girls. Furthermore, Indian male infants are fed more than females because it is important that sons grow strong enough to make a contribution to the family economy.

Although in most cultures mothers assign the chores of cooking, feeding younger children, and gardening to girls rather than to boys, there are always differences within a culture and, occasionally, a boy in a particular family is given these feminine assignments. Ember (1970) observed children 7½ to 16 years old in a Luo community in Kenya. The boys who had been assigned feminine work in the home were less masculine in their social behavior outside the home. They were less dominant, less likely to seek attention and recognition, and more likely to nurture others in a responsible manner. Thus, even within a culture with sharp sex-role differentiation, familial experiences that promote feminine behavior in the home can generalize and influence behavior outside the home. This result clearly establishes an important effect of individual experience on sex-role behavior.

The American mother tends to be more concerned with potential physical harm to her daughter than to her son. If a two-year-old girl wanders near the partly open door to the cellar, the mother is likely to warn her about the possible danger; she is less likely to warn her son in the same situation (Minton, Kagan, and Levine 1971). Similar warnings occur in different settings several times a day, seven days a week, month after month, and must have a strong influence on the child's tendencies toward fearfulness and inhibition. Moreover, the middle-class American mother is most critical of her firstborn daughter, setting higher standards for her, criticizing her for a less than perfect performance, and pressuring her for success (Rothbart 1971). As the drama of socialization unfolds, this consistent socialization presure is accompanied by a more harmoniously orchestrated relationship between mother and firstborn daughter than between mother and eldest son. If the mother makes a request, the girl usually obeys it. The boy is usually more resistant, and the relation with the mother less harmonious (Minton, Kagan, and Levine 1970).

Differences in parental behavior toward sons and daughters are partly determined by different reactive styles displayed by the infant. For example, an active child invites more vigorous reciprocal play, whereas a quiet infant provokes gentler handling. Since infant boys generally are more active than girls, we should not expect to see identical parental practices toward young children of different sexes. Nevertheless, a more important determinant of differential treatment derives from the parent's representation of the ideal boy or girl. Each parent possesses an idea of one perfect set of traits for males and another for females. These ideals are, of course, influenced by the values of the culture. The parents' actions usually are attempts to mold the child in accord with the cultural standards.

In one investigation, mothers of 3- or 4-year-olds listened to a taped voice of a child, and some mothers were led to believe the voice was that of a boy, whereas others believed it was the voice of a girl. The parents heard the taped voice make various statements involving disobedience and requests for help, and then wrote down how they would respond to that statement if the child were their own. The mothers composed more permissive replies to what they thought were boys than to girls; fathers were more permissive with daughters than with sons (Rothbart and Maccoby 1966).

It is likely that comparable parental practices interact either with biological traits of the child or with parental style to produce different effects in the two sexes, because boys and girls do not develop similar behaviors when treated similarly on a particular dimension.

The behavior of a large group of preschool middle-class children was observed over a five-month period in a nursery school setting. (In general, boys were more hostile, resistant, and dominant than girls.) The parents of the children were observed and interviewed at home. Following analyses of these data, the investigator assigned the parents to various "personality" types on the basis of their interaction with their children. Sons of parents rated as being highly authoritative were less hostile than sons of less authoritative parents, but the same relationship did not hold in the case of girls. In contrast, authoritativeness produced independence in girls and not in boys. But if, in addition to being authoritative, the parents were also nonconforming, then authoritativeness toward sons produced independence (Baumrind 1971).

This finding illustrates an instance in which similar parental practices produced dissimilar effects in boys and girls. Let us now consider a different situation in which a certain type of mother reacts differently toward her infant, depending upon its sex. During their first pregnancy, mothers were interviewed and rated for degree of excitement and enthusiasm detectable in their speech—a variable reflecting emotional expressiveness. Following the birth of the baby, the mother-child interaction was observed on three separate occasions during the first three months of life. The prenatally expressive mothers who had given birth to sons were physically affectionate with them, kissing and holding them frequently. Emotionally expressive mothers of daughters tended to provide the infant with visual and auditory stimulation, as if they were trying to accelerate its intellectual development (Moss, Robson, and Pedersen 1969).

Even this brief review of existing knowledge is persuasive of the conclusion that parents impose different patterns of treatment on sons and daughters from the very first weeks of the infant's life. It is probably impossible to find groups of boys and girls, especially in Western culture, who receive similar patterns of handling. It is not clear whether this is due solely to differential ego ideals parents hold for their children, or whether biological differences between boys and girls prevent parents from displaying identical treatment strategies toward their children. It is possible, finally, that even if we found boys and girls who received identical familial handling, the sexes would still differ because boys and girls react differently to the same experience, as a result of biological factors.

In sum, sex differences arise, in part, because each parent holds a representation of what the ideal boy or girl should be like as a young adult, and, in part as a result or the parents' theory of how to guide the child through infancy and childhood to adulthood. Since the ideals are different for the sexes, familial treatment will not be the same. Different patterns of experience gently but firmly push boys and girls in different psychological directions.

SYMBOLIC CONCEPTUALIZATION OF SEX ROLES

Another basis for sex differences derives from the fact that man is a "symbolic" creature who continually evaluates the congruence between his profile of attributes and his understanding of the concept "male and female" or "masculine and feminine." Certain human dimensions are so salient that they force every child to symbolize them. Two of these dimensions are age and sex. It is impossible for a culture to avoid inventing the opposing categories young versus old, male versus female, and every child knows that he or she is a member of these categories. A six-year-old boy knows that certain beliefs, wishes, and actions are most appropriate for the category young male, or more simply, *boy*. He has no choice but to tailor his psychology to the ideal definition of that category. Humans behave as if "what is, ought to be." Each child, therefore, unconsciously but continuously looks to his culture—his parents, his siblings, his friends, his teachers, and the mass media—to discover the psychological definitions of male and female.

Western society is at present changing those definitions at a rapid rate, and it is more difficult now than it was a decade earlier to formulate unambiguous psychological definitions for the sexes. The differences were clearer a decade or two ago, when a male was supposed to be able to defend himself physically, be competent at athletics, independent and autonomous, able to inhibit emotions like fear, sadness, and loneliness, and be heterosexually successful. Females were supposed to be socially skilled, noncompetitive, sexually attractive, and passive with males. Each child and young adult elaborated the definition which was presented to him and continually reinforced by his culture, his friends and parents, and by the fictional heroes promoted by schools and the media.

It is important to note that despite societal differences in standards, there is some minimal cross-cultural uniformity to the connotative understanding of *male* and *female* across the world.

In one cross-cultural study, various pairs of designs were shown to adults in six different cultural settings, and each individual was asked to decide which design best represented males and which females. Large objects were designated as male, small objects as female; dark-colored objects were male; light-colored objects were female; pointed objects were male; rounded objects were female (Osgood 1960). In a different investigation, young American children, five and six years of age, were found to make the same set of symbolic associations (Kagan, Hosken, and Watson 1961). Moreover, femininity is more closely linked to the symbolic dimension of naturalness than is masculinity.

Why is there this mysterious agreement on the symbolic dimensions of the concepts male and female? The association of maleness with size is a natural consequence of the fact that boys and men are almost always larger than girls or women. The association of masculinity with aggression probably derives from the fact that in most cultures males are more aggressive, either in the service of soldiering, hunting, fighting, or in rough-and-tumble play during childhood. The symbols of aggression, be they harm, fear, or terror are also preferentially linked to masculinity. Hence, darkness or pointedness is usually classified as masculine, and young children who select a pointed design as "more like their father than their mother" often explain their choice by saying "That can hurt you." The preferential link between female-ness and naturalness is understandable, because birth and nursing are quin-tessential natural functions, and it is easy for a child to come to the uncon-scious conclusion that to be female is to be closer to the experiences that nature intended.

The cross-cultural uniformity on these symbolic dimensions of mascu-linity-femininity has important implications. All individuals possess a set of basic assumptions about the essence of maleness and femaleness. Even if we could change the familial treatments to which children are exposed and could arrange the social environment so that all adults treated boys and girls equivalently, we might not totally eliminate sex differences, because of the symbolic interpretations of masculinity and femininity derived from irrevo-cable differences in size, strength, differential anatomy, and life functions.

Earlier in this chapter it was asserted that psychological differences be-tween the sexes are, in large measure, the result of differential socialization; nevertheless, the agreement on the content of some sex-role standards across many cultures suggests that different societies are responding in the same way to differences in physical qualities and normal life functions. As a result, they are constructing similar sets of sex-role standards.

SEX-ROLE IDENTITY AND CONFLICT

The symbolic dimensions associated with concepts of male and female lead directly to the meaning of the phrase *sex-role identity*. Sex-role identity is a belief concerning the degree to which a person's own biological and psychological characteristics are congruent with his or her idealized view of the concept male or female. The definition of the ideal is always influenced by the culture. A Japanese girl concludes that gentleness is an essential femi-nine quality; an American girl believes that physical beauty is a critical femi-nine trait. Once the boy's or girl's sex-role identity emerges, the child is vul-nerable to conflict, for he or she wants to avoid the display of behaviors or acknowledge the occurrence of thoughts and feelings that are incompatible with the idealized sex-role standard. Each violation weakens the integrity of the sex-role identity. As indicated earlier, aggressive and independent be-haviors are sex-typed in our culture, and, hence, there is greater conflict over hostile feelings and aggressive behavior among women, greater conflict over passive and dependent behavior and thoughts among men.

In one study, middle-class American men and women were shown a series of black-white pictures at extremely fast but varying speeds which ranged from .01 to 1.0 seconds. Each picture showed one adult acting either aggressively or dependently toward another. The subject described what he or she saw on each of seven exposures of the pictures. The women required longer exposure times to identify the aggressive scenes and describe them accurately. The men, on the other hand, required longer exposure times before they could describe the pictures illustrating dependent behavior. Each sex had greatest difficulty interpreting action that violated its own sex-role standards (Kagan and Moss 1962).

Although quality of intellectual performance is not as clearly a sex-typed attribute as are aggression or passivity, exceptional intellectual talent in science and mathematics is regarded as more appropriate for men and is, in fact, more common among males than females. One reason for this division is that today academic excellence at these skills facilitates vocational success and is, therefore, a more essential component of a male's sex-role identity. Moreover, adolescent girls are more anxious over excessive competitiveness than boys, and many females view intellectual striving as a form of hostility. Since hostility, competition, and aggression violate traditional sex-role standards for females, some young women inhibit intense intellectual effort in academic settings.

Horner (1968) asked college men and women to write a story in response to the following first sentence: "After first term finals, (Ann) or (John) finds himself/herself at the top of his/her medical school class." Women were much more likely than men to tell a story in which success seemed to produce anxiety. The stories contained indications that the girl was afraid of social rejection for deviation from the normal expected role for women. The following story is exemplary:

> Ann has planned for a long time to be a doctor. She has worked hard in her school work to enable her to learn better how to fulfill her dream. Now the hard work has paid off. Unfortunately, Ann suddenly no longer feels so certain that she really wants to be a doctor. She wonders if perhaps this isn't normal. . . . Ann decides not to continue with her medical work, but to continue with courses that she never allowed herself to take before, but that have a deeper personal meaning for her.

While they are in college, many capable, professionally oriented young women change their plans, shifting to less ambitious, more traditionally feminine roles (Tangri 1969), in order to preserve the integrity of their sex-role identity. A Wellesley student protested plans to admit undergraduate male students: "How can a girl maintain her role as a woman when she is in intense academic competition with men, especially if she is excelling? Many capable girls have faced the frustration of accusations of aggressiveness, lack of femininity and the desire to beat the boys, when they were in high school and college" (*Harvard Crimson* 1969).

It is interesting to note that in the primary grades girls in general are much more persistent and obtain better grades than boys in all subjects, including arithmetic. In the United States, the ratio of boys to girls with reading problems ranges from 3 to 1, to 6 to 1. It seems likely that the relative superiority of girls to boys in the primary grades derives from the fact that the average American six-year-old male perceives school as a feminine place. His introduction to the academic community is monitored by women. It is women who initiate the activities of painting and singing, and place a premium on obedience and suppression of restlessness and playful aggression. These are feminine values, and the young children of both sexes see the school as a feminine environment.

This conclusion is supported by results of the following experiment. Second-grade children were taught to assign one of three different nonsense syllables to pictures illustrating masculine objects, feminine objects, and farm-related objects. After the child had learned to do this well (about five minutes), he or she was shown pictures of objects found in classrooms, such as a blackboard or a page of arithmetic, and asked to assign one of the nonsense words to these pictures. Both boys and girls were most likely to associate the school pictures with the nonsense word they had assigned earlier to the feminine objects (Kagan 1964). If young boys perceive the mission of the school as feminine, they will resist complete involvement in classroom activity and, of course, will fall behind girls in academic progress. As boys approach adolescence, they begin to view acquisition of knowledge as appropriate to their sex because masculine vocational fields require intellectual skills taught by the school.

FIRMNESS OF SEX-ROLE IDENTITY

Real objects in the world are most often defined by their physical appearance, their functions, and the conceptual categories to which they belong. For example, a lemon is a small, round citrus fruit used for flavoring. Objective definitions of the human male and female emphasize a small set of biological and psychological characteristics, ranging from genetic constitution to hobbies. But man, unlike the lemon, defines himself to himself, and this view is not identical with the definition found in the dictionary. All men who are 5 feet 11 inches tall, have X and Y chromosomes and male genital anatomy, should, on the basis of sheer logic, regard themselves as equally masculine. However, the mind in its perversity does not trust these concrete, physical signs and insists on including psychological evidence in its final judgment. Therefore, a sex-role identity as a personal belief about one's own maleness or femaleness is not any simple derivative of how masculine or feminine his or her public appearance may be.

As a child matures, he comes to recognize the sex-role standards promoted by his reference group, and he senses the degree to which his characteristics match those standards. If the match is close, and he desires it to be, his sex-role identity will be firm. If the match is distant and he does not possess the sex-role characteristics he desires, his sexual identity will be fragile.

Differences among children in firmness of sex-role identity arise from several sources. First, most children believe they are more like their same-sex parent than any other adult, and tend, preferentially, to imitate that parent, especially if he or she possesses desirable traits. Galen of Pergamon was acutely aware of this process.

I cannot say how I got my nature. It was however my great fortune to have as my father a most good tempered, just, efficient, and benevolent man. My mother on the other hand was so irascible that she would sometimes bite her serving maids and she was constantly shouting at my father and quarreling with him, worse than Xantippe with Socrates. When I saw, then, the nobility of my father's conduct side by side with the shameful passions of my mother, I made up my mind to live and cleave to the former behavior and to hate and flee from the latter. And besides this enormous difference between my parents, I observed that he was never depressed over any affliction while my mother became annoyed at the merest bagatelle. You yourself doubtless know that boys imitate what they are fond of and avoid what they do not like to see. (Brock 1929, p. 171)

The boy whose father is skilled at tennis or golf is more likely to believe he has athletic talent than a boy whose father does not play any sports. Children are also strongly influenced by the definition of sex-role identity shared by their peer group. The boy who is clumsy on the baseball field is more likely to question his sex-role identity if his friends regard aptitude for baseball as an important masculine trait than if they value skill at chess.

Finally, the integrity of the sex-role identity is dependent on the quality of sexual interactions in adolescence. If the adolescent is unable to establish successful heterosexual relationships, he will begin to question his sex-role identity. The potential for attracting the affection of a member of the opposite sex and building a satisfactory sexual union is the quintessence of the sex-role standard for the adult. Each person tries to match his attributes to his notion of the ideal. If he believes he is close to his standards, his spirits are buoyed, and he makes further attempts to come even closer. If he feels his behavior is far from the standard, he may turn away from it and begin to accept the role of a feminine man or a masculine woman. Movement toward homosexuality, though laden with apprehension, often frees the person from the awesome responsibilities of heterosexuality. Acceptance of a culturally inappropriate sex role reduces the anxiety that comes from recognition of serious deviation from an ideal that cannot be attained. The only possible solution is to redefine the ideal in terms of what can be mastered.

Sex Differences in Early Infancy

We shall not summarize biological differences between the sexes here but, instead, will adopt a strategy that allows us to concentrate on infancy. Let us assume that the earlier a particular profile of sex differences occurs in ontogeny, the more likely it is to be heavily influenced by biological factors. If newborn infants differ in vigor of their reflexes, we are tempted to conclude that this variation is biological in origin, either genetic or the result of pre- or perinatal conditions. We shall use this strategy in examining early sex differences. The young infant has not been influenced by symbolic conceptualization of his role; and differences in parental treatment, although present, are less extreme during the first year than later. Rather than list in almanac style all of the known sex differences, we shall organize them around a few theoretical ideas.

SUSCEPTIBILITY TO FEAR

It appears that the infant female is a little more prone than the male to the distress state normally called fear. If a mother and her 6- to 12-month-old infant are taken to a strange room, a girl stays near or in contact with her mother for a longer period of time than does a boy. Mitchell (1968b) studied rhesus monkeys under similar circumstances and found that infant females stayed closer to their mothers than did males during the first 90 days of life. However, the rhesus mother tended to push her son away, while restraining her daughter, and hence the sex difference in behavior of infants does not derive solely from the fact that males are more likely to wander.

Human females show distress and upset to novel stimuli at an earlier age than males, for the young female infant under six months is more likely than the male to cry in a strange laboratory or unusual setting (Kagan 1971). Around three to four months of age, girls begin to inhibit active motoric responses in a strange situation; hence, if a toy is placed behind a barrier, the girl is less likely than the boy to reach for it. In one study, a mother and infant were situated behind a wire barrier, and, on a signal, the mother put the infant on the opposite side. Many one-year-old girls "froze" and began to cry. Boys were more likely to initiate some action. The boy might see a piece of lint on the floor and pick it up and examine it, or note the latch at the end of the barrier and explore it. Each of these responses diverted the boy from the source of the frustration or uncertainty. It is suggested that the action aborted his fear and prevented subsequent crying. As long as the child was involved in some action, or attending to some event, fear seemed to be held at bay (Kagan 1971).

If boys have a natural disposition to action in situations of uncertainty, even though the action may be task-irrelevant, the activity may protect them from overwhelming fear. The female's earlier display of fear, motor inhibition, and preference to stay close to the mother is not easily interpreted as a result of differential treatment by parents, and is certainly not a product of symbolic conceptualization of one's sex role.

One possible explanation for earlier display of fear in the female begins with the fact that the female is biologically precocious to the male. Growth of bone and of myelin sheath surrounding the nerves proceeds precociously, and the infant female seems to be a physically more mature organism. If this biological precocity contributed to or was accompanied by advanced psychological functioning, a set of important corollaries would follow.

COGNITIVE SCHEMATA

The first class of cognitive structures the infant develops are called *schemata*. A schema is an abstract cognitive representation of experience that allows the child to recognize past events. Before the end of the second month, the infant has already developed many schemata for objects in his life space. If females developed these schemata sooner than males, females would possess, at an earlier age, a better delineated representation of their world. An important principle of psychological dynamics states that a discrepant stimulus (that is, an event that is slightly different from the original that produced the schema) alerts the infant and provokes him to attempt to assimilate the unfamiliar event, to resolve the uncertainty it generates.

For example, a four-month-old baby who has schemata for his crib and room at home is brought to a different crib and room in the laboratory. The discrepancy alerts the infant, and one of two things can happen. The infant can either assimilate the discrepancy or deal with it by withdrawal. If either of these reactions occurs, he is able to cope successfully with the unusual stimulus, and the infant will relax, and may even smile. But if he cannot cope with the discrepancy, he will become afraid.

The early signs of fear displayed by the female infant in discrepant situations may reflect the fact that she has developed better-delineated schemata for her life-space than the boy and is, therefore, more likely to be alerted by new situations. The boy, who possesses less-articulated schemata, may not note the discrepancy. However, the girl may be immature in her "coping mechanisms" and have no way to deal with the primitive realization that she is not in a familiar context. Hence, she begins to cry. This argument is supported by the finding that girls who were most frightened in a laboratory setting when they were four months old played the most creatively with toys when they were one year old. This predictive continuity did not emerge among the boys (Kagan 1971).

It is possible that the infant female may pay for her early physical precocity with more frequent bouts of fear during the first year. In most young mammals, a prepotent reaction to fear is withdrawal. If the infant and child habitually withdraw in response to fear during the first year of life, a disposition to display withdrawal might be established. If this line of reasoning has merit, it would help explain the more frequent cautiousness and withdrawal of older girls in situations that are threatening.

On the other hand, the higher frequency of female withdrawal may result from innate response tendencies favoring retreat under conditions of fear arousal. If rhesus males and females are raised individually in isolated chambers and later brought together, the females withdraw and show more fear, while the males are more likely to attack (Mitchell 1968a). The actions are not the result of differential precocity of schemata, for both males and females were subadults at the time of testing. Hence, it is possible that the infant female is simply more strongly disposed to withdraw in response to threat. At the moment there is insufficient evidence to allow us to choose one of these hypotheses in preference to the other.

COGNITIVE FUNCTIONS

There is a second set of potential implications that follows from the fact that females are developmentally precocious to males. With growth, the paired cerebral hemispheres become increasingly asymmetric with respect to relative dominance. Gazzaniga (1970) suggests that the newborn is like a "split-brain" animal with equal hemispheric dominance, the left hemisphere gradually gaining dominance over the right with age. For most people, the left hemisphere is the major site of language functions. Some capacity for language comprehension is contained in the right hemisphere, but, if the left hemisphere is removed or damaged, expressive language is destroyed in a more serious way than if the right hemisphere is impaired. If the female is precocious, she might attain left-hemisphere dominance ahead of the boy owing, in part, to precocious myelination of the corpus callosum and the medial surface of the temporal lobe (Gazzaniga 1970; Lancaster 1968). As a result, the important speech functions of the left hemisphere might develop at a faster rate among girls. This fact might explain why girls usually begin to speak earlier than boys. However, the boy eventually develops a language as complex and rich as that of the girl. At 18 years of age, there are minimal sex differences in language ability.

An extensive longitudinal study of Caucasian children (4 to 27 months of age) suggested that, during the first year, nonmeaningful vocalizations—called babbling—were a better index of the state of excitability created by encounter with an interesting event among girls than boys (Kagan 1971). To illustrate, girls were more likely to vocalize differentially to stimuli of different interest potential. Further, when speech was played to eight-month-olds through a speaker baffle, the girls, who were more attentive during the stimulus presentation (as indexed by depth of heart deceleration), were more likely to vocalize for a few seconds when the speech terminated. This relation was absent for boys. Moreover, the girl's parental social class was an excellent predictor of the amount of increase in vocalization to interesting events during the last half of the first year. The boys' social class was unrelated to changes in vocalization over the same period.

In general, the infant girls who vocalized a lot during the last half of the first year were, at two years of age, more active, more excitable, and more impulsive than quiet female infants. However, there was no comparable relation among the boys. In still another study, four-month-old infants were shown an unusual three-dimensional stimulus in the laboratory. These infants were then exposed to different versions of the original stimulus at home for a period of three weeks. All infants returned to the laboratory after three weeks and were shown the original stimulus, which was now a little different from the one they viewed at home. The girls displayed increases in vocalization to this "interesting" event; the boys did not (Super et al. 1972).

These data suggest that vocalization in the girl may be a more sensitive index of intellectual excitement than it is in the boy, and this inference is in accord with the fact that vocalization scores derived from infant intelligence tests during the first year are better predictors of future intellectual functioning among preschool girls than among boys (Cameron, Livson, and Bayley 1967; Moore 1967).

SEX DIFFERENCES IN VARIABILITY

In addition to their precocious development as compared with boys, girls also show less variability for biological attributes. For example, there are more extreme instances on physical dimensions among males than females, i.e., more very tall and very short men than women, more very heavy and very light men than women. This greater variability among males also holds for intelligence. There are more men with very high and very low IQs than there are women. The greater male variability is accompanied by lower long-term predictability for psychological and physical variables. Height, weight, or number of ossification centers in the wrist show higher correlations from one age to a subsequent age among females than among males. Similarly, a child's relative rank for scores on vocabulary, IQ, and achievement tests is more stable over time for girls than for boys.

It is possible that the lower variability among females contributes to this firmer intraindividual stability of traits. Lyon (1962) has hypothesized that in the female there is buffering for the two X chromosomes. One of the female's X chromosomes is partially inactivated by the other X. That is to say, one of the X chromosomes is active, the other relatively inactive. However, chance determines whether the paternal or maternal X will be the less active one in any particular cell. Thus, if there is any allele on the X chromosome that contributes to an extreme psychological deviation, it will be buffered in the female but not in the male, since he possesses only one X chromosome. Some rare blood diseases carried on the X chromosome are fatal to males, but not to females. It is possible, therefore, that biological forces that produce extreme lethargy, activity, or irritability will be buffered in the female and lead to a more lawful relation between environmental experiences and psychological development. This hypothesis forms a nice bridge to the last theme.

SEX DIFFERENCES IN RELATION TO SOCIAL CLASS

Many independent studies of American infants have shown that there is closer covariation between indexes of cognitive development and social class for girls than for boys. It has generally been found that correlations between social class (as measured by education and occupation), on the one hand, and attentiveness in young infants or IQ scores in children of school age on the other, are higher for girls than for boys (Werner 1969; Hindley 1965; Kagan 1971). This is as true of black families as it is of white ones (Hess et al. 1968, 1969), *and* the same sex difference exists in rural Guatemalan Indians as in Spanish-speaking agricultural villages. How can we interpet this interesting phenomenon?

The sex differences noted in children of school age can be interpreted by assuming a stronger adoption of the family's values by girls than by boys. Since there is a major difference between less-well and well-educated parents with respect to concern with intellectual mastery, we would expect greater covariation between class and cognitive achievement for girls than for boys. Although this dynamic may be operating with school-age children, it is clearly not operating during the first year of life. At this early age, it is

likely that there is greater variability across social class levels in maternal reactions to daughters than to sons.

Most mothers in American culture, whether they be high school dropouts or college graduates, believe their sons will have to develop independence, responsibility, and a vocational expertise. When lower-middle-class
mothers of four-year-olds were asked to teach their children a new task, they
were more achievement-oriented and adopted a more businesslike attitude
toward sons than toward daughters (Hess, Shipman, Brophy, and Bear 1968,
1969). Lower-class mothers of daughters seem to project their greater sense
of impotence and inadequacy onto them and are less likely to stimulate, encourage, or reward their daughters' simple accomplishments. Observations
of lower-middle-class mothers of infants during the first two years affirm this
suggestion. Middle-class, in contrast to lower-middle-class, mothers spend
more time talking to and entertaining their daughters and chide them more
often for task incompetence (Rothbart 1971; Minton et al. 1971).

One group of mothers, whose children were 27 months of age, were observed at home with the children, and the observer recorded descriptive
statements related to all mother-child interactions. For most of the variables
there were no major class differences, but when a class difference in maternal behavior did emerge, it was likely to involve daughters rather than sons.
The most striking difference was that upper-middle-class mothers were
more likely to note and criticize incompetent behavior in daughters than in
sons (Minton et al. 1971). Well-educated mothers were three times more
likely than poorly educated ones to chide their daughters for failing to perform up to a standard held by the mother. There was no comparable class
difference for sons. This class difference in treatment of boys and girls was
specific to competence in performing specific tasks. Well-educated mothers
were generally more tolerant than lower-class mothers toward other categories of misdemeanor in daughters.

A recent study of five-year-olds from middle-class families that included
no other children of the same sex yielded similar results (Rothbart 1971). In
contrast to younger sisters, firstborn girls experienced the greatest pressure
for competent performance on a series of problems. Their mothers most
often reminded them of incompetent performance and were most intrusive
while the child was working at the problems (Rothbart 1971).

It is possible that American mothers from a broad range of educational
backgrounds are more divergent in their concern with proper behavior and
intellectual development in daughters than in sons. This phenomenon would
help to explain the closer relationship between maternal social class and
aspects of cognitive development among the girls than among the boys.

A second factor, alluded to earlier, assumes that there is less variability in temperamental dispositions among girls than boys and implies that there are more infant boys who are extremely irritable, alert, active, or lethargic than girls. Infants who, as a result of biological factors, are at either extreme of a particular psychological dimension, should be less influenced by specific caretaking experiences than those who are of a normative disposition. It is difficult to engage in long periods of reciprocal vocalization and joyful play with a highly mobile, extremely apathetic, or intensely irritable baby. Moreover, the mother who initiates these caretaking actions will influence the child less than one who initiates the same sequence with a less extreme child.

There is some empirical support for the notion that social experience affects girls' cognitive development in a more orderly fashion than it affects boys'. Observations of mothers and their three-month-old infants were made in the home, and the amount of face-to-face contact between the mother and child was quantified. Soon after the home observations, the infants were brought to the laboratory and shown representations of faces and geometric stimuli, and during presentation of these stimuli the infants' visual fixation time was coded. With respect to girls, there was a positive relation between the amount of face-to-face interaction with the mother at home and the infant's attentiveness to the faces among the girls, but no such relationship obtained for the boys (Moss 1967). On the other hand, the tendency to remain quiet at one month of age and to show low irritability at three months correlated with attentiveness for the boys, but not for the girls. One interpretation is that specific interaction experiences with the mother exert a major influence on the attentiveness of the girl, while temperament is more influential for boys (Moss and Robson 1970). The effect of familial experience on attention is more faithfully reflected in the infant female than in the infant male. Perhaps the greater male variability in both maturational development and display of temperamental attributes is responsible for this difference.

Summary

Differential physical precocity, decreased variability, symbolic representations of sex roles, different childrearing practices, and patterns of reward offered by extrafamilial peers and adults—all of these factors interact in affecting the psychological product we see among school-age children and adults. It is neither possible nor appropriate to state how much of a girl's language precocity or nonaggressiveness is caused by biology and how much by experience.

The attractiveness of any specific question about the sexes depends upon the questioner's theoretical interest. The social psychologist asks whether the culture is strong enough to offset the influence of biological vectors and to attenuate those sex differences that normally are the partial product of the biology-experience interaction. The biologist wants to know more about the physiological mechanisms that are functionally different for the sexes and how they might lead to differential growth under identical environmental experiences. The psychiatrist wants to understand how the differing standards that constitute sex-role identity make each sex selectively vulnerable to anxiety, and disposed to adopt particular defenses. The developmental psychologist is puzzled by the increasing differences between the sexes that accompany maturation, for males and females are more similar during the first week of life than they will ever be again.

Men and women in every society march to different pipers, are sensitized to different aspects of experience and gratified by different profiles of events. These differences do not preclude an egalitarian relation between the sexes, and the benevolent change in Western man's prejudiced attitude toward women over the past half-millennium is beautifully captured by two quotations written more than 400 years apart.

What else is a woman but a foe to friendship, an unescapable punishment, a necessary evil, a natural temptation, a desirable calamity, a domestic danger, a delectable detriment, an evil of nature painted with fair colors. Therefore, if it be a sin to divorce her when she ought to be kept, it is indeed a necessary torture for either we commit adultery by divorcing her or we must endure daily strife. . . . The tears of a woman are a deception for they may spring from true grief or they may be a snare. When a woman thinks alone, she thinks evil. (*Malleus Maleficarum*)

Our progress is surely apparent in Goldmund's advice to Narcissus, as he lies dying in his friend's arms, "But how will you die when your time comes, Narcissus, since you have no mother? Without a mother one cannot love. Without a mother one cannot die." (Hesse 1930.)

SEVEN

motives in development

Actions and thoughts are often directed at a goal, where a goal is simply a desired experience. A college senior enters the library after dinner; a ten-year-old teases his younger brother; a two-year-old carefully places a seventh block on a precarious tower of six. In all three cases, the person has some notion of a desired state of affairs—a goal. A motive is the mental representation of that goal. It is neither the action that gains the goal nor the feeling of excitement, tension, or distress that often accompanies the wish. Many children have thought of visiting Disneyland, yelling at their mother, or running away from home, but the motive was never acted upon and need not have been accompanied by a strong emotion. *The motive is simply the idea that stands for the desired experience.* Hence gratification, which is synonymous with the attainment of the goal, resembles the experience of finding a name that has been on the tip of one's tongue. Gratification is experiencing the match between the idea of the desired event and the event itself.

We need a concept like "motive" to understand human functioning because some of our actions are influenced by anticipations of the future. We need a concept to explain why a woman sitting in a quiet library suddenly rises from her chair, leaves the room, and returns after making a telephone call to arrange an after-dinner appointment. A representation of a future event provoked the action. If there is no internal physiological need or external pressure for the change in behavior, the cause is likely to be in the person's mind. When that cause is the idea of a future goal, the person is motivated. Unfortunately, a description of a person's actual behavior does not help us to understand its aim. The statement "John did not take the final exam" is too divorced from John's history to be of much value in understanding why John was absent for the test or in predicting John's behavior

Adapted from *Understanding Children* (New York: Harcourt Brace Jovanovich, 1971).

the next time a final exam is scheduled. No action, no matter how exact its description, contains enough information to allow us to infer its intention.

Motivated versus Nonmotivated Behavior

Not all behaviors are motivated. Many actions are simply reactions to the pressures of the immediate situation. A person sits quietly in a concert hall because that is the expected posture. He may have been motivated when he initially purchased a ticket for the concert, but his "act of sitting quietly" in the auditorium is controlled by the situation. A person's behavior should be viewed as composed of paragraphs. The first action, like the first sentence of a new paragraph, is often generated from within. But the initial action places a serious restriction on the next one, just as a topic sentence sets constraints on the sentences that follow. If we could tell when a person was beginning a new paragraph in his behavior, in contrast to when he was merely acting in the middle of one, we might be better able to understand his motives.

The social scientist's view of human nature has been strongly influenced by the nineteenth-century assumption held by physical scientists that every event in nature has a cause. For most of this century psychologists believed that their task was to find the causes of behavior. Sigmund Freud made this theme essential in his theory of human functioning. The basic human motives, which Freud called the id impulses, were regarded as the causes of behavior and neurotic symptoms. A person's motives were not always obvious to either himself or an observer, but there had to be a motive for all behavior.

Current conceptions of human behavior are not so uncritically wedded to the idea that all action derives from motives. This is not equivalent, however, to saying that an action has no cause. Actions like sneezing and coughing are the product of automatic reflexes. These behaviors are caused, but not by motives. Other actions are prompted by biological drives like hunger, thirst, pain, and the need for sleep. Still others are habits associated with subtle feeling states. For example, a professor talking to a group of students suddenly rises from his chair and walks around the room for a few moments. It is neither necessary nor reasonable to assume that he wanted to stand up, that there was a specific goal he wished to attain. Most likely, the professor stood up because this action had become a habitual response to a certain quality of excitement he experienced. Similarly, a four-month-old infant will babble in response to a smiling face. The infant does not want to babble nor is he necessarily gratified by this noisemaking.

The most common examples of nonmotivated behavior are learned reactions to particular situations. An American child sits in a chair to eat, a Japanese child kneels on a pillow, an international traveler in an airport stands at a lunch counter. The specific posture of sitting, kneeling, or standing is appropriate to the context in which the person is dining. A chair invites sitting, a pillow invites kneeling, a counter invites standing. The reader may reply that it is not the specific posture displayed that is motivated but the act of eating. Yet we know that a person often eats breakfast at 8:00 A.M., lunch at noon, and dinner at 7:00 P.M. not because he has any desire for food but because it is the appropriate time to eat. The context of the family seated at a table set with bacon and eggs at 8: A.M. calls for the act of sitting down for breakfast. Thus many actions are learned routines to particular contexts and not necessarily the product of a motive.

Awareness of Motives

Although a motive is an idea about a goal, it is not always fully conscious and well defined. It is typically not the state we experience when we instruct ourselves, "I must go to the post office, then to the barber, and be back at the office by 1:30." A motive can be a verbalized reminder, a fleeting image, or a fragmented version of either. We must distinguish, moreover, between the latent representation of the goal, or the motive, and the activation of that idea, which is called *motivation*. A motivational state is best viewed as an abstract mental set, where a mental set can be likened to the tuning of a radio or television. When the dial is moved to a particular setting, the amplifier becomes maximally receptive to one set of signals and minimally receptive to all others. Similarly, when a person sits down to watch a news broadcast or a replay of a Gary Cooper movie, he readies himself to receive certain sounds and sights; he is mentally preparing for a particular set of events. This preparation is the state called motivation.

A motive that is activated limits perception as well as action, for it acts like a governor on a motor or a program in a computer. The mind can be likened to a large collection of routines with an executive deciding which routine should be activated. The motive instructs the executive to focus more selectively on one set of routines and to ignore others. A simple illustration of the meaning of motivation as a set can be seen in the behavior of a man driving home after a day at work. The man leaves his office at 6:00 P.M., reminding himself briefly of where he is going. This self-instruction takes less than a second. His mind then turns to other matters—the evening's work, the problems of the next day, the unsolved crises at the office. He gets into his car, starts the ignition, leaves the parking lot, and automatically makes the correct set of turns to his house without ever thinking about his actions or about the goal toward which he is driving. Had he decided as he left the office that he was going to a restaurant on the opposite side of the city, he would have made a different set of correct turns and also arrived at his goal. There was a brief moment when a representation of a goal led the man to select a set of action routines that ran off automatically. The motive was the brief representation of the goal.

Each person possesses hundreds of thousands of representations of goals, most of which lie dormant in the shadow of unawareness. Some representations are capable of being activated into consciously experienced wishes. Others are less available to awareness, a fact that led Freud to invent the notion of *unconscious motives*. A motive is said to be unconscious when a person is unaware of a set of goals that he desires. But ideas may be partially conscious for brief periods of time, and it is possible for a person to experience only fragments of a wish.

Moreover, a person does not have to recognize the significance of his motives in order to act on them. The young child who performs poorly in school does not say to himself, "I hate my mother and want her to be unhappy; therefore, I will fail in school." The child might have a fleeting awareness of his mother crying and believe that failure to comply with her wishes would cause her to become upset. If he has learned that she is distressed by poor grades, a certain group of behaviors will be selected, much as the representation of home in the driver's mind led him to select the correct set of turns to his house. When a child is aware of a motive, he knows the goal he wants. The child who takes on chores in order to obtain money to purchase a bicycle can tell us why he is working after school. But if possession of the bicycle was a way of evoking his older brother's jealousy, by obtaining a prize the brother did not have, the boy would probably not be able to tell us about this wish. Although the child seems unaware of his desire to antagonize his brother, he may have had a fleeting idea of his brother's angry face. He does not label this brief bit of knowledge as meanness or hostility (psychologists do that), but its existence defines the motive. Unfortunately, we do not know how to detect these fragile, wish-laden representations. Since the child cannot verbalize them, we say that the motive is unconscious. But a fragmentary thought can be sufficient to activate a person toward attainment of a relevant goal.

An unconscious motive defines one end of a continuum of accessibility. At one extreme there is no awareness of a representation of a goal toward which a set of actions may be progressing. Thus the three-year-old, who is not aware of the rules of grammar, produces surprisingly correct sentences. We do not understand how a mental set can guide and order a group of complex behaviors. It is possible that the same factors that govern the relation between possession of rules of grammar and correct speech also apply to the relation between unconscious motives and behavior. For the selection of an action to gratify a motive is similar to the selection of a phrase for a sentence, or indeed a rule to solve a problem. A person possesses an abstract representation of a goal to be reached and, mysteriously, selects the right routine. In this sense, motivated behavior may be similar to the mental processes characteristic of all problem-solving. The essential ingredients are a representation of a goal and a set of strategies that might attain it.

Actions that seem to be obvious gratifications of one motive often turn out, upon analysis, to be gratifications of quite a different desire. Sometimes a person is fully aware of his desire for a certain goal but wishes to disguise it. He initiates behaviors that seem to be aimed at one goal, but his actions are intended for another. For example, a child wants to play with a toy another child possesses and offers the privileged one a substitute in the hope that he will attain the toy he wants. His clever bartering appears on the surface to be motivated by charitable impulses. On other occasions a person may believe that the goal-directed behavior he is engaging in is relevant to a conscious motive, but a primary motive, of which he is less aware, is the more significant cause of his action. For example, a college student emigrates to Canada to avoid the draft in the belief that he is motivated by a revulsion for the war in Vietnam. It is possible that his action is motivated by a desire to avoid a situation in which, as a soldier, he might lose control of himself. The student may be afraid that he would behave irrationally if an officer issued an arbitrary order. This uncertainty frightens him and he emigrates, unaware of the influence of the second motive. Similarly, the student protest movements of the 1960s attracted some young adults whose desire for power was salient. Their campus behavior was in the service of this motive, although they believed it was aimed at less narcissistic goals.

Some of the most poignant examples of the mismatch of motives and behavior are seen in the crises of middle age and the ideological confusion of adults. The disillusionment of many Western adults comes from a recognition that longstanding actions have been directed at goals that have suddenly become unattractive. When the motives become accessible and the relation of behavior to wish becomes clear, the person recognizes that the things he has been doing for ten years have not been leading to the goals he really wants.

Degree of Elaboration of Motives

Psychologists have traditionally described the quantitative dimension of a motive in terms of *strength,* as a predisposition to behave. But a mental representation of warm, blue-green surf does not have strength the way the blow of a hand does. Motives, like all ideas, are best described not as varying in strength but in *degree of elaboration* and *capacity to crowd out other motives*. The degree of elaboration of a motive depends on the number of different representations of a goal that can serve the motive. Consider a six-year-old who wants more attention from his mother. If the representations of that goal include a variety of well-defined reactions from the mother—kissing, playing, verbal teasing, a present, a pat on the head—the motive is highly elaborated. If there are few representations of the goal, the motive is poorly elaborated.

The degree of elaboration of a motive increases with age, for the acquisition of language, introspection, and the honing of wishes in the frustrating world of action all sharpen and amplify the representation of goals. One corollary of this developmental change is that the older the child becomes, the greater the substitutability of his goals. A two-year-old who wants attention from his mother will tolerate fewer kinds of maternal reactions than will the older child, who is likely to accept many different forms of attention. The five-year-old with a desire for power has limited ways to gratify it; the adult's power motive can be gratified by wealth, perfection of a valued skill, or identification with a group or person possessing this resource. A motive becomes elaborated as its goal states become more diversified. Adults, however, do possess some poorly elaborated motives. An uncomfortable restlessness and confusion of purpose are prevalent conditions in contemporary Western society. Many adults wonder about how they should conduct their lives, a state that has produced a poorly elaborated motive to "know oneself" and a spate of cartoons illustrating men climbing mountains to ask wrinkled gurus, "What do I want?"

The Motive Hierarchy

A person's motives, like all his ideas, exist in a hierarchy, and each can be dominant at different times. The notion of position in a hierarchy comes closest to the popular term "preoccupation." There are times when we become so concerned with a particular goal that it is impossible to suppress it. Even if we are successful in replacing it with another thought for a few moments, we soon find it has pushed the temporary visitor aside and reinstated itself in the front of consciousness.

Motives high in the hierarchy at a given time push a person to relate his immediate experience to the motive and to seek out experiences that are likely to be gratifying. Consider the consequences of different hierarchies of motives for two adolescent boys at a party. The motive for a sexual encounter is ascendant for one; the motive to attract the attention of the group is ascendant for the other. Each will be watching different people, have different thoughts during the evening, and react with different amounts of joy or anguish when the lights go out.

Motives change their position in the hierarchy if they are continually frustrated. A child who is always disappointed in his attempts to gain the affection of his parents may turn his attention to gratifying hostility toward peers. He now becomes preoccupied with hurting others, and the motive for parental affection becomes subordinate to the motive of hostility. Usually, only a few motives dominate thought at a given time, for it is difficult to set the switches of attention in many directions at once.

Although humans are motivated for a large number of different goals, ranging from political fame to monastic withdrawal from society, there are four primary motives that seem to be the basis for a great many secondary ones. These four motives—resolution of uncertainty, mastery, hostility, and sexuality—play an important role in helping us to understand the child's behavior in school. Let us now consider each of these motives in turn, devoting special attention to their relevance to the tasks of education.

The Motive to Resolve Uncertainty

One of man's primary motives is to resolve the uncertainty that is generated when he encounters deviations from his conception of the truth. People continually carve from the flux of experience ideas of what they believe to be the essential nature of the world. The child as well as the adult constructs representations of what he sees, hears, touches, and smells. These representations are the mind's way of coding reality. It takes only about ten weeks for an infant to create a representation of a human face, and once he does so he puts great faith in the essential correctness of that idea. Man is disposed to believe that "what is, ought to be." Whenever an experience disturbs his understanding of what ought to be, he is motivated to confront that disturbance and resolve it.

SOURCES OF UNCERTAINTY

The earliest source of uncertainty is the unfamiliar, where unfamiliarity implies a discrepancy between a mental representation of an aspect of experience and a specific event that is both similar to and different from the representation. The discrepant event can occur in the outside world—a strange animal or a friend's failure to smile; or it can originate within the body—an odd feeling in the chest or an intermittent throbbing in the forearm. These events alert the individual and generate uncertainty. If the unfamiliar experience cannot be explained or dealt with, fear or anxiety is likely to follow.

Once a mental representation of an object or event is established—for example, a young child's representation of "mother"—all other events in the world are seen as either related or unrelated to that idea. Most objects—a fish, a bottle, a tree—bear no relation to the original representation. A much smaller set of events—another woman, for example—is closely related. All variations of the mother are also obviously related to the original representation. If the child's mother were to change her hairstyle, wear an unusual dress, or acquire a scar, she would become a discrepant stimulus for him. Some of the features of the mother remain the same; others are different. These discrepancies attract the child's attention and alert him, as though the trigger of a gun had been cocked. The child is now in a special state of tension, or uncertainty, and something must happen. The child must be able to understand the discrepancy, act upon it, change it, or remove it. If the child can do any of these things quickly, within a few seconds, the state of alert tension disappears, and no strong emotion follows. However, if the child cannot cope with the discrepancy, a special state of tension emerges and maintains the motivation to resolve the uncertainty and reduce the uncomfortable feelings. The specific strategies initiated to cope with the discrepancy and alleviate the state many would call anxiety will depend on the child's unique history.

A second source of uncertainty is inconsistency between two ideas or between an idea and behavior. For example, a child who believes in God may be told by a friend that such an idea is silly. Or a child who believes his father to be wise and good may overhear a relative criticize the father's virtue. In each case, the child has two inconsistent beliefs and is uncertain as to which deserves credence; he cannot hold both and must do something to resolve the uncertainty. Two ideas claim the same degree of legitimacy, and the child must decide which one is the fraud. The conflict is usually resolved either by changing each idea a little, and accepting both as partially valid, or by rejecting one of the beliefs as untrue. Occasionally, the child will resolve the conflict simply by ignoring the inconsistency.

Inconsistency between a belief and behavior also generates uncertainty. A child feels he is honest, yet he has just told a lie. He believes he is brave, but he has just crossed the street to avoid running into a bully. His actions cast doubt on his beliefs about himself, and uncertainty follows. If the child cannot resolve the uncertainty, perhaps by rationalizing the inconsistency in some way, he will become emotionally upset. Depending on the nature of the inconsistency, he will experience anxiety, shame, or guilt. Man's dislike of inconsistency between his beliefs and behavior pushes him to invent rational bases for his actions, for if one irrational action is permitted expression, no matter how benevolent its effects, there is the danger that thousands of other irrational acts will demand equal recognition. And there will be no way to decide which ones are entitled to public display. Man likes to believe he acts out of rationality, and he continually arranges his world to make this possible.

A third source of uncertainty is the inability to predict the future, especially if the doubt hovers over potentially unpleasant events like punishment, physical harm, failure, or rejection. When a person is unable to predict the future—when he does not know what events will occur—he cannot know what behaviors and mental sets to activate in preparation for the future events. As a result, potentially incompatible tendencies are activated. To be unsure of the future affection of another is to entertain simultaneously the contradictory beliefs "She loves me—she loves me not."

Uncertainty over when psychological catastrophe will strike is one of man's most discomforting states. If he cannot ignore the doubt or reassure himself, anxiety will mount, often to an intensity that prevents him from initiating any productive action or idea, and he will be driven to resolve the uncertainty. An observation of a two-year-old boy is illustrative. The boy had put some freshly laundered linen into a toilet bowl. When his mother discovered what he had done, she lost her temper and hit the child severely, perhaps more harshly than she intended. The boy was obviously surprised, frightened, and in pain, and he cried for several minutes. It was a traumatic experience. The next day the boy found another pile of freshly laundered linen and again put it into the toilet bowl. He then walked into the kitchen where his mother was drinking coffee, stiffened his body to prepare for a spanking, and announced what he had done. His behavior in this situation was clearly not an act of revenge for yesterday's spanking. If it had been, the child would not have told his mother and prepared for punishment. The boy had been frightened by the unpredictably severe spanking he had received and needed to reduce the uncertainty. He had to attain control; he had to know when the knife was going to fall. So he committed the crime again and presented himself for justice. But on the second day he was controlling the time and location of the punishment. It was more important for him to reduce the uncertainty about the consequences of future play with laundry than to avoid a painful spanking. As we might expect, after this second punishment the child stopped dropping laundry in the toilet. He had gained the needed information.

The two-year-old pulls on curtains, brings a lamp into the kitchen, entangles himself in his mother's knitting, or plays with newly ironed napkins. The child's mother often regards this behavior as mischievious, and psychologists have on occasion called it aggressive. But these acts are not always impelled by hostile motives toward the mother. They may be the child's way of finding out what is right and wrong, of discovering how he can get his mother to respond to him, or of learning how to interact with his mother when he has violated a rule. The mischievous behavior is an attempt to obtain some information about the rules of living. A young child typically glances at his mother when he is about to commit an act whose legitimacy is questionable, whether it is touching a strange vase, taking a bite of a freshly baked cake, or teasing a baby sister. The child wants to know if what he is about to do is permissible. At the last moment, just before the action, the uncertainty becomes salient enough to force him to make a response.

Uncertainty over the presence of the parent is particularly salient for young children; hence "school phobia" is a common problem among six-year-olds. The child who suddenly develops a fear of going to school is usually afraid not of *school* but of *leaving home*. The child is not certain that his mother will be home when he returns from school. Children test limits with adults in order to find out what is permitted; they want to know the rules of each game, contest, or interaction so that they can more securely select future actions. Once the child knows what is right and wrong, he will try to match his behavior to that standard in order to keep uncertainty controlled.

REACTIONS TO UNCERTAINTY

Although uncertainty often generates unpleasant feelings of fear, anxiety, or guilt, it does so only when a person cannot interpret, modify, or act upon it. It is the inability to cope with uncertainty that produces the distress and subsequent attempts to attain goals that will provide some control. Many of the popular motives ascribed to people by psychologists or novelists are derivative of the primary motive to resolve uncertainty and its subsequent anguish. If a person can act upon the initial discrepancy or inconsistency—if he can interpret, ignore, or modify it—the uncertainty will be alleviated. This resolution of uncertainty and aborting of distress can be seen in many situations. If a ten-month-old infant is placed in a strange room alone, he typically cries. But if the infant crawls into the strange room from an adjoining room where his mother is sitting, he will not cry. He looks around, becomes alerted, and crawls back through the open door to his mother. Objectively, the situation in the strange room is the same. But in the first instance there was nothing the child could do in the unusual environment. In the second instance the infant had an effective action to perform when he was alerted by the discrepancy; he could crawl back through the door to his mother. This action blocked the fear.

Similarly, a one-year-old who watches his mother walk away from him in a strange room will not cry if his attention is absorbed in an activity. If he is doing nothing, he will cry. Uncertainty leads to anxiety only when there are no available reactions to cope with it or to detract attention from it. These simple observations of the infant's behavior reveal an essential principle about anxiety and its control. Man continually finds himself in unfamiliar rooms, but whether he is seized by anxiety or provoked to make a constructive defense against the uncertain depends on whether he sees an open door and believes he can reach that exit in a reasonable time.

Uncertainty is not always accompanied by unpleasant feelings of anxiety. On many occasions it is followed by a subtle and pleasant emotion that invites the label excitement. The critical factors that determine whether excitement or anxiety will follow uncertainty are, first, whether a person has responses available to deal with the uncertainty and, second, whether the uncertainty is self-generated or imposed from without. Anxiety occurs when the uncertainty is imposed on the individual and he has no reaction to cope with it. Excitement occurs when the person generates the uncertainty and possesses an action that can resolve it.

This distinction between uncertainty generated by the individual and uncertainty imposed from without has important implications. Dogs become helpless in a simple problem situation in which they experience a series of electric shocks that they initially cannot turn off, no matter what they do. They eventually become passive in this situation. When they are tested later, under conditions in which they can act to avoid the painful shocks, they continue to lie helplessly. Apparently the dogs learned that there was nothing they could do and hence did not try to solve the problem.

The uncertainty that accompanies excitement arises from a person's estimate of the potential effectiveness of a set of responses aimed at a goal. The uncertainty that accompanies anxiety results from the absence of any responses to deal with a discrepancy. *A person seeks uncertainty when he can deal with it; he avoids uncertainty when he cannot deal with it.* Thus we do not deny the obvious fact that man seeks challenge and fresh experiences. At first blush, this may seem to negate the view that the control of uncertainty is a primary motive. But man seeks adventure and new ideas only when he believes he has a set of actions and ideas appropriate to the challenge. He rarely seeks the novel when he does not believe he can handle it. The occurrence of anxiety or excitement hangs delicately on the availability of actions and thoughts to cope with the uncertain event. Man seeks this brand of uncertainty because he enjoys taming it.

The most extreme form of protection against uncertainty can be seen in the behavior of the schizophrenic. The schizophrenic patient is seriously withdrawn from others and frightened of physical or psychological contact with them. Every action announces his terror of relating to another person. When he is willing to talk about his feelings, we learn that he has split his physical body from his psychological self. He does not perceive what we call the "I" to be a part of his face, limbs, or trunk. And his speech is punctuated with irrational and often incomprehensible phrases. The schizophrenic might reply to the gentle question, "How are you feeling today?" with a cryptic, "Feeling, speeling; oranges and pie; I cut you a piece to help you live."

The psychiatrist R. D. Laing has suggested that these symptoms can be understood as an extreme reaction to the most profound sources of uncertainty any human being can experience. The schizophrenic is afraid both of being destroyed by others and of destroying them. He desires neither. His sense of self is so fragile that he lives with the continual fear that if anyone comes near him, he will lose whatever remnant of an identity he still holds. If someone were to show him the slightest kindness, he is sure he would psychologically dissolve into the nurturant person and be engulfed by the giver. Since he regards himself as evil, he is afraid that if he enters into any relationship, he will hurt or destroy the other person. The schizophrenic speaks illogically in order to avoid being understood; for to be understood is to be known, and this may tempt another to come closer. His "crazy" talk is functional, for it keeps others away.

The schizophrenic's fears are so overwhelming and his uncertainty so profound that his only protection against them is to deny that the self exists. He may kill himself so that no one else can do it first. The dramatic defense of the schizophrenic bears some resemblance to the boy who dropped the laundry into the toilet and announced his crime. The child, like the schizophrenic, placed himself in control, even though the cost in terms of psychic pain was enormous.

The fact that other people are a greater source of uncertainty for modern man than the physical environment has led to an elaboration of motives surrounding people. It is perhaps not surprising that over the last thousand years there has been a growing tendency to regard people, rather than demons, spirits, poisons, herbs, or bodily humors, as the primary cause of mental illness. Thus modern psychiatrists believe that a mother's treatment of her child or the social conditions in a city are critical determinants of childhood violence or adult schizophrenia, whereas ancient Greek or medieval physicians placed the blame for these afflictions on impersonal, demonic, or biological forces.

SECONDARY MOTIVES

Each of these sources of uncertainty—discrepancy, inconsistency, and unpredictability—leads to the primary motive to resolve it in some way. There are many ways to accomplish this goal, and they vary with age, culture, and personal history. Some children learn that staying close to a parent alleviates uncertainty; such children are called dependent. Others try to get praise for painting, a report card, or a clean room; these children are said to seek attention and recognition. The wish to dominate can also be motivated by uncertainty. When a child feels he is subordinate to another, he can never be sure when the dominant one will place demands on him or coerce him into performing some action. The subordinate role always contains more uncertainty than the dominant one. Hence most people want to assume a dominant position with others.

Wishes for praise, dominance, or closeness to others—and their accompanying actions—that result from the primary motive to resolve uncertainty are called *secondary motives.* Since most adults are capable of helping the child reduce uncertainty, children usually want to withdraw from adults when they are anxious and uncertain because they have not had the experience of having adults help them control uncertainty and fear, or because they are not sure how adults will treat them.

Absorption in an activity is another way to alleviate uncertainty. In an ingenious experiment, monkeys were taught to press a lever to avoid painful electric shocks. When the experimenter subsequently eliminated the shocks for long periods of time, the monkeys pressed the lever more often than when the shocks were present. That is, when shock became an uncertain event, they used the response that was most effective in the past—pressing the lever. An action directed at a goal diverts the mind and aborts the discomfort of apprehension. The therapeutic value of work is based on this idea.

This principle also helps us to understand the behavior of teachers and administrators who have been made uneasy by the critical attitude of both parents and press toward the school's practices and apparent failures. Educators are anxious because they are not sure what they should do. This anxiety has led them to become preoccupied with change in any form as a way of buffering the uneasiness.

Many school systems eagerly await the announcement of any new curriculum, and a great deal of busywork follows. The new curriculum keeps teachers, principals, and supervisors occupied. They are doing something, and this activity keeps anxiety muted. As might be expected, many teachers and administrators have developed a motive for devising new curricula. For the act of constructing, perfecting, implementing, evaluating, and finally discarding curricula dilutes uncertainty and becomes an attractive goal in its own right.

The young teacher may be anxious about the poor progress of her pupils, the noise in the room, the unruly boy in the back row. She is prone to leap at simple solutions. Drill work, ordering children to the office, and trying a new reading program seem to be the answer to her troubles. The teacher busies herself with mastery of the program and introduces it into her classroom. The involvement in the curriculum diverts her attention from her uncertainty and anxiety, and she feels better about her work. If her anxiety remains low, she will seek out new educational procedures regularly whenever she feels uneasy. In time she will develop a motive for this activity.

This is not to imply that curriculum changes are of no value. New curricula are helpful and, if successful, will make educators more willing to try new ideas. Moreover, even if a new curriculum is not superior to an older one, the emotional involvement in finding and mastering it alleviates the teacher's uncertainty and she will view it as beneficial. Who is to say it is not?

The child's love of play is not unlike the teacher's devotion to devising or changing curricula. Young children do not like to sit and think. They actively seek variety in experience and through games. Although there is as much uncertainty in the child's world as in the world of the adult, the adult has a richer store of knowledge that he can use to analyze his doubts and reassure himself. The child is less able to use this defense of intellectual analysis and therefore chooses play, which can be so totally absorbing that it effectively prevents him from dwelling too long on uncomfortable uncertainties. During the long work periods in school the child is confronted with many sources of uncertainty. But he knows that afternoon games, with their fixed rules, are only a few hours away, and he is eager to begin them.

The varied schools of psychotherapy offer another example of the way in which involvement in an activity can alleviate anxiety. Each school of therapy seems to be effective with particular symptoms and patients. Yet the means by which each method attains its results are dramatically different. Consider the treatment of a woman who is afraid of crowds. Every time she is in a crowd her heart beats fast, her breathing becomes short, her palms sweat profusely, and she feels terrified. If she sees a psychoanalyst, he may tell her, after a certain number of sessions, that she is afraid of suddenly losing control of herself and undressing in public. He reassures her that she can control these impulses and that there is nothing to fear and suggests that she tell herself this the next time she is in a crowd. The woman believes the doctor's interpretation, for it matches her current understanding of her personality and her theory of mental life. The next time she is in a crowd and senses anxiety mounting, she is reminded of the analyst's interpretation. She thinks about it and reassures herself that she is capable of inhibiting her urge to undress in public. As she becomes engrossed in these thoughts her anxiety diminishes. "Thinking about the interpretation" recruits her attention, and her fear is reduced. The woman feels better, and both doctor and patient are convinced of the validity of the explanation that produced the cure.

The same woman might have made an appointment with a modern behavior therapist, rather than with the psychoanalyst. This doctor tells her that her fears are conditioned reactions to crowds. It is not necessary to know why the fears originally developed; it is essential only to break the conditioned habit, to decondition her. The doctor tells the woman that this deconditioning can be accomplished by learning to relax when one is in a fearful state. The feeling of relaxation will become conditioned to the sight of the crowd, and the fear will be extinguished. The doctor suggests that one way to become more relaxed is by controlling one's breathing, and he tutors the patient in the breathing exercises to be used when she is afraid. The woman believes the therapist's prescription, for his suggestion matches her theoretical understanding of the cause of her symptoms. The next time she is in a crowd and feels fear rising, she reminds herself of the doctor's suggestion and begins to concentrate on her breathing. As her attention becomes recruited to the task of relaxing, her fear recedes. The anxiety yields as she concentrates on her breathing.

The essential similarity between these two therapy procedures is that the patient believed in the effectiveness of an engrossing action or thought sequence and implemented it. The action required concentration and made it difficult to dwell on the feelings of anxiety. Thus it is possible that the fundamental basis for the cure in each case was not the specific nature of the therapy but the fact that the woman implemented a routine that she believed would help her.* The therapist might have told the woman to think of God, read the Bible, have a child, fall in love, take a Caribbean vacation, or work for civil rights. If the woman believed in the rationale behind any of

---

* Professor S. Valins has demonstrated that a woman who believed that her heart rate did not change while she looked at pictures of dangerous snakes subsequently showed less fear to a live snake. Presumably the subject's conclusion that she was not afraid stemmed from her belief that a steady heartbeat means low fear; however, the evidence for the steady heartbeat was coming not from her own body but from a tape recorder.

these suggestions—that is, if she believed that the actions would allay her fear—and if she trusted the doctor and followed his suggestions, her anxiety would probably diminish.

Study of the enormous variety of "therapeutic" procedures used in different societies suggests that the essential curative agent in psychotherapy is the resolution of uncertainty through the provision of rituals that engage the patient's faith. Members of a mountainous Peruvian community believe that if a person, with the help of a healer, can display courage while hallucinating that a boa constrictor is entering his body, he must be emotionally strong enough to recover from his psychological symptoms. Among the Yoruba of Nigeria the healer—called the *babalawo*—functions very much like an American psychiatrist. He explains each illness and suggests remedies by relating the symptoms to folktales and myths, rather than to early childhood trauma, as we do in the United States. The healer may tell a patient that he has developed certain symptoms because he was destined to be a diviner but failed to assume his responsibility. He can be cured if he becomes initiated into the cult of diviners. This initiation totally involves the patient's energies, for he must memorize long sections of folktales and poetry. In modern Japan a new form of psychotherapy, called Morita therapy, is gaining adherents. The curative regime consists of a brief initial period of enforced rest followed by work. The patient is told that he should evaluate himself by the products of his work rather than by his symptoms.

In each of these therapeutic procedures—which seem to be equally effective—the patient implements an ideology and a set of behaviors that he believes will help him. Since all cultures differ in their local theories of mental illness, the specific therapeutic regimes they select also differ. But in every case the curative value of the therapy seems to be based on the same basic processes—the adoption of a coherent set of ideas and the implementation of a set of actions that the patient believes will resolve his psychic distress.

The social institutions of most societies are conveniently organized procedures to provide action routines to cope with uncertainty. In our society, marriage, work, and school provide complex, ritualized involvements that bind our attention and turn us away from preoccupation with the daily discrepancies, inconsistencies, and doubts that cannot be easily interpreted or acted upon. Similarly, sexual behavior is often used unconsciously to resolve uncertainty, for an affair can be as totally absorbing an enterprise as work, investing in the stock market, yachting, or caring for three young children. Each of these routines fills the vitally human need for absorption in an activity with manageable uncertainty. A college sophomore captured this delicate tension: "I am afraid to stop studying or going to class, for these rituals keep me from the terror of saying, 'The hell with it all.' . . . Then where would I be? I'm scared of not believing in anything."

THE FAILURE OF TRADITIONAL SOLUTIONS

Many of our traditional methods of dealing with uncertainty are failing because a large portion of the population has stopped believing in their effectiveness. Young people are confronted with the discrepant experience of knowing large numbers of people to whom they feel similar but with whom they do not share beliefs about the rituals that heal. This inconsistency is toxic to the effectiveness of an ideology or behavioral routine. Hence some high school and college students are caught in a strangling web of apathy. They are confronted with all three sources of uncertainty—an unpredictable future, bizarre headlines, and doubt about the simple truths they have heard from their parents. But they have no effective set of ideas or actions to deal with these puzzles.

If young people had another goal to school and career, there would be less alarm, for there would be less apathy. But they do not; the young are searching for an effective substitute. Several candidates are gaining popularity on high school and college campuses. The wish to test the depth and strength of one's emotional capacities has become one alternative. Some young people ask themselves a question earlier generations never thought of: "How much pounding and expansion can my emotional shield accept?" The motive to master this challenge is likely to expend itself in a short while, for the total intensity and variety of experience is soon exhausted, the answer to the original question is clear, and the uncertainty is resolved. One will have learned how tough or fragile the inner self is.

A second goal gaining advocates is the search for honesty and intimacy in human encounters. Any ritual that carries the flimsiest decoration of artificiality is shunned, for it prevents contact and dehumanizes by forcing unnatural roles on unwilling actors who do not like the game of pretend. This ethic is more viable, for it is profoundly human. Since it is, in the extreme, unattainable, it is forever laced with some uncertainty and therefore satisfies the main requirement for permanence. Fortunately, it is a more healing motive than the individualistic competitiveness that captured the energy of earlier generations. If our society can nurture this freshly born objective, our 20 million young adults may be able to find a more comfortable and involving morality that will be toxic to the infectious boredom being carried into our institutional structures each day.

When human beings are motivated to resolve uncertainty, they are not deprived of a state called certainty, in the same sense that they are deprived of warmth when cold or water when thirsty. Psychological uncertainty is characterized by a particular organization of ideas and is accompanied by a physiological state of "alertness." This state has an inherent lability and is usually followed by the activation of mental processes that produce a different organization of ideas and a dissolution of the alerted state. The new arrangement is neither a reduction nor an attenuation of the first, but a different set of ideas. Some people may feel that the phrase "resolving uncertainty" is defensive, that it implies that people dislike the unknown and avoid new challenges. At the moment, the choice of words is a matter of taste. Given the sparsity of data on this issue, "the motive to know" might just as well be substituted for "the motive to resolve uncertainty." Although the first phrase is more flattering to us than the second, the logic and implications of the argument seem to this writer to be almost identical.

The Motive for Mastery

The motive for mastery—the wish to enhance one's knowledge, skill, or talent—is related to the motive to resolve uncertainty. There are, however, two major differences. First, the mastery motive is activated when a person generates a discrepancy between his level of accomplishment and the level to which he aspires. Uncertainty occurs when another person or event imposes a discrepancy between what the person believes to be true and reality. Second, the mastery motive does not always have a distinct alerting state that precedes the wish. A four-year-old may see a pile of blocks in the corner of a room and quietly sit down and build an elaborate house. If we ask him to stop, he does not; if we try to make him stop, he becomes angry. He is deeply involved in what he is doing. But it is unlikely that the child experienced any strong tension as he walked to the blocks, or even as he began building the house.

The desire to perfect a skill, finish a task, or solve a challenging problem can, of course, arise as a secondary motive based on the wish to resolve uncertainty. For example, a child may work hard in school to avoid criticism from teachers or parents—that is, to resolve the uncertainty surrounding adult acceptance. An adolescent girl may strive for better grades to maintain her father's affection; an adolescent boy may perfect his ability to fight in order to become the leader of a gang. Mastery often serves as a secondary motive to gain acceptance, love, and power. Perhaps the purest expression of this dynamic is captured in a statement made by a young woman following the anguish of an abortion: "I wish I could be what everyone wants."

Although the motive for mastery can arise as a secondary motive, it also has a set of primary foundations, which are based on three goals: the desire to match behavior to a standard, the desire to predict the environment, and the wish to define the self.

As noted earlier, the child is continually acquiring ideas about the world—how tall people are, how many feet cows have, how cold snow is, how fast cars travel. Once he decides on the true characteristics of these phenomena he comes to believe in his decisions, and he tries hard to maintain them. A child builds up a storehouse of beliefs and expectations about how the world should be. Some of these rules about the world he has experienced directly. He knows that milk is white, that chairs are for sitting, that dogs bark. The child is also aware of other rules that he has not experienced. He has been told that mountains have snow in the summer, that Hong Kong is a crowded city, that alligators have long snouts. These rules are like compasses that guide behavior and reasoning.

The child tries to simulate, by construction or imitation, some of these idealized states. The four-year-old builds a house of blocks because he has an idea of what such a house should look like, and blocks are available. A man climbs a mountain because he has a representation of what it might look like from the top, and there are mountains available. However, it is obviously fallacious to predict that any time a child sees some blocks he will stop and build a house. There has to be an additional element of *uncertainty about reaching the idealized state.* The child must have some doubt about his ability to match his actions to the ideal. If he is perfectly certain he can build a house of blocks, he will have no motivation to build it. Similarly, if he is perfectly certain he *cannot* build the house, he will not be motivated to try. The motive for mastery is generated only when the child is a little unsure. Hence one condition for activation of the mastery motive is possession of an idea about some idealized experience (called the *standard*) and some uncertainty about being able to match one's feelings, thoughts, or behaviors to that standard.

A second basis for the mastery motive is the desire to predict future events. Adults spend much of each day unconsciously estimating what the weather will be like, what the boss's attitude will be, how tired they will feel at 6:00 P.M., how much traffic they will encounter on the highway. The child too is caught up in the obsessiveness of prediction. He tries to predict what will happen in school, how his friends will behave toward him, how well he will do in the afternoon baseball game, how soon the recess bell will ring.

The child wants to predict events accurately because it gives him a feeling of control over them, just as the boy who threw a pile of laundry into the toilet confessed to his mother in order to be able to predict when punishment would occur. Every person wants to be in control of events rather than a pawn; he wants to be able to anticipate when, where, or how unpleasant events will occur in order to prepare for them. This desire leads to many forms of mastery behavior. A man who invests in stocks may be testing his ability to predict the rise and fall of prices, and his behavior is driven as much by this motive as by a desire for increased wealth. The child spends much of his first two years in school trying to predict what will happen and how he will be evaluated. Once he is able to do this, usually by the fifth grade, his involvement in school tasks diminishes. He has figured out the tasks and wants to turn to more challenging enigmas.

A child's behavior with a new game is one of the best examples of how the desire to predict uncertain outcomes fuels mastery behavior. If the child is unable to predict his performance, he is likely to work harder at the game. Once he has mastered it, he can turn his attention to another activity. The behavior of an infant with a new toy provides another illustration. A one-year-old discovers a toy xylophone and begins to play it. It makes different sounds and he explores, clumsily and inefficiently perhaps, the pattern of sounds. He begins to grow tired of the toy when nothing new happens, when he has exhausted the possibilities and is surprised no more. Each man's life consists of a series of attempts to predict his reactions in uncertain contexts. When performance in one context becomes predictable, he moves on to another. The joy is in mastering the unknown challenge, in the activity rather than in the product.

Emotion is most intense when a person is gaining predictive control, not when it has been gained. A newly graduated physicist goes to work for an electronics firm. He gains knowledge and experience and eventually accepts the responsibility for building six plants. Finally, at age 38, with the six plants completed, he tells his boss that he is bored. The man became most apathetic at the moment when we would expect him to be experiencing maximal satisfaction because his involvement in his work derived from his desire to predict and control the many uncertain outcomes of his job. Although a motive for mastery is activated when a person tries to attain an outcome with some uncertainty, *he only picks uncertain goals for which he has a response to make.* Uncertainties that generate no appropriate action are usually followed by anxiety.

A third basis for the mastery motive is the desire for self-definition. Every person wants to know his outstanding characteristics, the traits that define the self-as-object to the self-as-person. This desire is the essential component of the wish to gain information about the self, to know who one is. A college student remembers thinking before his first experience with a drug, "If I did not subject myself to this experience at least once, I might be missing something potentially enlightening."

Since the specific information that is valued depends on the culture, the child will turn toward society to discover the characteristics he should master. Contemporary Western society celebrates the significance of "knowing yourself," and young adults seek life experiences that they hope will provide partial answers to this puzzling question. For many young people this motive even pushes sexuality to a secondary position. They postpone marriage or sever a sexually gratifying relationship because they believe it will interfere with their search for self-definition. One young woman explains why she allowed the man she loves to leave her:

> I guess I'm just at the point of feeling able to develop some of my other talents apart from the housewife and mother roles which I know so well and could so easily get completely sucked into. But I mustn't stop now—I just now see myself as able to develop a significance of my own and I think I'm afraid that for awhile anyway marriage might divert my attention too much. . . . My primary purpose has been to understand myself, for if that task is not accomplished I fail to understand how I can be of value to anyone else. (Goethals and Klos, p. 181)

Some questions about the self can be resolved without anyone else's help. But in most cases the only way to evaluate oneself is to be with others. The culture tells a girl she should be beautiful. But how can she know how attractive she is unless she is pursued by men she values and can compare herself with a wide range of women who define beauty? The social group decides who is attractive, seductive, plain, or homely. A young black woman writes:

> There is always the problem of the white woman and her standard of beauty. It is her world. She stares out of billboards and *Mademoiselle* with all the cool and self-possession of the adored. And we of long arms, liquid eyes, and full lips want to be acknowledged. . . . If only our [black] men would stop chasing the white quasi-goddess. We wait . . . and I know few girls who give a damn about the current beauty standards. Beauty is a state of mind. Black women are reaching for that state of mind. But beauty takes a man to tell you. . . . Any woman needs a man to realize herself fully, sexually and emotionally. And the same is true of a man. (Goethals and Klos, p. 152)

Gratification of the desire to know the self too often requires a comparison with others. Our infamous tests of intellectual ability—be they the Binet IQ or college board scores—present the student not with an absolute score but with a rating that tells him how well he performed in relation to all the other students who took the test that day. Perhaps psychological maturity should be defined as that time in life when a person has established such a well-articulated understanding of self that he or she can decide on the quality or morality of an action without showing it to anyone or comparing it with the actions of others. A few fortunate adults come close to attaining this precious state; most do not. Children are clearly not capable of making completely independent evaluations of the degree to which they possess culturally valued attributes. Unfortunately, the child must use his friends to decide how big, strong, kind, attractive, smart, honest, or artistic he is. Since the child wants to know his assets and limitations, he is motivated to master difficult tasks in order to obtain some feedback on how well he is doing. The child wants an identity, and it is composed in part of his profile of talents. In order to develop a well-delineated positive identity he must master certain tasks. One of the critical factors in this process is the uniqueness of the skill to be mastered. There is minimal advantage in acquiring a talent that everyone possesses. The ability to walk, hold a fork, open a door, or make rhymes adds little to the self-definition. These skills enable the child to feel similar to others, but they do not permit him to feel different from others. Thus the child is moved to acquire skills that other children do not have or to develop exceptional competence at an everyday skill. The representation to be attained is the perception of self as more competent than another. The more unique the profile of competences, the better delineated the self-concept.

Anger and the Motive of Hostility

The emotion of anger arises from conditions that are almost the reverse of those that produce uncertainty, for anger is provoked when one is certain that a person or object is imposing—or may impose—a threat or frustration. There is a parallel between the subtle emotional feeling of uncertainty and the subsequent motive to resolve it and the emotion of anger and the subsequent motive of hostility. Two types of experiences are likely to provoke anger, and once this emotion is aroused the person will want to remove, hurt, or injure the individual or object that he believes caused his anger. This motive is called *hostility*.

SOURCES OF ANGER

A major source of anger is the interruption of a response routine. Any interruption—actual or potential—of a sequence of behavior directed at a goal can provoke anger. For example, a child is watching television and his brother changes the channel; or the older brother simply warns the child that he is going to take the television away in 20 minutes. The internal sensations created by such an interruption are one component of anger. A second component is the child's perception of the cause of the interruption. If he thinks he knows the source of the frustration, anger develops and is likely to be accompanied by a hostile wish to hurt, physically or psychologically, the cause of the interruption. Let us note again the parallel with uncertainty. Just as a discrepant event that cannot be handled provokes the altered state of uncertainty, so the blocking of a goal-directed action provokes anger. Uncertainty leads to a motive to resolve it; anger leads to the motive of hostility.

A second source of anger is a threat or challenge to a person's standards—to what he believes to be both true and good. Name-calling is a classic illustration. A ten-year-old becomes angry if he is called stupid, ugly, or afraid because he has been prevented from carrying out a potential response routine. A person's actions flow from his beliefs, and a threat to the validity of these beliefs leaves his behavior without rational foundation. A child would not study if he believed he was unintelligent and could not master a subject. An adolescent boy would not try to establish a relationship with a girl if he were sure he was unattractive. The undermining of standards is always a potential block to future action.

Most of the occasions for anger and hostility arise when we are prevented from behaving in a way that matches our desires or our preferred beliefs about ourselves. This mismatch breeds resentment, for we want our behavior and beliefs to be in harmonious accord. As the child matures, his anger becomes increasingly directed at people who are potential threats to the attainment of a goal or to standards that he would like to maintain. It is generally the case that we become angry only at people who threaten us— either by frustrating our desires or by preventing us from holding standards that we find pleasing. Most people are indifferent to the vast majority of others they meet; they are angry or hostile toward a very small proportion of the people they know.

An adolescent boy feels intense hatred for the young man who he suspects may steal his girlfriend. A young college woman resents her mother's excessive concern with clothes and appearance because she wants to believe her family cares about socially important issues. The mother's behavior threatens the daughter's standards. Whenever someone is a potential threat to the attainment of a desired goal or to the maintenance of a standard, anger and hostility are likely to develop. Since beauty, love, power, wealth, and status are among the prized goals in our society, the people who control access to these prizes are usually targets of hostility.

The simmering of anger between husbands and wives is usually due to the inability of each partner to gratify the motives of the other. The wife may want continuing reassurance that she is loved and is vital to the functioning of the family. If her husband does not allow her to hold this standard, she grows resentful. The husband may need to believe he is the final arbiter of decisions or the stabilizing figure in the home. If his wife does not support this belief, he too grows angry. Our culture's emphasis on the significance of sexual pleasure may lead each partner to feel the other is inadequate and to blame the other for a frustration that is, in all likelihood, of mutual origin.

ANGER VERSUS ANXIETY

An unpleasant feeling-tone following a discrepant event is common to both anxiety and anger. If the source of the feeling cannot be specified, or there is uncertainty over its termination, anxiety is generated. If the source can be specified and the outcome is predictable, anger is the dominant reaction. For example, if a person is not sure why he failed a task, he becomes anxious. If someone suggests that he is basically incompetent, he becomes angry. Anger occurs when a person mobilizes his attention on a relatively specific cause of discomfort, or more accurately, on what he believes to be the cause of the discomfort.

Anger does not always occur whenever a child's actions are interrupted. If he does not know what interrupted his behavior—what caused the tower to fall—he may become afraid rather than angry. If someone takes a toy from him, he begins to rage and protest. However, if someone were to gradually lift the toy away from him, as if by an invisible force, the child will become alerted and uncertain and will probably display fear rather than anger. Consider a man's experience with a door that will not open. The man will feel anger at another person if he believes that someone locked the door from the other side. He will become angry with himself if he believes that the door is stuck because he failed to oil the lock before the winter began. But if the man is sure that the door is neither locked nor stuck, and unsure as to why it will not open, uncertainty and anxiety will occur. The door becomes a discrepant event that he cannot explain.

Whether anxiety or anger arises in a particular situation depends on the person's interpretation of the experience. Anxiety occurs when he has no immediate explanation for a discrepant event that blocks a response routine. Anger occurs when he believes that he knows the cause of the thwarting of his actions. Several intriguing implications follow from this analysis. People who do not reflect upon possible explanations of frustrating events are apt to become angry; people who pause to analyze the situation are likely to become anxious. The national unrest in America prior to the 1968 presidential election made many intellectuals anxious because they realized that no one person or group was to blame for the strife that was tearing at the nation's spirit. "The conditions and the times" were held responsible, but people cannot become angry with an entity as abstract as "the conditions and the times." Other segments of the population became angry at the hippies, the blacks, college students, or all three groups, because they believed these people were the cause of social unrest. Many citizens voted for George Wallace out of anger with and hostility toward those who wanted Humphrey or McCarthy elected. They wanted to hurt those citizens who had frustrated them. The more knowledge a person has about a frustrating situation that has no clear or simple cause, the less likely he will be to respond with anger. But the more knowledge he has about a situation that does have a clear cause, the more likely he is to become angry, especially if the cause is human.

The child passes through developmental stages during which the balance of anger and anxiety changes. During the first three years, when the child has few explanations for unusual actions, he is likely to become frightened, not angry, at human behavior that he finds strange or unfamiliar. As he approaches school age and develops some fixed ideas as to causes, the balance shifts toward anger as a more common reaction to the uncomfortable feelings generated by discrepant actions in others. The eight-year-old cruelly teases a child who limps, throws stones at a bus carrying black children to his school, or rages at his failure to be included in a play group. The three-year-old, in contrast, does not become angry in any of these situations. The older child is more prone to anger because he places the source of his uncertainty and discomfort in the external world. A child's mood will quickly change from fear to anger if he realizes, or persuades himself, that the sudden turning off of the light in his room, which he cannot understand, is a trick perpetrated by someone. When the initially frightened child realizes that the source of his discomfort is human, he complains angrily, "Why did you scare me?"

The child is often uncomfortable and anxious in school because he cannot do the assigned work. However, it is easy for him to decide that parents or teachers are the source of his discomfort. Any anxiety he may have felt initially will be dispelled and replaced by resentment toward them, for if they had not forced him to go to school and to work at problems he could not solve, he would not feel so uncomfortable. The child may blame his parents and teachers for his "being in school" and have an unconscious desire to hurt them for this frustration. This wish can find expression in inattention in school or unruliness at home. The most serious threat to the child is the possibility of failure. Some children will be unable to blame either the teacher or the parent for the frustration of failure, and they will become anxious. Similarly, if the child cannot gain acceptance by his peer group and cannot blame anyone for this failure, he will become anxious. If the source of his rejection is specifiable, he may become angry and devise ways to injure or annoy his persecutor.

The teacher is also prone to anger. A noisy child interrupts her lesson; a bright child cannot learn the lesson she prepared. The teacher's anger often leads to hostility because she believes that she knows the source of her irritation. And she acts to eliminate it. She sends the noisy boy to the office; she tells the bright child he is not paying attention; she keeps the class after school. She scolds and scolds and scolds. She blames the size of the class, the absence of curriculum materials, the long hours—everything and everyone but herself. If the teacher understood more clearly the complexity of the classroom environment and made a more careful diagnosis of the cause of her irritations, she might be more constructive.

The anger of many college students arises from their beliefs about the causes of their frustration and distress. The average 19-year-old is unsure of his future and of the values he should adopt. He is plagued by uncertainty and vague feelings of isolation. Like the young child, he is confronted with many specifiable sources of frustration—examinations, term papers, indifferent professors, large classes, and social injustice. Since each of these phenomena also elicits discomfort, he unconsciously places the full blame for his dyspeptic mood on these immediately accessible targets. He is angry and wants to hurt those who he believes are the sources of his anguish. He openly criticizes his courses, his professors, his university, and the institutions of society. On occasion he attacks their property. Although his anger at these targets is not without some justification, it is amplifed by the additional anguish generated by the personal uncertainties of his daily life.

As indicated earlier, the wish to hurt the irritating object is the most likely consequence of anger. It is relatively easy for hostility to follow anger because of the close relation in time and space between the uncomfortable feeling of anger and the object or person causing it. The source of anger is usually present and specifiable. Since human beings continually frustrate or threaten others, by intention or accident, it is inevitable that hostility will develop. As people crowd together in smaller and smaller living areas, it becomes increasingly easy to blame others for personal distress, and anger and hostility may come to displace anxiety as a prepotent reaction to the daily discomforts of everyday living.

SECONDARY MOTIVES

Like uncertainty, hostility also leads to a variety of secondary motives, including mastery, power, recognition, affection, and dominance. There are many ways to hurt another person. Direct physical attack is the most obvious, but teasing, criticism, and threat are also effective. Less frequently the achievement of mastery and recognition, the acquisition of power and wealth, and sexual behavior can gratify a hostile wish. Let us consider how each of these apparently nonaggressive behaviors might gratify hostility.

A ten-year-old boy resents a less intelligent classmate who bullies him continually. The boy might strive for good grades in school in order to threaten the bully by making him feel he is less intelligent than his victim. The acquisition of power can be used to humble another who covets status. A person "gets even" with another by gaining more of what the enemy values, be it strength, power, money, or honorary degrees. Sexual behavior can also gratify hostility. A woman with an inattentive husband initiates an affair out of anger; a man who hates women uses sexual behavior to defile them. This writer recalls talking with a 19-year-old college woman who was engaging in promiscuous sexual behavior with older male friends of her father in the hope that he would discover her actions. She wanted to "shake him up" for his past indifference toward her.

Thus the same motives and goal-related actions that resolve uncertainty can also serve to gratify hostility. The child can work hard in school to reduce anxiety over parental displeasure or to displace a younger brother and cause him grief. An adolescent can obtain a power position with his peers in order to be free of the uncertainty he feels when others dominate him or to frustrate a rival who wishes to control the group. An adolescent girl may do poorly in school because she wants to avoid the responsibility and uncertainty of being placed in a situation in which consistently high performance will be expected of her or because she wants to disappoint her aloof, demanding mother. The public goal sought by the child is rarely a faithful clue to his basic intentions. This is one reason why some books of parental advice are of questionable value.

How shall we regard the goal-directed behaviors that seem to be aimed at gaining mastery, power, dominance, affection, sexual pleasure, or recognition? For example, should an action that hurts another person be called aggressive even though the intention is not to injure anyone? Should any action that serves hostility be called aggressive, even though it does not hurt anyone? We probably should not use the word "aggressive" to describe such behavior, for it implies a hostile intention that may not be present. The same suggestion is relevant for dependent behavior. All dependent acts are not the product of anxiety. Behavior is most profitably described—or categorized—by diagnosing its intention and noting its context, rather than by examining its final effect in the world. We call all acts of adolescent crime aggressive because they seem to have the common effect of injuring property or people. But these behaviors can stem from many different motives and can occur under different circumstances. We regard drug taking as indicative of a motive for escape and ignore the many other possible reasons for the action and the situation in which the action occurs. Taking heroin in a party setting in order to avoid teasing by friends is different in an important way from shooting heroin alone in order to escape depression. We must always ask about the primary intentions of the action and the situations that provoked the motive and maintained the behavior.

Sexual Motives

It may seem odd that sexual motivation is the last rather than the first motive to be discussed, considering Freud's emphasis on sexuality. Sexual motivation is important in childhood, but is probably not as relevant as control of uncertainty, mastery, and hostility to the work of the school. An important distinction between sexuality and the other three motives is the sensory qualities of the former.

There is a small set of sensations that people report as pleasant, and the source of the pleasure can be traced to the discharge of specific receptor areas on or within the body. A sweet taste, cessation of pain, warmth, genital stimulation, and orgasm are among this group. The mental representations of these sensory states are called *sensory motives*. Although it is obvious that people wish to repeat events that are physically pleasant (one four-year-old boy refers to his penis as "happiness"), the conditions that determine pleasantness are usually associated with the other motives just considered.

The primary goal of sexual motivation is the sensory pleasure derived from genital stimulation. The primary goal for the other three motives is not a sensory experience but a cognitive state. Of course, cognitive representations of symbolic goals do become associated with the sensory pleasure of sexuality. A man may experience sexual excitement when he sees a female undressed, when he hears a sexy joke, or when a perfumed woman brushes up against him. An infinite number of events and ideas can become linked with sexual excitement, and each can serve as a goal for the primary sexual motive. Moreover, the primary motive is not synonymous with the desire to be masculine or feminine or the motives for dating, marriage, love, and promiscuity. Each of these secondary motives and relevant actions can serve the primary sexual motive but can also gratify the motives discussed earlier.

SEXUAL BEHAVIOR IN PREADOLESCENCE

Although the primary sexual motive for sensory pleasure probably does not undergo much change with development, the secondary motives associated with it do. During the preschool and early school years many children develop affectionate relations with the parent of the opposite sex, and secondary motives to see the parent nude or to obtain physical affection become ascendant.

These sexual motives are important aspects of the affectionate bond between the child and the parent of the opposite sex, and they make the child more receptive to adopting the values of that parent. However, the anxiety generated by sexual feelings toward the parent can create conflict and symptoms like phobias and nightmares. Sexual wishes and masturbatory behavior can conflict with a standard (inconsistency between two beliefs, or between a belief and a behavior) and may generate anxiety and the subsequent desire to alleviate the distress. The child expects punishment for these motives, and his preferred reaction is to behave in a way that will make parental punishment unlikely. The strategy is to become obedient to parental requests, do well in school, or become responsible, honest, trustworthy, or virtuous—depending on what values the parents promote. There is only one danger in this dynamic. If the anxiety over sexual motivation is unusually intense and the accompanying guilt pervasive, the child may deprecate himself and come to the conclusion that he cannot do anything well. Excessive guilt over sexual motives can provoke the child to seek punishment. The child may misbehave in unusual and inexplicable ways. He may become irritatingly mischievous or annoying, and his behavior may be puzzling to his parents. These reactions can be the child's way of inviting punishment as an atonement for his violations of prohibited thoughts and actions.

SEXUAL BEHAVIOR IN ADOLESCENCE

During the early adolescent years the dominant secondary motive is the desire to establish heterosexual relationships. The adolescent combines the strong desire for sexual gratification with wishes for psychological intimacy with others and for relationships that will enhance his self-concept.

There is much concern over the permissive attitude toward sexual behavior held by contemporary adolescents. But even if we could produce statistics that reflect the relative frequency of sexual acts for young adults in 1970, 1950, 1930, and 1910, the number of episodes of intercourse would not give us insight into the essential issue. The attitude toward the act and its functional role in human interaction are the important themes. The grand-parents of today's young adults sanctified sexual behavior in marriage and vilified it before marriage. This arbitrary blend of values distorts sexuality and removes it from the realm of everyday human activity. Contemporary young adults have repaired this astigmatism. They have stripped sexual be-havior of both the sacredness and the shame that is characteristic of the atti-tude of older generations.

There is much health in this attitude. The price to be paid, if any, con-cerns the depth of the relation between the partners. Bonds between adults are often self-serving and fragile, kept taut by illusion. Sexuality has been an important component of that illusion. The sanctification of sexual behavior, though perhaps unnatural, constrains action and retards the inevitable wear-ing away of the sexual mystique. If the discoveries of sexual joy are made many years before a marriage partner is selected, it is less likely that intense passion will, like ambrosia, persuade the partners that they are privileged to a precious rite.

The Relationship between Motives and Behavior

DEVELOPMENTAL CHANGES IN MOTIVES

Since the desire to keep uncertainty within a narrow band is a pervasive human trait, the dominant motives during any period of life are often cen-tered on those goals whose gratification is a little uncertain. Hence we can better understand the changing motives of the growing child by examining the major sources of uncertainty. If a person is certain that a goal can or can-not be had with ease, there will be no activation of the motive for that goal. The motives that are preoccupying are usually those linked to goals that one is uncertain of attaining. These foci of doubt change as the child matures.

Infancy and Early Childhood • During the first four months of life the infant has few, if any, mental representations of future goals and therefore no motives. The causes of his actions reside in other forces. A newly hatched turtle crawls over yards of wet sand toward the sea with no image of the sea and no idea of where it is going. The conditions of light and shadow created by the moonlight on the water elicit the directional locomotion. So too with the very young infant. Some objects or situations invite responses because they are attractive in appearance or produce pleasant, exciting stimulation. The movement of a mobile is sufficient incentive to elicit hitting it. It does not help us to understand the child's response if we say that he *wanted* to hit it. Many events can elicit specific actions from the infant, but these actions are not necessarily guided by an idea of a desired goal.

As the child approaches the second half of the first year his first motives emerge. An example of this new maturity is seen in the nine-month-old child who reaches for a toy he saw hidden under a pillow, as if he knew it was there. When he shows surprise that it is gone, he is telling us that he expected to find the toy, that he had a mental representation of the object. We therefore infer that he was motivated. The young child in a typical family is certain of food and warm clothing and unaware of the problem of peer acceptance; thus he is not preoccupied with attaining these goals. He is uncertain, however, about the presence of his parents and their affection. Desire for these goals becomes dominant during the second year. When a child is in a strange house and cannot see or touch his mother, he becomes distressed if she does not return. His need for her presence dominates his consciousness, and no other prize, no matter how attractive, can lead him to forget his fear.

As the child enters his third year he learns to reassure himself that his mother's absence is temporary, and this source of uncertainty diminishes. But now a related motive becomes dominant. The child becomes uncertain about his mother's attitude toward him, her signs of approval, disapproval, punishment, and rejection. He becomes sensitive to any information about her feelings for him. The desire for some sign of positive evaluation dominates his earlier wish for her presence. This motive remains dominant until the fourth year of life, when a new source of uncertainty emerges. The four-year-old becomes concerned with his power and autonomy in relation to parents and siblings. His mother orders him to go to bed, to eat, to wash, to stop making noise, to stop teasing his sister, to stop picking at his meat. The constraints on his actions are frustrating, and he cannot predict when they will occur. His uncertainty over these events pushes the motives for autonomy and dominance to the top of the hierarchy. The child becomes preoccupied with whether he will be able to resist intrusions into his activity, whether he will be coerced into submission, whether he will be able to control others. He is still motivated for affection and positive evaluation but is now a little more certain of these prizes. Hence, when the issue of autonomy and dominance arises, the motive for affection takes a subordinate position.

The struggle to preserve one's autonomy of action and choice is threatened most seriously during the preschool years, and the need to control this potential threat becomes of paramount concern to the child. The desire to dominate others is based on the need to reduce uncertainty over future interactions with other people. The child rebels at the tension of not knowing whether the next person he will meet will force him into submission, will intrude upon his actions, or more seriously, will attack him in some way. When he is assured of a dominant position in the interaction, his uncertainty is quieted.

The Early School Years • As the child approaches school age he begins to base his conception of himself on his competence at culturally valued skills. The one-year-old who learns to walk, talk, and run is perfecting a set of coordinations that are natural to all children and hence easy to attain. School-related skills, however, are less natural—millions of children all over the world never learn to read, write, or add—and more difficult to attain. Children evaluate their competence at these skills in part by comparing themselves with others. Unfortunately, the child assumes that if he is less talented than another, he is also less worthy. The child is not sure he can read, spell, or play baseball, and he wants to know once and for all whether he is able to gain expertise at these skills. He is also uncertain about his ability to form friendships. Hence competence and peer acceptance become major sources of uncertainty during the early school years, and the motives to attain these goals are ascendant in the motive hierarchy.

Adolescence • During early adolescence sexual motives make an initial claim for salience. Western culture has persuaded every 14-year-old that sexual attractiveness is important, and the young adolescent is unsure of this new challenge. The first dates of the adolescent are exquisite illustrations of the attempt to determine sexual effectiveness, poise, and responsiveness. A new source of uncertainty breaks the surface of awareness, and the motives for praise, dominance, mastery, and acceptance move over and give this new wish a central place in the psychic space.

The young adolescent also feels uncertain about the integrity of his beliefs and about whether he holds a coherent set of moral principles that can guide action. He worries about the fact that he believes in God but some of his friends do not, and he broods about which conclusion is correct. He wants to base his moral decisions on his own values, rather than on the opinions of his parents, but he is not sure what his moral principles are. In short, the adolescent experiences uncertainty over his ideology. Campus unrest, the damning of adult authority, and occasional apathy are the consequences of this moral void. These disquieting phenomena will continue until young adults find a code of values to which they are willing to give spiritual commitment.

It is helpful to conceptualize stages in human development in terms of changing foci of uncertainty. The major uncertainties, like irritants, force the system to deal with them and, in the process of coping, produce change. As the child matures, his goals become more symbolic and less dependent on overt action. The three-year-old wants to be hugged; the eight-year-old wants some sign or indication that he is valued. The four-year-old wants to see his brother cry; the fourteen-year-old merely wants to know that his brother is upset. When an adult has gratified a motive it is usually the case that he has finally experienced the thought he wanted—or the thought that he thought he wanted.

EXPRESSING MOTIVES IN ACTION

As noted earlier, there is neither a simple nor a necessary relation between a motive and an action aimed at gratifying it. First, a motive need not lead to any behavior. A boy can be motivated to date a girl but may make no attempt to gratify the wish. Second, an action can serve any one of several motives. The primary motive behind a particular response is rarely obvious. One boy may set fire to a school in order to experience sexual excitement and orgasm; another to express hostility to a teacher; a third to be caught and to obtain notoriety among his friends. The external act of arson is the same, but the motives are dramatically different.

There are five major factors that determine whether or not a motive will be expressed in action. These factors are (1) the likelihood that a situation will activate the motive; (2) the degree to which strong feelings accompany the motive; (3) the availability of actions that can gratify the motive; (4) freedom from the anxiety and conflict that inhibit action; and (5) the person's confidence that the action will lead to a desired goal.

Activation of the Motive • Motives, like all ideas, exist in either latent or active form. Every person has hundreds of thousands of ideas that lie dormant until he happens to encounter a scene that evokes them. A man may know that Nepal is in northern India but may never call upon that fact until someone asks him or he reads a headline about fighting on the Indian border. Even the most hostile child does not walk around all day hating people. The motive is activated only when he is thwarted or threatened, and hostile action is most likely to occur following activation of the motive.

As the child matures, the activation of motives become less dependent on external circumstances and more closely related to his thoughts. The four-year-old sees someone with an ice-cream cone and wants one; he sees his mother caring for his infant sister and suddenly craves attention. The adult's motives are more independent of immediate events in the environment. A young man who has been wronged by a friend may be driven for years by a desire for revenge, without benefit of seeing the target of his hate. Of course, not all the adult's motives are completely independent of the external environment. A pretty girl, a traffic jam, or a challenging golf course can jar a motive from latent to active form.

The teacher can activate the child's motive for mastery by linking it to existing motives that are ascendant for him. For example, the average first-grader wants the teacher's praise and acceptance. He believes that a positive response from this "good" person implies that he is also "good." The child wants the teacher to approve of his performance and, by implication, of him. He wishes to avoid her disapproval, for it implies that he is bad. If adults are viewed as good, or at least as more good than bad, the profile of actions and objects that adults praise will help the child to decide which things in the world, including himself, are good. This "laying on" of value works like King Midas's golden touch.

One of the serious liabilities of building larger and larger school units in the service of economy and efficiency is that it increases the depersonalization within the school. A ten-year-old is lost in the midst of 150 other ten-year-olds whose art teacher attends all five fifth grades. College undergraduates are protesting against this terrible sacrifice to size, and many colleges must begin to create new structures. Elementary schools and high schools should begin to break up larger units into smaller ones. If a new elementary school for a thousand pupils is being planned, it should not be given one name and viewed as one institution. Rather, it should be given six names and regarded as six separate schools that happen to be on the same property. Thus a first-grade child will be in the only "grade" in his school, and upon graduation there will be six valedictorians rather than one, six prize-winning poems rather than one, and six times as many opportunities for students to participate in the creative and constructive activities of the school. Such a procedure would enable more children to believe in their individual worth. The more the child actively shares in the prizes that the community values, the more salient his motive for mastery and the healthier the school atmosphere.

Accompaniment of Strong Feelings • Motives are often accompanied by strongly felt sensations from the heart, stomach, muscles, and skin. These feelings form the basis of the emotions we call anger, loneliness, sadness, passion, and excitement. We are more aware of our motives when they are accompanied by strong feelings, for the distinctive experience of joy, pain, anger, or sexual excitement cannot be ignored. These emotions activate motives—thoughts appropriate to certain goals—and maintain our attention on them. As a result, action is likely to occur. When our motives are not accompanied by strong feelings, we tend to forget about related goals and concentrate on other domains of interest.

A person is not always aware of the motives to which his emotions properly belong, and a strong emotion can provoke a variety of behaviors. A four-year-old child may be irritable because he is hungry but may not be aware of the source of his irritation. If the feeling occurs during a quarrel with an older brother, it is likely to increase the child's hostility toward him. Every mother has an awareness of this phenomenon, for she excuses aggressive or mischievous behavior at 11:30 that she would not excuse earlier in the morning by noting, "It is close to Johnny's lunchtime and he always gets nasty then."

The number of basic emotional states is a continuing puzzle to psychologists. Some people argue that there are as many emotions as there are words for different kinds of feelings. Thus "sad," "depressed," "mournful," "grief-stricken," and "apathetic" refer to different emotions, for we have a different association to each of these words. Psychologists are generally disquieted by this casual attitude toward emotion, however, for it allows us to make up new emotional states each day merely by finding new names to describe how we feel. An alternative and more reasonable view is that there is a small set of emotional states that can be differentiated, and that all other emotions are derivatives of this basic set. If this assumption is true, how can we determine the basic set? Observations of infants, complemented by studies of chimpanzees, suggest at least six basic emotional states: distress, fear, anger, depression, excitement, and contentment. These six emotions may be primary because of their distinctive feeling tone and characteristic association with certain bodily postures, facial expressions, and vocal sounds.

Distress and Fear • Both infants and young chimpanzees whine and whimper when they are removed from their mother, are in pain, or are in a situation that is physically uncomfortable. This distress state occurs in all mammals. Fear is aroused by situations that are discrepant or that directly threaten the physical integrity of the animal. These conditions elicit tendencies to withdraw and characteristic facial expressions. The chimpanzee shows retraction of the ears and lips; the child shows widening of the eyes and retraction of the skin on the forehead. Spontaneous defecation and urination often occur when animal or child is intensely fearful.

Anger • As we have seen, anger is generated when a goal-directed action is either interrupted or threatened. Such a situation usually leads to increased motor action, lowering of the eyes, staring, and often a vocal outburst. The rage displayed by a chimpanzee who has been chased from an eating area resembles the kicking and thrashing of a three-year-old who has been carried forcefully from the backyard into the house. Chimpanzees also seem to show reactions that resemble human jealousy. Jane Goodall reports that a female chimpanzee being attended by half a dozen males bristled with anger when a younger female came into the area. The males quickly turned their attention to the younger animal. Following the unexpected rejection, the older female's hair stood erect—a reaction typically seen in anger—and she sauntered over to the younger female and began poking at her.

Depression • The emotion of depression, or apathy, is occasioned by loss of an object of attachment. Both chimpanzee and child show lassitude, loss of appetite, and sluggishness when they lose their parent—a combination of traits that we associate with depression. This syndrome occurs when the child knows the goal he wants but is unable to attain it, when he is helpless to obtain a desired goal. Depression thus contrasts nicely with anger, which is an active response to the thwarting of a desired goal. The shift from anger to sadness is often seen when two people sever a love relation. Initially, one partner is angry at the rejection and may even make an attempt to restore the tie. If he is unsuccessful, and still in love, he is likely to become depressed, if only temporarily.

Excitement and Contentment • Excitement is a pleasant emotion that most often occurs when the child encounters a discrepant event that he can assimilate because he has an appropriate response to make. A ten-month-old child watches a small car roll down a wooden incline, hit a doll at the bottom, and knock it down. During the first five or six occurrences of this event the child looks puzzled; he is quiet, subdued, and attentive. By the ninth occurrence he smiles as the car rolls down the incline, on the tenth he laughs, and on the eleventh he is laughing, babbling, and highly excited. The child finally understands the event and can integrate it into his experience. This simple example captures the essence of excitement. The child feels eager anticipation on the first day of school or before a carnival, a date, or a plane trip. In each case, an unusual event has occurred or is about to occur, and the child is prepared to deal with it. Fear and excitement are both preceded by the unusual. But fear arises when there is no available way of coping with the event; excitement occurs when the person is prepared. Contentment can be seen in the purring of a cat, the murmuring of a chimpanzee when he is being groomed, the smile of pleasure in a baby when he is being stroked or fed, and the relaxed mood following orgasm. The major difference between contentment and excitement is the level of arousal.

Possession of Appropriate Responses • The possession of responses that can gratify a motive also controls the child's behavior. It should be obvious that a one-year-old cannot effectively hurt his older brother or play baseball, even if he were motivated to do so. He does not possess the actions that might gratify the wish. Many behaviors are learned by watching others and by inferring the relation between motive and action. Thus the five-year-old learns that teasing can hurt; that yelling is an effective way to threaten others; that confession is a means of avoiding punishment.

Freedom from Anxiety and Conflict • Anxiety is a continual threat to the expression of goal-directed behavior. The changing mores on sexual behavior are a good example of this principle. In earlier generations adolescent girls were aroused sexually and possessed relevant behaviors, but sexual expression violated their standards and elicited anxiety, and they were led to inhibit sexual action. Contemporary adolescent girls engage more frequently in sexual behavior primarily because they feel less anxiety over its expression, not because the motive has become more salient or passion stronger.

Anxiety over motivated actions that violate standards builds through the first decade of life and then stabilizes. Hence during the period from three to ten years of age there is apt to be an increasingly disguised relation between a child's motives and his behavior. During adolescence anxiety over gratifying certain motives attenuates as the adolescent persuades himself that it is childish to be afraid of expressing resentment toward a parent or sexual wishes toward a love object. The relation between the adolescent's motives and his actions becomes more direct.

As noted earlier, inconsistency between two ideas is an important source of uncertainty and anxiety. When the inconsistent ideas are motives, the person is said to be in *conflict*. Many conflicts that derive from contradictory wishes can influence behavior in the classroom. For example, the desire for a teacher's approval is opposed by a motive "to be mature," which is characterized by independence from adults and a coolness to their praise. A young girl's wish to perform well in mathematics is opposed by her desire to maintain sex-role standards, which emphasize unusual competence at mathematics as a masculine trait. The wish to get better grades in order to gain recognition contradicts a motive to be cooperative rather than excessively competitive with others. Or the wish to excel may be opposed by the fear that one will not be able to perform continually at a high level. In sum, the motives for praise, recognition, mastery, and power, which push the child to work in school, often conflict with motives with an opposite set of goals. This conflict produces uncertainty, anxiety, and eventually inhibition.

Sex-Role Conflict • During the primary grades a young boy's reluctance to violate sex-role standards can interfere with his involvement in school. Most children view the school as a feminine place because women run the classroom. This perception violates the boy's desire to make his talents and behavior congruent with a masculine standard, and his zeal for school mastery is diluted. The college student's involvement in school is also affected by the desire to maintain sex-role standards. Masculine standards place preferential value on pragmatic knowledge and on special competence in mechanics, mathematics, science, and business. Academic subjects that have little instrumental effect on the world or that are primarily verbal—such as English, history, and foreign languages—are viewed as feminine. Thus it is not uncommon for a young man to be doing well in physics but failing history or English, while his female counterpart is doing fine in English but is unable to pass her physical-science requirement.

It is an unfortunate fact that the legitimacy of domains of knowledge is influenced by sex-role standards, and the teacher should be aware of potential conflicts. One useful suggestion is to masculinize the primary-grade classroom so that more boys can be persuaded that school is "man's" work as much as "woman's." The optimal strategy is to place male as well as female teachers in the classroom. Since this is difficult to do at the present time, the teacher might segregate her students for some part of the day so that reading and number lessons are held in all-boy or all-girl settings. The teacher can then introduce materials that are maximally interesting to boys or to girls, rather than using texts and problems that attempt to appeal to both sexes and are often insipid.

It is possible that the changing sex-role values of our culture will minimize this conflict in the years ahead and make these suggestions obsolete. But at the moment a large proportion of boys in the first few grades, especially those whose fathers are not in academic or professional vocations, view the school enterprise as feminine. We should try to remedy this maladaptive perception.

Conflict over Autonomy • The young boy's desire to develop a sense of autonomy as well as a masculine sex-role identity often leads him to resist complete obedience to the teacher, for he views the act of passive submission as both childish and feminine. He is pushed to defy the teacher occasionally and to resist conforming to her requests.

The desire for autonomy also creates conflicts for the college student. For example, a young woman who has worked diligently since school entrance and has an excellent record suddenly decides two months before graduation that she is going to withdraw from college to write a novel, join the Peace Corps, or work for civil rights—each a commendable and socially relevant action. But a few hours of friendly talk reveal the root cause of this decision. The young woman believes that her diligence was motivated in part by a desire to please her parents. She feels she has worked for them, and that graduation is their victory, not hers. Thus to graduate is to admit that she allowed fear of her parents' displeasure to motivate her, and she feels childish. The young woman holds a standard for maturity and autonomy that dictates, "There should be no fear of adult disapproval; one must work for personal goals." She cannot decide if she wants to graduate because she wants the degree or because she desires her parents' approval. The doubt grows and cannot be resolved, and the decision to withdraw is an escape from the uncertainty.

Some of the defiance of the college student also arises from doubts over autonomy. The student suspects his motives: Is he studying biology because he wants to be a doctor or because he wants to obtain the approval of his parents and teachers? It is much like fighting ghosts in a dark room, as if someone heard the command "Breathe" and was not sure if breathing were his idea or another's. It is frightening to work for a goal and to be unsure of why one is seeking it. Escape is one defense.

Since the young child also wants to establish his own values, it is advantageous to persuade the six-year-old of the value and importance of learning intellectual skills. The child is more likely to become motivated to do schoolwork if he believes that the investment of effort is his decision, not the teacher's. For example, the primary-grade teacher might persuade her students of the importance of learning to read by announcing that during one recess period each day no child will be allowed to play with another unless he can first read the child's printed name on the blackboard. The value of clear writing might be promoted by announcing one short period during the day when no child is allowed to speak, and any communication to another must be done by written note. These simple procedures can persuade the child of the desirability of academic skills. If the child decides that these skills are valuable—for him—his motivation to master them will be enhanced.

Conflict over Power and Status • Some children learn to devalue power. Since excellence in school occasionally brings recognition and a position of power and prestige among one's peers, the child may inhibit academic effort in order to avoid assuming a status role with others. There are two major ways in which such a devaluation of power can occur. First, the child may not trust his competence and may fear that if he gains recognition, adults will come to expect outstanding performance from him continually. He is not sure he can deliver excellence all the time and so prefers to remain unnoticed. Second, the child may grow up in a peer or sibling structure in which he is always the scapegoat. As a result, he will develop a negative attitude toward those who rule, who have power over others. The child may decide that the bad rule, the good are ruled. Or he may rationalize his lack of power by deciding that those who have power are corrupt, that no one can attain status, respect, or fame without corrupting his basic values. Thus attainment of power is de facto proof of a tainted character. Children and adolescents who have developed a negative view of power may not invest maximal effort in school, for they do not want the recognition and status that unusual talent can bring. Such children must be persuaded that attainment of power can on occasion be beneficial. For most children, of course, the task is just the opposite—they must be persuaded that academic mastery can bring the recognition and status that they value and desire.

Expectancy of Success • Even if a motive is activated, feelings are strong, and the child has a set of effective responses to make, he may not display the responses if he does not believe they will attain the desired goal. For example, most children want to learn to read, but many do not expect to succeed and hence do not involve themselves in the task. A ten-year-old girl who has lived in five foster homes since birth wants affection desperately and knows how to solicit it, but she does not approach others because she is sure her overtures will be rejected.

The belief that an action will gratify a motive determines not only whether the action will be taken but also the ascendancy of the motive in the child's mind. If the child continually expects his desire for friends to be frustrated, the motive will eventually become subordinate to others, and attempts to gain friendship will be rare. As early as three years of age the child learns the pain of failure and wants to avoid it. This aversion stems both from fear of punishment by others and from anxiety over not meeting internalized standards of performance.

The child as well as the adult erects strong defenses against possible failure. For example, a group of four-year-old children was shown a set of ten pictures and asked to recall as many pictures as possible. This is a difficult task for a young child, and most four-year-olds cannot remember more than three pictures. After recalling two pictures, one girl said, "I think I will just tell you one more and then we should do something else." When asked if he could recall any more pictures, a boy replied, "I can't, my mother won't let me, she'd be mad if I said any more."

Compare these statements with those of a 21-year-old college senior who was writing a thesis that would qualify her for graduation with honors. She had written the first chapter, and the instructor, impressed with its quality, praised her excessively and suggested that the final thesis would be outstanding. Four days later the student told the instructor that she would not be able to finish the thesis because she was not feeling well. After 20 minutes of conversation, the young woman admitted that the earlier praise had frightened her; she had become convinced that she would not be able to produce five additional chapters of equal quality and was afraid of disappointing the instructor and herself. Despite the potential delights of graduating with honors, her fear overpowered her desire for success. We would much rather avoid the pain of failure than taste the sweetness of victory, for when both are possible, we often prefer the former.

Most children in all cultures are driven by the primary motives of control of uncertainty, mastery, hostility, and sexuality. Since this is a rather limited set of motives, we might expect all children to be more similar in psychological structures and behavior than they appear to be. However, there is marked divergence in the secondary motives that flow from these primary forces. The specific goals of the secondary motives are taught by the society and differ across ethnic and cultural groups. The ten-year-old, middle-class child in Evanston, Illinois, is motivated to attain good grades; the ten-year-old child in Guatemala wants to be a better coffee cutter.

EIGHT

THE CONTINUING ENIGMA of INTELLIGENCE

T HE TENDENCY has always been strong to believe that whatever received a name must be an entity of being, having an independent existence of its own. And if no real entity answering to the name could be found, men did not for that reason suppose that none existed, but imagined that it was something peculiarly abstruse and mysterious."

John Stuart Mill may have been thinking of that enigmatic concept, intelligence, when he wrote those sentences, for "intelligence" has become one of the most controversial words in our lexicon. It was inevitable that many societies would invent the idea of intelligence, since man requires an explanation for the obvious differences among persons in their ability to adapt to the problems posed by particular environments. Intelligence is the psychic analogue of physical endurance. In those societies where the critical environmental challenges remain relatively constant over long periods of time, there is usually social consensus on the characteristics that define a "smart person," although one culture may emphasize activity level, another quality of memory, a third the capacity for pensive reflection. Fewer than 100 years ago, Sir Francis Galton believed that intelligence could be measured by evaluating visual and auditory acuity. That definition has been abandoned in favor of size of vocabulary, ability to solve arithmetic problems, and inferential reasoning.

Despite the lack of unanimity among scientists or cultures as to how intelligence should be assessed, many Americans believe that differences in mental capability—no matter what tests are used—are due, in large measure, to biological factors. Hence they are not very critical in evaluating the quality of the scientific evidence that supports that belief. I hope that this essay will persuade some readers that the evidence surrounding the inheritance of IQ does not permit strong statements about the degree to which biology or experience contributes to variation in IQ score. There is good reason to doubt the truth of the widely publicized statement that 80 percent of intelligence is inherited. May I add that this essay neither defends social egalitarianism nor evaluates the morality of those respectable scientists who have argued for a genetic interpretation of variation in IQ scores.

Let us begin by asking why the IQ test became the most popular method of measuring the concept of intelligence. Many scientists assume a complementary relation between the psychological processes of mind and the biochemical processes of brain. However, scientists who reject a concept like "overall efficiency of the brain" are less troubled by the concept "general intellectual ability" and are willing to believe that the IQ score may capture that characteristic. One group of psychologists is openly critical of the idea of general intelligence and favors separate measurement of functions like memory, perception, and reasoning. A second group, led by Professor Jean Piaget, regards use of special rules of reasoning as the best index of intelligence and deemphasizes the importance of the language skills that make up the heart of the intelligence test. A final group assumes that the ease with which a child or adult learns a totally new skill or concept should be the essential criterion of intelligence; the IQ test does not assess that ability.

Since scientists hold varied conceptions of intelligence, one would think that we would have developed different tests of this attribute. Why does one test dominate? The answer goes back to the first decade of this century, when school progress became the criterion against which the value of the intelligence test would be judged. Once that decision had been made, and it was made self-consciously by the inventors of the test, the history of the last 65 years was inevitable. Since questions that did not predict progress in reading, arithmetic, and composition were purposely omitted from the intelligence test, it is not surprising that a high IQ score predicts school and college grades. The test was constructed to guarantee that relation. Since satisfactory grades are a major requirement for college admission and subsequent entry into professional vocations that allow accumulation of status, power, and wealth, it is again necessarily true that the IQ score would predict a more successful adaptation in our society. However, the original basis for selecting the test questions has been forgotten. The causal relation between IQ and eventual success has been turned on its head, and it is argued that doctors, bankers and lawyers have higher IQs than cab drivers, plumbers, or house painters because they possess biologically better ner-

vous systems, rather than because the circumstances of their rearing familiarized them with the language and class of problem presented on the IQ
test.

We shall examine the anatomy of the IQ test to determine the plausibil-
ity of the statement that correct answers measure a basic capacity to learn
and manipulate new ideas, to remember past experience, and to reason
coherently—processes often regarded as the essence of intelligence. The
two most popular intelligence tests are the Stanford-Binet, used most often
from age two through adolescence, and the Wechsler Scales, used from age
five through adulthood. Since the tests are similar in content, we shall
discuss the Wechsler Scale, which is more widely used and covers a broader
age range.

The Wechsler Scale consists of eleven subtests, six of which seem to be
more verbal in nature than the remaining five. All 11 tests use words, pictures, and materials that are more familiar to middle-class, white Americans
than to any other social or ethnic group. Three of the subtests require knowledge of factual information—the definition of a word, an author, or a socially
acceptable rule of behavior. Other tests require remembering a series of
numbers, detecting the similarity between two concepts, discovering a missing element in a line drawing, arranging blocks in a design and pictures into
a coherent story, solving a puzzle, and, finally, decoding and copying a series
of simple designs. Scores on the vocabulary and information tests—which
are most predictive of the total IQ score—are most likely to be influenced by
what one reads and whom one talks with since they ask only for factual information. The tests that require the most active thought (constructing designs,
remembering numbers, and solving puzzles) have the lowest relation with
the total IQ and show less evidence of genetic control than knowledge of
facts. Thus we arrive at our first paradox. If IQ is a biologically influenced
characteristic, why is knowledge of arbitrary items of factual information the
best index of that dynamic trait?

Table 8.1 lists five questions taken from the vocabulary or information
tests of the Wechsler Scale and five questions taken from a test devised by

Table 8 · 1   Questions from Wechsler and Dove Tests

Wechsler Test	Dove Test
Who wrote *Hamlet?*	In C. C. Ryder, what does C. C. stand for?
Who wrote *The Iliad?*	What is a gashead?
What is the Koran?	What is Willie Mays' last name?
What does *audacious* mean?	What does "handkerchief head" mean?
What does *plagiarize* mean?	Whom did "Stagger Lee" kill in the famous blues legend?

Adrian Dove. Dove's questions were selected to be familiar to urban, poor blacks; the Wechsler questions to be familiar to middle-class, white Americans.

It is unreasonable to ask whether high scores on either test measure anything to do with basic mental capacity. A person's score reflects the probability that he has been exposed to the information requested.

Consider a related example. Janet Fjellman worked in Kenya with a group of children living in a rural area and an urban group living in Nairobi. The rural adults make a distinction between domestic and wild animals which adults in Nairobi ignore. When the unschooled rural children were asked to sort an array of animal pictures into conceptually similar categories, they divided them on the basis of domestic versus wild; the city children sorted by color. The assumption behind the scoring and interpretation of intelligence tests would have classified the city children as nonabstract and, by implication, less intelligent than the rural children. Since this decision violates our intuitions concerning the nature of intelligence and the role of schools in promoting abstract thought, we are forced to the reasonable interpretation that differential familiarity with the concept "domestic versus wild animal" was responsible for the products of the two groups. This explanation is supported by the fact that the city children produced more abstract categories when geometric shapes like circles and squares were the materials manipulated.

If the Wechsler Scales were translated into Spanish, Swahili, and Chinese and given to every ten-year-old in Latin America, East Africa, or China, the majority would obtain IQ scores in the mentally retarded range. It strains intuition to conclude that most of the children in the world are mentally retarded, with the exception of middle-class Americans and Europeans. Persuasive support for the cultural bias of the test comes from an examination of protocols from black children who are part of a longitudinal study conducted by the Child Growth and Development Center at Johns Hopkins University, under the direction of Dr. Janet Hardy. I examined these protocols and noted that many children were failing some questions because they did not comprehend the syntax of the question, the pronunciation of words, or the intention of the question. Their answers were reasonable, but they received no credit. The staff then performed an experiment. After administering the Wechsler to a large number of these children using standard procedures, they conducted a detailed inquiry to determine, if possible, why the children gave incorrect answers. They confirmed the initial suspicion that many children had given reasonable replies for which the scoring manual denies credit or failed to give correct answers because they did not understand the question. As a result many of them lost ten to fifteen IQ points.

The profound cultural bias in the test is perhaps best revealed by answers to the question "What is the thing to do if a child much smaller than yourself starts to fight with you?" The middle-class child, who usually indicates that he would try to avoid a fight, receives maximal credit. Many of the black children said they would retaliate. When asked why, a typical reply was, "My mother say if someone mess with you, you mess 'em back." Clearly, each group is telling the examiner what he believes to be the correct action in such a conflict. To call the first answer more intelligent than the second is to make mental capacity equivalent to morality.

A second source of error is the result of differential familiarity with the grammar or vocabulary that carries the question. Many black children who could not answer the inquiry "What must you do to make water boil?" replied correctly during the inquiry when the examiner said, "How do you boil water?" The poor black child, unfamiliar with the verb form "must you do," behaved as if he were addressed in a foreign language.

A third source of error stems from misperception of the examiner's pronunciation. When asked to define "fur," some said, "That's what happens when you light a match." Clearly, the child had interpreted the word to be "fire." When asked to define "sword," their replies suggested that they heard the word "saw." These examples, which comprise only a small proportion of all the sources of error that could be documented, suggest that the IQ test is a biased instrument almost guaranteeing that middle-class whites will obtain higher scores than any other group in the country, and that the more similar the life experiences of two people, the more similar their IQ scores.

If this conclusion is intuitively appealing, why do many people believe that 80 percent of the variation in intelligence is inherited? There seem to be two reasons for this view. Since the genetic differences among humans probably influence some aspects of mental functioning, it seems like such a small leap to the stronger statement that differences in IQ are primarily genetic in origin. However true the first statement, the second does not necessarily follow. Heredity also controls the amount and distribution of the hair on our heads, but the distribution of facial hair in Harvard Square is primarily attributable to cultural mores, not to biology.

Hence a more serious basis for the genetic argument is the undeniable fact that the closer the genetic relation between two people, the more similar their IQ scores. Since this fact is the principal, rational support for the conclusion that a person's IQ is 80 percent due to heredity, we must examine the bases for that fact to see if that inference is reasonable.

In order to appreciate the argument, it is necessary to consider some statistics. When the IQs of parents and children or brothers and sisters are correlated, the values tend to hover near the theoretically expected value of 0.5. Correlations between the IQs of pairs of genetically unrelated people chosen at random are close to the theoretically expected value of 0.0. Although the difference between 0.5 and 0.0 may seem sufficient to implicate genetics, one must not forget that in most of these studies the parents, children, and siblings resided in the same home, neighborhood, and community and, hence, shared similar values, motives, and knowledge. On this basis alone we would expect these genetically related people to be more similar in IQ.

Scientists quickly reply that the more critical tests of the genetic hypothesis are contained in comparisons of the IQ scores of identical and non-identical twins reared in the same environment and the scores of identical twins reared in different environments. It is true that the IQs of identical twins, who have the same set of genes, are more similar than those of non-identical twins who are of different genetic structure. However, Richard Smith, who compared 90 pairs of identical and 74 pairs of nonidentical twins, found that the identical twins, especially females, were also more similar in behaviors that are likely to be the result of similar experience, not heredity. For example, identical twins were more likely to study and do their homework together, to have the same set of very close friends, and to have similar food preferences. Smith concluded, ". . . there is a difference in the overall environment of the two types of twins which will, in turn, influence intrapair differences . . . it seems evident that the assumption of a common environment for monozygotic and dizygotic twins is of doubtful validity and, therefore, the role of environment needs to be more fully evaluated in twin studies."

However, since the IQs of identical twins reared in different environments are also more similar than those of people selected at random, the role of heredity seems certain, and the role of environment ambiguous. But that conclusion requires a condition that is rarely met; namely, that the twins be reared in different home environments and encounter radically different values and treatments. Since officials responsible for the placing of children in foster homes try to place them in similar settings, it is possible that most of the twin pairs were sent to families of similar religious, linguistic, racial, and social class background and, as a result, were exposed to similar experiences.

There are four major studies of identical twins reared in different homes. In one study, 41 percent of the twin pairs grew up in homes that were highly similar socioeconomically; only 26 percent (12 twin pairs) were sent to families markedly different in social class. In 9 of these 12 pairs, the twin who lived in the upper-middle-class home had a higher IQ than the twin adopted by the working-class home.

In another study, only 4 of 19 pairs of separated twins (21 percent) grew up in homes with large differences in educational attainment. Let us see what happened to these children. In one pair, one girl had five years of schooling; her sister three years of college. In two pairs, one finished high school; the other the eighth grade. In the most dramatic pair, one sister with an IQ of 92 only finished third grade; the other with an IQ of 116 had a college degree. Now it is less clear that the similarity in IQ score between identical twins reared apart is primarily a result of common heredity.

Robert McCall has found that the correlation between pairs of genetically unrelated white children from the same social class is not 0.0, but 0.3. Since the correlation between brothers and sisters living in the same home is only 0.5, it is reasonable to suggest that the similarity in IQ scores between siblings or separated twins should not be interpreted as primarily genetic in origin. We have recently analyzed some data that provide additional support for this view.

The data were supplied by Drs. Janet Hardy and Doris Welcher of the Johns Hopkins Child Growth and Development Study. They selected a random sample from their records of more than 400 children, all of whom had been administered a Wechsler IQ test when they were about seven years old. Most of the children were from poor black families residing in a relatively homogeneous ghetto environment. When pairs of black children were selected at random, the correlation between their IQ scores was low, and the average difference in their IQs a little more than 12 points. However, when pairs of children were selected so that each pair was of the same sex and their mothers of similar age and years of education, the average difference in IQ dropped to nine points, which is only a little larger than the average difference of seven points reported for the 122 pairs of identical twins reared in different homes, and smaller than the average difference of fourteen points found for one set of twins when IQ equivalents for their scores were computed. More specifically, among the genetically unrelated pairs of same-sex children matched only on maternal age and education, 43 percent had IQ differences of six points or less. This degree of similarity approaches that found for two of the studies of separated identical twins, where the comparable proportions were 47 and 50 percent. Since matching genetically unrelated children on maternal age and schooling markedly increased the similarity of their IQs, it is reasonable to argue that the similiar IQ scores of separated twins could be the partial result of placement in similar home environments.

Let us assume that number of years in school (which typically varied between seven and twelve years for this ghetto population) reflects primarily the mother's concern with traditional academic accomplishment, rather than her biological ability to do schoolwork. If that motivation was reflected in the treatment of her children, the similarity in IQ for these matched pairs would argue for the profound effect of environment on IQ.

Those who favor the genetic hypothesis reply that social class is correlated with IQ because biologically more intelligent people rise in social class. Hence matching children on mother's education is equivalent to matching them on basic intelligence. This statement ignores the fact that the first generation of European Catholic and Jewish immigrants who came to America typically did not attain any more formal schooling or higher IQ scores than contemporary blacks, Puerto Ricans, and Mexican-Americans. Today the distribution of IQ scores of Jews and Catholics is similar to that of the dominant group of white Protestants. Since it is unlikely that the "genes governing intelligence" in these ethnic groups have changed during the last 50 years, it is fair to question the assumption that being low on the social class ladder at a particular time is primarily the result of hereditary factors.

Moreover, if the genetic interpretation of social class differences were correct, we should not see any major class differences in the parental treatment of young children, for the IQ differences between middle- and lower-class parents and children are presumably the product of internal biological forces, not differential socialization. Any evidence of social class differences in parental treatment that was theoretically concordant with different IQs would weaken the genetic position.

Fortunately, recent studies have found dramatic differences in the mother's treatment of her child as a function of her education and her husband's occupation, differences that imply that better-educated parents create experiences for their children that facilitate good performance on IQ tests. Steven Tulkin observed white working- and middle-class mothers of ten-month-old infants and found that middle-class mothers engaged in reciprocal verbal interaction with their infants more often than working-class mothers. It is reasonable to assume that this language stimulation would facilitate the high vocabulary scores middle-class children attain on an IQ test. Several years ago I observed two-year-old children from working- and middle-class homes and found that the working-class mothers issued more arbitrary prohibitions and were more likely to remind their children of their faults and the possibility of potential punishment. This experience is likely to impair self-confidence—a personality characteristic that affects performance on an IQ test. These results—suggesting that the relation between parental social class and IQ reflects the role of differential experience—weaken the view that social class and IQ are positively related because the middle class contains a greater proportion of people with biologically better nervous systems.

A third point of vulnerability in the genetic argument concerns the legitimacy of the *heritability ratio* to assess the magnitude of hereditary influence. Estimates of the heritability ratio are usually based on the difference in the IQ correlation between identical and nonidentical twins. The ratio is based on the assumption that the causes of variation in IQ can be added together, some being due to environment and some to heredity. A serious criticism of the use of the heritability ratio is that its proponents have ignored the possibility that heredity and environment might be highly correlated in their computations. There is good reason to believe that aspects of the young child's temperament are treated differently by middle- and lower-class parents, and, as a result, the qualities measured by IQ tests are enhanced in middle-class homes and, perhaps, suppressed in working-class homes. If this were true, current heritability values might be spuriously high.

Consider a concrete illustration of this issue. I recently completed a longitudinal study of a large group of firstborn, white children who were followed from 4 through 27 months of age. There was a major difference among the four-month-olds in the tendency to babble spontaneously—some infants were extremely quiet while others were continuously cooing. Let us assume that biological factors are partially responsible for this variation in infant "vocalization." Observations in the homes of these children revealed that college-educated mothers were much more responsive to their infants' babbling than mothers with less than a high school education. The middle-class mothers talked back to their infants, and long reciprocal dialogues ensued. At 27 months, the girls who were the most talkative and had the largest vocabularies (by inference, the highest IQ scores) had been highly vocal infants reared by college-educated mothers. Highly vocal infants raised by lower-middle-class mothers were significantly less proficient verbally.

Since social class is typically correlated with IQ score, it is reasonable to suggest that the heritability values, which are interpreted as reflecting genetic factors, are spuriously inflated by a strong relation between particular temperamental traits and social class differences in parental responsivity to these traits.

There are, therefore, three bases for doubting the provocative statement that heredity accounts for most of the variation in IQ score. The IQ test is a culturally biased instrument; the similar IQ scores of genetically related people can be simulated in genetically unrelated people who live in similar environments; and, finally, the probable correlation between heredity and environment is ignored in current interpretations of the heritability ratio.

Why, then, do many scientists and parents continue to believe in the inheritance of IQ (excluding the small proportion of children with specific forms of severe mental retardation resulting from known genetic factors)? Perhaps one reason derives from the belief that in order to maintain stability, a small group must possess some power over the mass of the citizenry. In most instances the psychological traits of those in power become, with time, the explanation for the differences in status and privilege. Tenth-century Europe awarded power to those who were assumed to be more religious than their brothers. The presumption of a capacity for more intense religiosity provided a rationale that allowed the larger society to accept the fact that a privileged few were permitted entry into marble halls. In the isolated Mayan Indian village in which I have worked, the men tell us that women must never be given responsibility because they are born fearful and cannot make decisions. Being born male is the village's explanation of differential ability to wield power. Contemporary American society explains its unequal distribution of status as a partial product of differential intelligence, rather than innate religiosity or sex, and it makes the same genetic arguments. Intelligence is America's modern interpretation of saintliness, religiosity, courage, or moral intensity, and it has become the basis for the awarding of prizes.

American parents are deeply concerned with the intellectual development of their children. Indeed, intelligence is regarded as if it were a primary psychological organ. The requirements for entrance into all major status-awarding institutions consist primarily of mental examinations and past intellectual performance. There is no assessment of physical prowess, religious attitudes, or emotional stability, although there is some acknowledgment of the relevance of motivation, honesty, and character as revealed through letters of recommendation. But the Scholastic Achievement Test and Graduate Record, medical, and law entrance examinations are purely cognitive in content. This practice announces the culture's assumption that if one is intelligent, it is likely he also will make technically correct and morally appropriate decisions in any position of trust and responsibility.

This prejudice is reminiscent of Plato's conviction that a person possessing correct knowledge cannot help but make morally proper choices. It is also reflected in the writings of the decade following the Revolutionary War when Robert Coram, Noah Webster, and others wrote that education was the best prophylaxis against despotism. If a person knew the law, he would obey it. Salvation, too, was dependent on proper tutoring, for no one could appreciate the principles of Christianity without proper education. Thus the ignorant were likely to be full of vice and susceptible to the devil's temptations. A half-century ago we regarded mentally retarded people as moral defectives, for a weak intellect made a child vulnerable to impulsive and morally devious actions. In the years before the Civil War it was assumed that vice and corruptibility were a product of ignorance and that education and knowledge could alleviate these stains. The twin attitudes that vice is established early and education can uproot it are expressed in Noah Webster's "Education of Youth":

> The only practical method to reform mankind is to begin with children, to banish, if possible, from their company every low bred drunken immoral character. . . . Virtue and vice will not grow together in a great degree, but they will grow where they are planted and when one has taken root it is not easily supplanted by the other. The great art of correcting mankind therefore consists in prepossessing the mind with good principles. For this reason society requires that the education of youth should be watched with the most scrupulous attention. Education in a great measure forms the moral characters of men and morals are the basis of government. (Rudolph 1965, p. 67)

Robert Coram affirmed Webster's views: "Information is fatal to despotism. . . . In a republican government . . . every class of people should know and love the laws. This knowledge should be diffused by means of schools and newspapers and attachment to the laws may be formed by early impressions upon the mind" (Rudolph 1965).

For Coram, as for Plato, to know what is true is synonymous with being moral. Knowledge is the key to morality, and preparedness for acquiring knowledge requires intelligence.

We want our politicians, judges, doctors, lawyers, and teachers to be intelligent. Halberstam captures this American bias in *The Best and the Brightest*. McNamara, Bundy, Rostow, and others who surrounded John Kennedy in the early 1960s were chosen because they were intelligent, rational, and dispassionate, not because they knew how to manage a defense department or run an antiguerrilla war in Vietnam. Deep in our souls lies the belief that an intelligent person can analyze any complex situation by breaking it down into logically rational categories. And if those categories can be placed in mathematical form, decisions can be made without the interference of sentimental prejudice. Those who can perform this mental activity with alacrity are assumed to have a special biological quality that can be applied, like a wizard's baton, to all troublesome situations. They are good shamans who deserve our respect, reverence, and awe. We reject the

Greek view that emotion should moderate a penetrating rationality. The less colored by affect, the firmer and more reliable the intellectual conclusion. To be smart is to possess a basic biological attribute that cannot be lost easily.

Why and how did we acquire this reverence for analytic, dispassionate, quantitative rationality and make priests of those who display this competence in one area of thought? The answer may lie partly in our desire to believe in a generalized mental ability that transcends specific domains of skill. Moreover, we want to maximize certainty and minimize errors. A society preoccupied with the investments of large material resources must avoid mistakes that are costly of capital. A society concerned primarily with political ideology, or an agricultural community dependent on rain and sunshine, has less to risk in a less rational decision and is a little more likely to award intuition and external agents more power.

America emphasizes a rational intelligence over most other human attributes in part because it recognizes that opinions and philosophies are culturally determined. We have been taught to be tolerant of other people's beliefs because they are presumed to be largely the product of the vicissitudes of experience. But intelligence is supposed to be made of different stuff. Despite the longing of many Americans that variation in all important psychological qualities be the consequence of experience, most, including some libertarians, believe that mental ability is influenced at least in part by biology. Therefore, level of intellectual talent reflects profoundly an aspect of each person's essence. Intelligence is seen as a psychological manifestation of a physical entity, the way beauty is tightly yoked to the arrangement of eyes, nose, and mouth on the frame of the face. Intelligence may be the only human trait that the contemporary West regards in absolute terms, in contrast to the more relativistic attitude our society takes toward individual variations in feelings, motives and values. Our attitude toward the nature of intelligence conflicts with the equally strong desire to prove that Locke was right and to arrange environments so that all can be competent.

We readily acknowledge differences in opinions about sexuality, God, work, and courage. When we meet someone who prefers a Catholic to a Protestant, adultery to fidelity, or a bureaucratic job to an entrepreneurial one, we do not assume that those preferences were fixed by neural tissue but rather that they were molded by an accumulation of encounters. There is a tacit consensus that each person can potentially believe anything. Since we cannot easily delegitimize the opinions of others, evaluating a person's virtue by his beliefs is regarded as intolerant and bigoted. But in formulating a theory of life and society, we need one absolute in a sea of relativism, one buoy to keep us from drowning. We have made intelligence that absolute.

We are helped in this prejudice by our knowledge that some diseases associated with mental deficiency are biological in origin. It is natural to go beyond this limited information and assume that most variability in intellectual talent derives from biology.

Additionally, morality and character seem to be products of our will. We have the sense that we can be honest and kind if we choose. But insight, an elegant metaphor, or a creative invention seem beyond volition. That is one reason why we award more respect to Kant, Beethoven, or Einstein than we do to the most honest of men. The belief that elegant intellectual products cannot be created through simple persistence, despite Edison's epigram about the ratio of perspiration to inspiration, is based on the faith that forces beyond our control are contributing to mental ability. In a society that respects rational, material explanations that can be confirmed or refuted in empirical observation, it is reasonable to suppose that biological forces emanating from heredity would constitute that special force.

If we believe we can affect change in a personal quality, we are likely to award formative power to the environment. If we have the sense that motivation is insufficient, we are more prepared to award influence either to external forces like social prejudice or to biological factors like heredity. Most societies award a special potency to qualities that cannot simply be willed, like the ability to trance or being born with a caul. Moreover, rare qualities are more exciting than common ones; thus a flower seems more beautiful than a leaf; a heron more lovely than a robin. (Of course, some rarities, such as mental retardation and schizophrenia, are devalued but that is because they violate basic assumptions about proper behavior.) Human qualities that are infrequent and seem beyond our sphere of personal influence have a special power either to awe or to frighten us. We are tempted, quite naturally, to attribute their occurrence to lawful, legitimate forces we cannot control. Since we do not want to believe that the attainment of power and status, which we have come to eroticize, is arbitrary, we satisfy our twin desires to be democratic and egalitarian while retaining orderly procedures for the transfer of power from one generation to the next by using intelligence as a basis for awarding access to positions of status. Since status is correlated with virtue in the West, the intelligent are likely to be regarded as morally pure.

In Confucian China, men strove to achieve morality, not power, and the source of morality was not knowledge but external circumstances. We believe that humans are born with unequal intelligence, but the Taoists and Confucianists assumed that all were born with equal merit and equal potential to be "jen"—the ideal person. The reasons why the West stressed intelligence and the East ethics are unclear. Economy, social structure, heterogeneity of values, contact with other groups probably all influenced the different emphases. But each culture has some choice as to the qualities it selects as primary (the attributes that unlock the door to power and dignity) and the theory it uses to explain how those attributes are gained.

Since most Americans believe that unequal levels of intelligence contribute to differential power, wealth, and dignity, American parents worry a great deal about the integrity of their child's mind. There is less concern with physical appearance, vigor, health—even happiness. The amount of shame or pride an American middle-class mother feels about a body blemish or a happy disposition is small when compared with the emotion felt when she learns her child is intellectually behind or a genius. We have placed a special stigmata on any impairment of intellect because access to power in the West requires education, and education requires intelligence. Hence early signs of intellectual impairment, no matter how mild, conjure up images of hoboes and ditchdiggers—doomed to spend their lives with shovel and pick. Most Americans have little sympathy for Minsky's interpretation of intelligence: "My own view is that this is more of an aesthetic question, or one of sense of dignity, than a technical matter. To me intelligence seems to denote little more than the complex of performances which we happen to respect but do not understand."

What, then, should we conclude about the meaning of intelligence and the causes of differences among people in the efficiency and quality of their language, reasoning, and ability to solve challenging problems? The basic capacity to remember, to symbolize, to reason, to abstract, and to categorize is present in all human beings. My work in Guatemala suggests that ten-year-old children living in extremely isolated agricultural villages show a potential capacity for symbolism, memory, and conceptual inference comparable to that displayed by middle-class American children. Furthermore, it is useful to talk about competence in the separate mental processes that constitute mental life rather than about a generalized intelligence. Some people possess an excellent memory for visual scenes but have difficulty learning a new language. J. P. Guilford has argued for many years that a mental profile should be assigned to each person rather than a summary number that is presumed to reflect overall mental prowess. The concept of "general intelligence" is, in my opinion, theoretically useless because it distorts the nature of cognitive functioning.

As for the bases of the differences in quality of thought, I remain puzzled. Existing scientific data do not permit strong statements about the degree of genetic or environmental control. The differences in IQ between blacks and whites can best be explained as a result of experience and the serious bias in the tests. The high degree of similarity between genetically related people could be the partial product of similar experiences. Future research is likely to reveal that heredity makes a contribution to the different profiles of human talent. But available knowledge is simply too faulty to permit any firm conclusion. Those who must have an answer to this question will have to be more patient. When I was a student, Down's syndrome, which was then called Mongolism, was regarded as nongenetic. We now know that this defect is caused by a chromosomal anomaly. Nature is an elusive teacher, and we must not allow what we want to believe to distort our interpretation of the messages she has supplied us with up to now.

NINE

ON CULTURAL dEPRIVATION

Introduction

EVERY society presents its members with a set of psychological requirements and a calendar announcing the approximate age of expected
appointments. The substance of the requirements is a function of the unstated, and often unconscious, presuppositions of the culture as well as
the pragmatic skills and characterological traits most citizens recognize are
necessary to maintain the society's functions. Most families in a given community are aware of these values and prepare their young children for their
future evaluation during adolescence and early adulthood. The fifth-century
Athenians esteemed physical coordination, eighteenth-century colonial
Americans valued Christian piety and conformity, the Utku Eskimo of Hudson Bay, control of aggression. The families in these settings tried to socialize
the locally sacred qualities in their young. But despite a consensual proto-
type toward which all move, there is always variation in the level of attainment or perfection of the profile of prized attributes. Indeed, if a characteristic was equally perfected in all adults it would not be among the cherished
dimensions, for it would be of no value in differentiating among citizens.
That is why an erect posture and a pleasing manner, though appreciated, are
rarely high in the hieararchy of special qualities. They are too easy to obtain.

If modern families are a correct guide to the past, it was probably the
case then, as it is now, that children from families with greater power, status,
and wealth were in firmer possession of the important characteristics than
were the less privileged. This is the puzzle we seek to understand. Is this
because the former had different genetic constitutions, treated their children
differently, were more confident that they could influence their children's

From *Genetics, environment and intelligence*, ed. A. Oliverio (Elsevier/North Holland Bio-
medical Press, 1977), pp. 371–84.

future, were more effective role models, or is the difference due to a combination of these factors?

All societies invent categories that simulataneously describe and explain the 10 to 20 percent of children whose profile of behavioral accomplishment is least pleasing. In trying to understand this variation, the community can select from a limited number of interpretations: luck, supernatural power, diet, illness, heredity, family practices, peer experiences, and institutional practices, each of which is seen as potentially influencing the abilities, skills, motivation, energy, or emotions of the child. Since some of these forces will be either inconsistent with the society's cosmology or just plain absent, in practice, the adult community has only a few choices. In modern Mayan Indian villages in northwest Guatemala, the valued traits include physical endurance, alertness to opportunity, and responsibility. A failure to obtain some semblance of these qualities by ten years of age is usually blamed on the date of birth, demons, or failure of the family to train the seven- and eight-year-old properly. Rarely is luck, heredity, or peer experience called upon to account for success or failure. In North America and Western Europe, the valued traits from three competence-performance pairs—intelligence and academic success, an affection for people and effective habits of social interaction, and a desire for autonomy and behavioral independence. Although the latter two are prized, the community beleives that the first pair, intellectual competence and school success, is most important for the attainment of economic security and status and, hence, awards it a special salience.

Since there is such obvious diversity in the cognitive, attitudinal, and motivational qualities of preadolescents who score in the lowest twentieth percentile of the norm-referenced instruments we use to evaluate intellectual and academic skills, it is reasonable to invent nominal classifications that will simultaneously separate the heterogenous group into more homogenous subpopulations and imply the reason for the deviance of each population.

The organically mentally retarded are the smallest group. It is presumed that they have a defect in central nervous system function, owing to a genetic or at least biological etiology, that leads to poor cognitive performance. A second group, called minimally brain damaged, is assumed to have a subtle central nervous system impairment, either cell damage, slower development of the central nervous system, or biochemical disturbance, that cannot be localized, but that impairs cognitive functioning. A third group, called the physically handicapped, has obvious sensory or physical impairments that can be expected to impede cognitive development because of the facilitating function that keen sight and hearing have for cognitive work. A fourth group, classified as emotionally disturbed, presumably has an intact biological system but is held to be anxious, hostile, or inattentive because of unknown psychological experiences encountered during the first half-dozen years. After these four groups have been set aside, there is still a sizable group of children who still score in the lowest twentieth percentile, perhaps half of the original sample. They are not evenly distributed across the society and are more often found in urban than in rural areas and in families which are not only economically less secure than the majority but also hold a value system different from the majority, two characteristics that define the term "ethnic minority."

In the United States and Western Europe, children from ethnic minorities always make up the majority of the group who fail in school and obtain low scores on tests of intellectual capacity. Given the cosmology of the modern West, only two reasonable interpretations are possible. One assumes that these children are biologically incapable of learning academic skills easily and effecively; the second is that experiences in the family and neighborhood did not establish a properly rich repertoire of language or an appropriate profile of motivation, standards, and styles of problem solving. The educated citizens in our contemporary society who are egalitarian in philosophy are reluctant to blame the child for his plight. Hence they invented a term that lifted the responsibility from the child and family and placed it in a nether world between the home and the national legislature, somewhere in the "culture." During the 1960s this child was called "culturally deprived," meaning he was deprived of psychological stimulation as an infant, encouragement as a preschool child, and proper cultural experiences as a preadolescent. The unstated referent was a middle-class growth experience. But the term "cultural deprivation," which was only invented 20 years ago, became obsolescent when ethnic minorities resented the implication that their children were deficient in anything. They insisted their children were merely different. Hence the term "learning disabled" or "academically handicapped" has increased in usage. But whatever the term, we should not continue to quarrel about the label to apply to these children; it always involves a reference to cognitive ability.

It is interesting to note that the current, presumably sophisticated discussion of the different intellectual profiles of lower-class black and middle-class white children has a close analogue in the debates among Colonial Americans in the late eighteenth century. Thomas Jefferson believed, like Arthur Jensen, that the memory competence of Negroes was equal to that of the whites, but the black was deficient in reasoning and imagination.

Comparing them by their faculties of memory, reason and imagination it appears to me that in memory they [Negroes] are equal to whites; in reason much inferior, as I think one could scarcely be found capable of tracing and comprehending the investigations of Euclid; and that imagination they are dull, tasteless and anomolous . . . some have been liberally educated and all have lived in countries where the arts and sciences are cultivated to a considerable degree. . . . But never yet could I find that a black had uttered a thought above the level of plain narration; never see an elementary trait of painting or sculpture. (*Notes on Virginia*, pp. 139–40; from Jordan 1969, pp. 436–37.)

The contemporary debate on the nature and cause of differences in cognitive ability contains an old refrain with roots deep in the past, for the same two issues emerge again and again. Do populations in a society differ on a general intellectual skill or on specified talents? Are the group differences innate or acquired? Jefferson, like J. P. Guilford, believed in a profile of specific abilities, but, like Jensen, believed that the deficiency in reasoning was innate. Benjamin Rush and Samuel Smith, among others, believed the deficiences to be complex but a product of slavery and, therefore, remedial (Jordan 1969). It is interesting that Jefferson did not suggest that other equally obvious psychological differences between Negro slave and free white were innate. The differences in cleanliness and thievery between slave and slaveowner were regarded as acquired because eighteenth-century Americans assumed that the creator had to have given all men morality since a sense of right and wrong was necessary for suvival. Reasoning and imagination, it was implied, were less essential; presumably some could get along without them. Additionally, grace of phrase and keeness of mind brought a special status to the holder that could not be attained by simple honesty. There is a final reason why the argument for innateness is always easier to propose for intellectual than for other qualities. Morality and character seem to be products of our will. We have the sense that we can be honest and kind if we choose. But insight, an elegant metaphor, or a creative invention seem beyond volition and due to a special force. In a society that respects rational, material explanations that can be confirmed or refuted in empirical observation, it is reasonable to suppose that biological forces emanating from heredity would constitute that special force.

If we believe we can effect change in a personal quality, we are likely to award formative power to the environment. If we have the sense that consciousness is insufficient, we are more prepared to award influence either to external forces, like social prejudice, or to biological factors, like heredity. Most societies award a special potency to qualities that cannot simply be willed, like the ability to trance or being born with a cawl. Moreover, rare qualities are more exciting than common ones. A leaf seems less beautiful than a flower; a robin not as lovely as a heron, not because of symmetry of form but, we suggest, because the second instance is less common. (Of course some rarities are devalued, mental retardation, schizophrenia among them, but that is because they violate basic assumptions about proper behavior.) Thus, those valued human qualities that are less frequent and seem beyond our sphere of personal domination have a special power to either awe or frighten us. We are tempted, quite naturally, to attribute their occurrence to forces we cannot alter. In this sense the environmental explanation of cultural deprivation is intuitively more difficult to defend than the biological one. Given the paucity of firm evidence, it is likely that a committed defense of the nurture explanation of differences in cognitive ability derives its strength, in part, from a wish to believe that an egalitarian society can be achieved.

The Problem

The problem is to understand why the children of economically disadvantaged minority families attain lower scores on local tests of intellectual ability and master school tasks more slowly. The problem can be simplified by noting that being a member of an ethnic minority adds only a little to the functional relation. Relative poverty is the major predictor of both intelligence test scores and grades. Moreover, the relation between relative poverty and cognitive ability is even found in small, isolated, subsistence farming villages in Latin America and Africa where the range of wealth between poor and middle class is $50 a year rather than $15,000, and where all families are impoverished by American standards.

The Presumed Explanations

The candidates for explanation of the relation between poverty and academic progress fall into four complementary, not mutually exclusive, categories. All four presumed etiologies are hypothetical essences which, like Newton's aether, may turn out to be invalid ideas.

COGNITIVE ABILITY—A UNIFIED INTELLIGENCE VERSUS AN ORCHESTRATION OF TALENTS

One presumed cause of failure on academic and IQ tests is "deficient intelligence." That statement might have meaning if the referent for the nondeficient pole could be specified absolutely. The sentence "John's eyesight is deficient" has meaning, for the diagnosis of impairment is relative to an absolute criterion of 20–20 vision. With operations and corrective lenses, most children could have adequate eyesight, at least theoretically. But deficient intelligence is diagnosed with respect to the ability of other children. Although the scores on IQ tests seem to imply an absolute criterion, because 100 is claimed to be the average score, all the tests are age-graded and based upon a particular norming sample. Hence it is not possible for all children to be of adequate intelligence. Success on a certain set of questions on either the Stanford-Binet or the Wechsler intelligence tests has no meaning apart from the age, nationality, and language of the child taking the test.

But let us ignore this problem and assume for the moment that the IQ score does indeed reflect a biological quality of the child, best defined as "the ability to profit from new experiences and the ability to learn new symbolic information quickly," a definition with which few would quarrel. The difficulty with that definition is that there is often no relation between the child's IQ score, the presumed index of his intelligence, and the ease with which the child learns a new set of symbolic codes (Holtzman et al. 1975). Moreover, investigations of cognitive functioning which sample a very broad set of mental abilities do not always find uniformly high correlations among test scores (Stevenson et al. 1976). This is not only true of modern societies; it is true of children in nonmodern communities as well. Rogoff has found no relation between quality of recognition memory for objects and recall of sentences in eight to nine–year-old children living in an Indian villge on Lake Atitlan (1976). The lack of unity in a varied battery of cognitive performances, which holds at all ages, is inconsistent with a position that assumes all children possess differing amounts of some hypothetical mental competence. The postulation of a general intellectual factor is based on the results of factor analyses of mental test data which typically reveal that the first factor contains more variance than any other. But this is not reason enough to posit a "general intelligence." The first factor could just as well index a generalized factor of motivation, linguistic knowledge, or expectation of success that was common to all the test performances.

The alternative view, promoted most extensively by J. P. Guilford (1967), argues for specificity in intellectual functions. Guilford posits 120 different types of abilities based on cognitive processes, nature of information coded and manipulated, and final products. This view is not popular because of the complexity of the conclusion and the awkwardness of its practical implications. No one wants to contemplate administering 120 different tests to children to discover their talents. We prefer the aesthetic simplicity of a single concept and are willing to distort reality, up to a point, to obtain it. Like most poets, when scientists must choose between a beautiful but slightly less accurate statement and a less beautiful but more accurate one, they are tempted to choose the former if they can get away with it. The cognitive profiles of academically retarded children of poverty are more supportive of Guilford than of Spearman, for these children are not consistently less adept than middle-class, academically competent children on varied aspects of intellectual functioning, including memory, perceptual analysis, reasoning, and evaluation.

We believe that the poor school-performance of lower-class children is due to a few very specific cognitive impairments, exacerbated by motivational factors. Use and comprehension of the language of the society is one of these central competences. The correlation between school progress and scores on standard vocabulary tests is consistently high and has the highest correlation with school grades of any cognitive ability. Failure to develop the vocabulary forms and language style of the school environment is usually a correlate of school failure. The academically retarded child typically has a less sophisticated repertoire of the linguistic forms used by the school and by the middle-class majority. It is still not clear whether the lower-class child has, in an absolute sense, a limited language reservoir and limited ability to process language or just a different set of language forms. High school dropouts who obtain lower scores than middle-class, academically talented children on the vocabulary scales of the standard intelligence tests obtain higher scores than the middle class when they are asked about the meaning of street argot.

Since reading ability, which is the cornerstone of school success, is dependent on language resources, it is at least reasonable to suppose that the causes of the academic deficiency lie with the language repertoire of the lower-class child rather than with his ability to learn the symbolic meaning of visual forms. We recently tried to teach some isolated, illiterate Indian children nine years of age the semantic meaning of 20 logograms (Kagan et al. 1976). Most learned the meaning of the 20 symbols in fewer than half a dozen exposures and were able to read lengthy "sentences" composed of these logograms (see also Gleitman and Rozin 1973).

MINIMAL BRAIN DAMAGE

A second presumed cause of academic failure among poor children is a subtle anatomical or biochemical lesion in the central nervous system. These children are called "minimally brain damaged" (Wender 1971). The adjective "minimal" is used because it has been difficult to locate the site of the lesion. The bases for the diagnosis are hyperactivity, clumsiness, and poor performance on tests that require copying designs and perceptual analysis, a syndrome that some believe reflects damage to brain-stem areas and, hence, difficulty in concentration and motor coordination. We should note here the paradox that although the main problem in school progress is linguistic, most who believe that academically retarded children are minimally brain damaged do not believe the lesion is in the language hemisphere.

The problem with this explanation of academic retardation is that children diagnosed as minimally brain damaged perform similarly to academically retarded children who are diagnosed as biologically intact (Mattis et al. 1975). Moreover, children diagnosed as brain damaged perform more poorly on subscales of intelligence tests measuring language and acquired knowledge than they do on questions requiring more dynamic cognitive processes like memory and reasoning. The hypothesis of minimal brain damage gains its greatest strength from the established fact that there is more disease and greater reproductive risk accompanying pregnancy and delivery among lower-class than among middle-class parents. Since toxemia, prematurity, and anoxia at delivery can lead to damage to the central nervous system, it is logical to assume that the poor child is subject to greater risk for central nervous system trauma during the pre-, peri-, and early postnatal periods.

DEVELOPMENTAL RETARDATION

A third candidate for explanation is a slower rate of development of those parts of the brain that are involved in cognitive functions, especially language, or slower development of monitoring cognitive functions as a result of lack of environmental challenge.

One specific form of immaturity is a delay in the normal dominance of that part of the left hemisphere primarily responsible for detecting and comprehending language. Dominance of the left or right hemisphere of the brain with respect to language is often assessed by putting earphones on a child and simultaneously presenting two different words to the two ears, and then asking the child which word he heard. If he consistently reports the word played to his right ear, he is regarded as having left-hemisphere dominance for language; if he reports the word played to his left ear, he is regarded as having right-hemisphere dominance for language. It is believed that this is because there is a stronger neurological connection between each ear and the opposite side of the brain (i.e., the right ear and the left hemisphere, the left ear and the right hemisphere).

The results of experiments comparing normal and reading retarded children are inconclusive. In one study, for example, five- and six-year-old children with serious delays in speech were compared with normal children. They heard 40 different word pairs, differing in one phonetic element (for example "leg" versus "led"). The 40 different word pairs were read to the child as well as 40 pairs or trios of numbers. Although the language-retarded children differed from the normal children in reporting the numbers (they reported more digits heard in the left ear than the right), they did not differ from normals in reporting words. Both normal and language-retarded children reported two-thirds of the words they heard in the right ear, indicating normal left-hemisphere dominance for language. But the difference in reporting of numbers implies a possible difference in brain functioning between the two groups (Sommer and Taylor 1972).

Some believe that a child whose left-hemisphere areas were slower to mature (myelination of the areas of the temporal lobe typically occur later in development) would be slower in mastering the competence necessary for reading. The child would eventually develop these skills, but perhaps a year or two late. Presumably if one could identify these children in kindergarten, the schools could either begin some simple tutoring in reading skills or, at the least, refrain from coming to the premature conclusion that the children were permanently unable to master school skills. In one study (Satz et al. 1974) diagnostic tests were initially given to a large number of boys entering kindergarten. Two years later the scientists assessed the boys' reading levels at the end of grade 1. Eighteen children were diagnosed as being severely retarded in reading at the end of grade 1 (four percent of the entire group), and the kindergarten tests had predicted low levels of mastery for all eighteen of these children. The most sensitive tests were (1) knowledge of the alphabet, (2) a test that seemed to measure reflectivity-impulsivity, and (3) a test in which the child first had to learn numbers for each of the fingers on his hands; the examiner then touched one finger or several fingers (the child could not see his own hand), and the child had to say the number of the finger or fingers touched by the examiner. This test required the coordination of both perception and memory. The child had to detect which finger was touched, remember the numbers that corresponded to each of the fingers, and finally coordinate these pieces of information. Eventually all children perform well on these tests, but five- and six-year-olds who have difficulty with them are likely to become reading problems.

Another argument put forward to support delayed maturity as one explantion for early reading difficulty is the fact that in the United States young girls' scores on reading readiness and primary grade reading achievement tests are typicaly higher than those of boys (Balow 1963; Dykstra and Tinney 1969).

Since girls develop faster than boys physically, it is not unreasonable to assume that their psychological development may also be precocious. Hence girls may be temporarily more prepared for reading instruction than boys. A study of reading achievement scores in Germany, however, revealed that boys' scores were higher than those of girls. Moreover, in the German sample there was no preponderance of boys over girls who scored in the lowest tenth percentile on the reading tests. (In the United States, you will remember, more boys than girls generally obtain very low scores on reading tests, see Preston 1962.)

These results suggest either that the reading superiority of American girls is not due to earlier biological maturation, or else that cultural factors have the power to overcome slight differences in biological maturity between the sexes. In any case, the German data imply that American teachers should not tacitly accept the boys' greater difficulty in mastering reading as inevitable.

We will have to wait for future research to determine how much retardation in the attainment of left-hemisphere dominance for language is a major cause of reading and language deficit. At present, the hypothesis that reading disabilities are due to a lag in the development of the normal dominance of the left hemisphere of the brain and associated cognitive functions seems reasonable, although it is certainly not proven beyond dispute.

A second form of the immaturity hypothesis is concerned with the rate of development of cognitive systems involved in complex monitoring functions. It is fairly well established that between the ages of five and ten, a set of cognitive processes emerge that is necessary for school progress. The time of appearance of thse functions can vary by as much as three to five years. These executive functions include: (1) reflecting on one's thought and the consequences of actions, (2) recognizing a problem and adjusting effort so that it is in accord with the difficulty of the problem, (3), maintaining flexibility; ability to give up initially incorrect solutions, (4) activating strategies of organization, rehearsal, and retrieval, (5) controlling anxiety and resisting distraction, (6) faith in the power of thought, (7) relating information to a larger structure or network.

Some of these executive functions facilitate recall memory. We recently found that Guatemalan children growing up in extremely isolated villages were three to four years late in activating the strategies necessary for remembering a lengthy series of pictures or words. Middle-class American children can remember a string of 12 words or 12 pictures by eight or nine years of age, while the isolated Indian children did not perform at that level of competence until several years later. One interpretation of the three- to four-year lag is that the American child experiences more frequent challenges in school and both earlier and greater encouragement to develop intellectual skills than do the isolated Guatemalan children. These experiences facilitate the development of these executive functions.

It is likely that a larger proportion of lower- than middle-class children develop some of these executive competences late, owing to the family's lack of encouragement and reward of intellectual progress; hence they enter school less well prepared.

MOTIVES, STANDARDS, AND EXPECTATIONS

A final presumed cause of slower academic progress, which is the most difficult to specify, is psychodynamic in nature. It is believed that many lower-class children care less about academic success and/or are less confident of mastery. This explanation, which is as hypothetical as intelligence, minimal brain damage, or delayed maturation, requires an analysis of what is meant by the terms "motive," "standard," and "expectation," and a statement of how these processes interact. All children and adults possess a hierarchically organized cognitive representation of goals they want to attain. The set of representations is a motive hierarchy. Each of the goals in the hierarchy is associated, to differing degrees, with an evaluative dimension that defines its moral standing (a standard), and subjective estimate of the probability of attaining the goal. Other things equal, motives that are closely linked to standards take precedence over those minimally linked to standards. But that statement should not be taken to mean that the latter will never ascend the hierarchy and dominate the child's thought and actions, for the child will often play with sand rather than seek affirmation of his worth from his family. Thus the hierarchy of motives is not constant from hour to hour, and we need a principle that tells us how and when the hierarchy is altered, if even temporarily.

One process that affects the motive hierarchy is uncertainty. When the child is temporarily uncertain about attainment of a goal, that goal will ascend in the hiearchy and remain there until the uncertainty is partially resolved. Uncertainty is synonymous with expectation of goal attainment. Both the subjective belief in easy attainment of a goal as well as a belief that the goal is unattainable are associated with minimal uncertainty. Uncertainty is maximal when the child does not have a firm expectation of either attainment or frustration. The salience of the motive in the hieararchy bears a curvilinear relation to uncertainty of attainment and a linear relation to the strength of the link to the evaluative component. A combination of these two functional relations implies that a motive is most likely to remain high in the hieararchy when the child is uncertain of attaining a goal which is strongly linked to a positive standard. Let us now apply these simple principles to the school progress of lower- and middle-class children.

We assume first that all children are uncertain about the receipt of parental approval and punishments. They want affirmation of their value and minimal restriction, punishment, and signs of disfavor. All children, especially those of school age, are sensitive to the assignments that parents give them, the qualities they should attain in order to keep uncertainty low. Middle-class parents are more likely than lower-class parents to make intellectual talent and school progress requirements for continued approval. Lower-class parents are more likely to make obedience and inhibition of aggression requirements for family acceptance, even though both groups of children are concerned with both school progress and obedience. The motivation to perform well in school is less salient among lower-class children than the motive to avoid disapproval and punishment from adults. To volunteer answers or to move ahead in the workbook are a little dangerous, for these behaviors increase the probability one might provoke chastisement or punishment.

The school context adds another ingredient. The child is acutely sensitive to his talents and qualities vis-à-vis other children his age. Seven-year-olds are remarkably accurate in ranking the abilities of their peers and in placing themselves in that rank order. As early as the second grade, the child perceives how capable he is in school tasks in comparison with others. Since a lower-class child enters school both less prepared intellectually and less highly motivated, he quickly falls behind the middle-class child. In a year or two he realizes he is not as academically competent as the former and concludes that he can never be. The only standard he has to judge his competence is the performance of the other children. By the fourth and fifth grade the lower-class child has become relatively certain he cannot meet the requirements of the school's tasks. Since motivational salience is linked to uncertainy, the motivation to work at school tasks drops in the hierarchy, for uncertainty over mastery has become resolved. The divergence in talent increases rapidly after that decision, and by adolescence the chasm between middle- and lower-class children becomes enormous.

The child from an economically improverished family develops a different profile of psychological qualities from infancy. He learns a different vocabulary, perhaps a less rich one, is not socialized in a manner that makes intellectual and academic progress salient in his hierarchy of motives, is at risk for subtle central nervous system insult, and is consistently exposed to chidlren who have more of what the society values. It is a case in which "different" does not have the connotation of "equally valuable."

Class Differences in Infancy

The class differences in developmental history appear early, usually by the second year of life (McCall, in press). We have found that day care versus home rearing was far less important than ethnicity or class in a group of Chinese and Caucasian infants seen over the period 3 to 29 months of age. Working-class children, both Chinese and Caucasian, performed less well than middle-class children on tests of linguistic sophistication at 2.5 years of age, although the middle- and lower-class children were equivalent on tests of memory for location and perceptual analysis.

The early influence of class on young children was also revealed in a follow-up investigation of 75 Caucasian, firstborn, ten-years-olds who had been seen a decade earlier for extensive assessments at 4, 8, 13, and 27 months. Wechsler IQ scores and reading ability at age ten were correlated with social class of the child's family ($r = 0.5$), while variation during infancy in attentiveness, activity, and quality of play had little or no predictive power to these school-related dependent variables.

The power of social class to predict IQ was seen in most dramatic form in a study of more than 25,000 lower- and middle-class infants who were assessed regularly from birth through age four and for whom extensive biological information on child and mother was available from before birth. The correlation between maternal education and the family's social class, on the one hand, and the Stanford-Binet IQ at age four, on the other, was $+0.42$ for the Caucasian children. When a large and varied set of relevant prenatal and neonatal biological variables was added to the stepwise regression equation, including birth weight, anoxia, and mother's health, the correlation increased by only a small amount to $+0.46$. For the black children, the comparable correlations were $+0.26$ for class with IQ and $+0.32$ when all the biological variables were added to the regression equation. This result is not to be interpreted as indicating that toxemia, apnea, birth weight, or mother's health are unimportant for intellectual talent, but rather that when IQ is the criterion, social class has most of the variance (Broman et al. 1975).

Why does class predict intellectual ability better than any other psychological dimension psychologists have devised, whether the setting be America, England, or a Guatemalan village where intelligence is not the most valued human quality? What is happening in the home of the less poor that gives their children a cognitive advantage? We suggest that one factor is a belief, held by both parent and child, that each can meet challenges and solve them. In any community, those with more of what is valued, be it land, cattle, money, lineage, form of birth, property, or intelligence, feel more potent. They hold the illusion that they are in greater control of each day than those with less of the valued entities. The privileged are more likely to communicate this mood to their children. Wiener has suggested that adults interpret success or failure on tasks as attributable to either internal factors (ability and motivation) or to external factors (task difficulty and luck). The family with greater status in the community is more likely to persuade its children that the internal factor of effort is effective and that they have greater ability than their peers in the community. The middle-class parents persuade their children that each is an agent of personal effectance. The family's enhanced status is viewed as a partial validation of that assumption. The less potent families, unwilling to acknowledge they are less able or lazier, are more likely to attribute their disadvantaged position to external forces beyond their control, to the difficulty of tasks set by others and to luck. Such beliefs discourage individual effort. Many observers of lower-class children have suggested that an important difference is in the attitude each adopts toward a new task. The middle-class child is the unrealistic optimist persuaded of the value of persistence and motivation; the poor child doubts his capability to do what is demanded. Of course the prophecy is self-fulfilling, and the cycle continues. One of the nicest supports for this suggestion comes from the difference in school progress between first and later-born children of the same sex growing up in middle-class families. The firstborn typically obtains better IQ scores and grades than the later-born because the latter, exposed daily to the more competent older sibling, develops doubts about his ability to master difficult tasks.

Recommendations

Since part of the problem of the lower-class child is inherent in the inevitable ranking in comparison of self with others, it may be impossible to remove completely class differences in intellectual progress. We can only alleviate them by reducing the range of performance. The presumed causes we have listed imply three remedial actions. First, the lower-class family should be exhorted to encourage the development of language skills in their children and to make intellectual talent and school progress a more central value. Since the lower-class child is more at risk for academic failure, a program of early detection instituted around four to five years of age might be useful. Such a program could diagnose the children most likely to have difficulty and offer them one-to-one tutoring prior to entrance in the first grade. Third, schools with a large number of poor children might be given more of the community's resources than they now receive. Finally, the society might decide to celebrate, in a serious way, a broader array of talents. Suppose the school gave as much status and prestige to artistic, musical, and physical skills as it does to reading and mathematics. Such a change in emphasis might help to persuade the lower-class child that he has important areas of talent. That realization might buffer the expectation of failure that surrounds the assessment of intellectual skills. Of course this is an ethical issue. The larger community believes that intellectual competences are sacred and is not prepared, at the moment, to alter those priorities to help the less-advantaged child. Much of the West is still committed to a modern form of social Darwinism that is not so much prejudiced against the poor as it is convinced that not all can survive. Some must fail; it is nature's way. As long as the West believes its morality should be in accord with natural law and remains convinced that the jungle is a proper metaphor for human society, we will continue to have more culturally deprived children than we need to. It is useful to end with a fable.

There once was a kingdom called Nretsew. During an early era it is said that all the citizens believed in a force called *nis* which, like dust, was everywhere. It was important to avoid any contact with *nis*, especially contact with the eyes. The people had learned, over the centuries, how to walk and work with their eyes partially closed, and all citizens made cotton overings for their eyes to minimize contact with *nis*. By the time a person had reached adolescence, each had learned a large number of strategies to avoid contact with *nis* and all felt virtuous and safe. And then a strange thing happened. A family who was regarded as a little eccentric started to work with their eyes open. They burned their eye covers and did nothing to protect themselves against *nis*. But to everyone's surprise the family did not become ill; rather they seemed happy, healthy, and began to prosper. Soon other families began to question the old fear, and after many generations, the belief in *nis* had become a cause for laughter. Indeed the few families who still walked and worked with their eyes partially closed were scoffed at and humiliated in public. In time, no one believed in *nis* anymore. By this time, a period of many generations, the kin of the original, eccentric family, who were now revered by the society, had invented special eye exercises that were believed to lead to health, virtue, and wealth. When friends inquired about the exercises, the family gave individual sessions to a select few. In time everyone wanted to learn these exercises, but few had the opportunity, so the exercises became institutionalized. Instruction took place in large areas in the parks of large cities, and a special vocabulary grew up around the exercises. Instructors would utter phrases like "external rectus verticalis" or "occiput oblique" during the half-hour sessions in the parks, where instruction occurred daily at 10:00 and again at 2:00. Those who lived in the periphery of the kingdom became resigned to never learning the exercises. They told their children that they could live a happy and satisfying life if they did not learn the exercises, but if they could manage to gain this special knowledge, complex as it was, they would have a much richer life. When an outlying villager managed to get to the city where the instruction occurred, he returned home dimayed because he could not understand the instructions. This unhappy situation persited for many generations until a most extraordinary thing happened. A strange epidemic struck the kingdom. Feverish bands of villagers roamed into the city parks and began dancing during the periods of eye instruction. At first these disruptive citizens were evicted by local authority. But soon their numbers became so large that in some parks it was impossible to proceed with the exercises. Authorities decided to solve the problem by dividing the park into sections; one for dancing, the other reserved for the instruction in eye exercises. We have no record of what happened after that legislative decision, only one remnant of a speech made by a member of the original family denouncing dancing as an evil force that interfered with the effectiveness of the exercises.

TEN

THE child iN THE family

SCHOLARS have a fetish for positing hypothetical entities, assuming their reality, and spending too long a time debating their definition. Social scientists today debate the meaning of "morality," "emotion," "intelligence," and "family," just as physical scientists in the past quarreled over the nature of aether and phlogiston. The physical sciences find it a little easier to relinquish devotion to specific essences because they are able to gather empirical data that are sufficiently persuasive to reveal the inaccuracies of their original conceptions. The less potent social sciences are burdened with too many crusty words that over time have come to have a life of their own—floating free of reality in hallowed halls that seem inviolate. Social scientists spend too much time arguing over the preferred definition of an entity and too little time seeking the functional relations among the relevant events, for the entity is merely an abstraction that holds the realities in a coherent relation to one another.

Since social scientists probe dynamic processes, they are disposed to orient toward the future and to find the hidden functions of their intellectual inventions. Unfortunately, they frequently assume that there is one "best" function to be discovered, rather than acknowledge that "purpose" depends upon the perspective of the target. In *The Eternal Smile*, Lagerquist has God reply to an interrogator, who asks, "What purpose did you have in mind when you created man?," with "I only intended that man would never be satisfied with nothing."

These problems of definition and inferred function plague any discussion that deals with the family. Inquiring into the purposes of the family is not unlike asking about the purposes of a poem. The answer depends on the

From The family, *Daedalus*, Spring 1977, pp. 35–56.

This paper was prepared while the author was a Belding Scholar of the Foundation for Child Development. The research reported in it was supported by grants from NICHD, Office of Child Development, the Carnegie Corporation of New York, and the Spencer Foundation.

position of the respondent, whether poet, professor, publisher, or critic. In both modern and less modern communities, the functions of the family depend upon the perspective taken—that of the state, husband, wife, or child.

The Functions of the Family

THE STATE'S PERSPECTIVE

Most government officials in America—elected or appointed—believe that the family, not the state, is the preferable unit for nurturing and socializing the child because they assume that most families try to do the best they can for their children and because it is more economical for the state if the family has this responsibility. The state will be both less efficient and less benevolent. A second purpose of the family is thought to be that it keeps employment steady. Husbands and wives will retain their jobs with the same employers for long periods of time because they feel responsible for the family's economic welfare. If they do not have that responsibility, they might be more prone to occupational mobility and erratic patterns of employment.

THE PARENTS' PERSPECTIVE

From the perspective of the parents, the family offers a different set of resources. It can be a locus of solace and psychic relief—a space where anger, depression, and despair are permitted more open expression than they are outside the walls of the home. In what is seen to be an increasingly impersonal and mutually suspicious environment, the family provides each adult with an opportunity to feel needed and useful. The family provides conditions that invite its adult members to serve and to minister to a mission that transcends the self—the opportunity to beget and raise a child. Adults, like children, are naturally disposed to exploit their basic abilities. The child walks when he has the necessary physical coordination, talks when his temporal lobe has sufficiently matured. Nature has awarded the adult, especially the mother, a unique capability: although not all women are curious to exploit that talent, most are eager to test their effectiveness as a sculptor of new life.

Raising children has another psychological benefit: It offers parents an opportunity to validate the value system they brought to adulthood. Sometimes it is similar to the one they took from their families two decades earlier, sometimes it is a radical transformation, struck from intense childhood pain and carried to adulthood in a vow not to visit upon the next generation the destructive practices and philosophies that scarred their lives. Each parent has a chance to promote a hard-won set of ethics and to test the utility of standards that took many years to create. In a sense, each parent is a scientist testing a personal theory of human development with each child.

THE CHILD'S PERSPECTIVE

The intent of this essay is to examine the family from the child's perspective; there the family participates directly in at least three basic processes. It provides the first targets for identification and attachment, and it disseminates information regarding the profile of actions, appearances, and thoughts that the child must command if he is to attain a sense of virtue and competence. These are intrafamilial processes, the effects of which are mediated by direct psychological contact between the child and other family members. But each family is not just a continuing set of human interactions; it is also a structure, defined in part by the number and functions of its members and embedded in a larger network. In societies stratified by class, as ours is, the family's socioeconomic position exerts a profound influence on many aspects of the child's development.

The text of this paper follows a simple plan. We shall first consider the intrafamilial mechanisms of identification and attachment, and then the ways in which the child extracts information regarding his value and talent. Next we shall summarize some of the developmental correlates of class membership, and, finally, deal with the intriguing consequences of one aspect of family structure—namely, the child's ordinal position.

The Family as a Model for Identification

During the first half of their second year, children acquire a sense of the symbolic. An indication of this new competence is usually seen in their play with toys. Now, but not six months earlier, a little girl will treat a piece of clay as if it were a cookie and pour imaginary tea from a small teapot into an even smaller cup. This new capacity, which is soon amplified by language, leads the child to apply symbolic labels, many of which have a strong evaluative connotation, to herself and others. Children learn the language categories for age and sex, come to appreciate that they have the same last name as the rest of the family, and realize that they share anatomical and psychological qualities with their parents, especially with the parent of the same sex. It is as natural for the child as it is for the adult to group objects or events that are similar into a common category. Indeed, as early as 12 months of age some American children will treat dolls, toy animals, and foods of different kinds, sizes, shapes, and colors as members of discrete conceptual categories, suggesting that the one-year-old has the capacity to extract invariant attributes from an array of events and create a symbolic home for them.[1]

The process of noting shared qualities among objects is applied to the self and members of the family, and by age three or four children are likely to believe they are more similar to their parents than to any other adult they know. Young children also believe they share more attributes with the same-sex than with the opposite-sex parent, an understanding that is articulated at the level of metaphor. When they are shown pairs of designs differing in size, hue, or angularity and are asked to select the one that typifies each parent, most boys and girls agree that the father is larger, darker, and more angular than the mother. And young boys regard themselves as larger, darker, and more angular than girls.[2]

Although the belief that one is similar to another is the most important component of identification, the child's evaluation of the parents' desirable and undesirable attributes is a dimension of particular importance. For most young children, the parent is perceived to be physically stronger and psychologically more competent, powerful, and nurturant than the child—regardless of the parents' actual strength or competence vis-à-vis other adults in the community. These attributes are also regarded as desirable by the child. The third ingredient in the process of identification is the child's assumption that if he were to become even more similar to his parents, he would be able to share vicariously in the affective consequences of their desirable resources and experiences with greater intensity. He would feel stronger, more competent, and more powerful. The child's belief that he shares basic qualities with a parental model, together with the vicarious sharing of the model's inferred affective states, make up the formal definition of identification.

During the early school years, the child comes to appreciate—often for the first time—the attributes the wider society values or derogates. The American child realizes that material wealth, a certain pattern of cognitive abilities, and particular vocations are valued; excessive drinking, an unskilled job, a home in disrepair, and an inability to read or write are undesirable, and therefore potential sources of shame and humiliation. That knowledge produces a sharp change in the child's conception both of his parents and of himself, for the insight regarding society's evaluation of his parents is taken as a diagnosis of the self. Hence the family's social class position and the specific psychological characteristics of parents and siblings influence the degree to which the child's conceptualization of himself is positive or negative.

The Family as a Source of Protection and Target of Attachment

The family provides alleviation of distress from the moment of birth, but, as infants approach the second half of the first year, they begin to seek out parents and others who care for them when they are apprehensive or uncomfortable. This disposition to seek proximity to particular people in times of distress has acquired the name "attachment." The major implication of this phenomenon is that only a limited number of people possess the power to allay the infant's distress quickly. Those who hold this power are precisely the ones the infant looks to or moves toward when it is uncomfortable.

A child can be attached to more than one caretaker, and most children have a stable hierarchy of preferences that is tied to the quality of the interaction rather than to its duration. The results of two recent studies support the assertion that the biological parent in the Western nuclear family has a mysterious ability to remain the preferred target of attachment, even for young children who spend a considerable amount of time with substitute caretakers outside the home.

The first of these studies was an investigation of the effect of group care on Chinese and Caucasian children during the first 2½ years of life.[3] One group attended a day-care center in Boston five days a week from age 3½ months through age 30 months. Each child attending the center was matched by ethnicity, social class, and sex with a child being reared at home. When the children were 20 months old, they were placed in an unfamiliar setting with the mother, an unfamiliar woman, and, for the day-care children, the primary day-care teacher, but, for the children raised at home, a friend of the family. During the 45 minutes of observation, the child was deliberately made uncertain on two occasions by having the three adults suddenly exchange seats. All the children—those raised only at home as well as those attending the day-care center—went to their mother for comfort when they were tired, bored, or apprehensive because of the unexpected provocation. There were no important differences between the behavior of the children raised at home and those attending the center. If the child approached anyone at all, it was typically the mother. This does not mean that the day-care children were not attached to their caretakers, for if the mother was absent, as she was when the child was at the center, they sought the primary caretaker.

In a related investigation,[4] Nathan Fox observed children living in infant houses on Israeli kibbutzim. The infants visited the parents' homes for only a few hours each day around the dinner hour, spending the rest of their time in the infant house with a *metapelet*. These children were observed individually in an unfamiliar room on the kibbutz with the mother, an unfamiliar woman, and their *metapelet*. The children were more secure when they were left with the mother and a stranger than they were with the *metapelet* and stranger—as evidenced by the greater amount of time they spent playing, and less time spent hovering near the familiar adult caretaker. Both of these studies imply that the number of hours a child is cared for by an adult is not the critical dimension that produces a strong attachment. There is something special about the mother-infant relationship. The parent appears to be more salient than substitute caretakers to the child. It is not clear why this is so.

One possibility is that the parent is both more affective and more unpredictable with the young child and, hence, is a greater source of uncertainty. A conscientious and sympathetic caretaker of a group of children outside the home is aware both of the psychological diversity among the children under her care and of the differences in values between each parent and herself. As a result, she is unlikely to hold rigid standards for such things as talkativeness, cooperativeness, cleanliness, aggression, quality of play, or the age at which particular developmental milestones should appear. Because she is less profoundly involved with the children than are the parents, she will be more relaxed than they are about these standards. It is neither a source of pleasure if one child is precocious in learning to drink from a cup, nor a source of apprehension if another spills his milk. This tolerance for diversity leads the caretaker to allow each child considerably more latitude than the parent would to behave in accordance with his temperament and relative level of maturity, especially in Western countries. With the exception of extremely destructive or regressed children, the caretaker does not ordinarily impose constraints when the child seems occupied and happy. As a result, the caretaker does not become a source of uncertainty for the child. Finally, group-care settings are typically more routinized than the home, and the actions of caretakers therefore are apt to be more predictable.

By contrast, the typical mother is emotionally involved with her infant and more likely to display strong affection and to convey emotionally charged messages. In addition, she holds standards by which she judges the child's development, and she watches for deviations from them. One mother may believe that any defiance of her authority is a sign of future rebelliousness, and she quickly reacts to it with disapproval or punishment. Most American mothers hold standards for cleanliness and against destruction of property, physically dangerous acts, and aggression toward others, as well as notions of the proper ages for walking and talking. The mother diagnoses the deviations of the child's developing profile from her idealized standards; when they become too large, she intrudes and attempts to shape behavior so that it conforms more closely to her understanding of what is appropriate. Each intrusion, whether punishment, praise, or command, punctuates the child's behavior and consciousness and creates a temporary state of uncertainty that alerts the child to the mother and to the action the child has just issued. The next time the child is in a similar situation or entertains the possibility of initiating an action associated with prior intrusions, he remembers that intrusion and again experiences uncertainty. Only after parental response to a particular class of actions has been consistently repeated will the child establish a firm expectation, and only then will his uncertainty subside. This line of speculation suggests that the typical mother is a more frequent and distinctive source of uncertainty for her child than the usual surrogate caretaker. The parent is less predictable, more difficult to understand, and a more frequent source of joy and excitement. Psychoanalytic theorists would say that the mother was more highly "cathected" than the caretaker; in the more modern language of cognitive psychology, the mother would be described as more "salient."

The Communication of Information to the Child

The salience of the mother, as revealed in studies of attachment phenomena, raises the more general question of what constitutes psychological information for the child. There is no doubting that parental practices and attitudes, whether viewed as rewards and punishments or simply as communications, influence the child's development. Therefore, we need to determine the relation between what the family members do and say, on the one hand, and the child's representations of what they do and say, on the other. The form of that relation is at present enigmatic.

Conceptualization of the relation between physical energy and psychological sensation was absolute during the latter part of the nineteenth century, when it was assumed that visual sensation was a function of the absolute amount of light energy impinging on the retina. We now know that homogeneous stimulation of the retina results only in a constant experience of illumination that is independent of the wave length and intensity of the physical stimulus.[5] Similarly, if one immerses a finger in a jar of mercury which produces a constant pressure against the skin, there is no perception of pressure on the finger. The recognition of pressure is felt only at the surface, where there is a transition from mercury to air. It is at the transition—at the point of contrast—that one processes information about the physical sensations coming from the two parts of the finger.

The perception of information thus depends on change and contrast. Hence, it is not surprising that a young infant's attention is drawn to visual events that move or have contour contrast and to auditory events that are rhythmic and rich in transitions. Indeed, it is believed that we perceive hunger when blood-sugar level changes rather than at any absolute blood-sugar level. It might be productive to assume that the conceptualization of self and others is monitored by a similar principle. The child may most easily draw psychological conclusions about the quality of self and others when he detects nodes of contrast between himself and someone else, or among others, in either objective or symbolic attributes. This hypothesis assumes that the most effective influences on the child are contained in perceived contrasts.

Consider an example: For a child who is rarely chastised, a sharp rebuke for a new misdemeanor is an important piece of information which should lead to future inhibition of that action. For the child who is continually chastised, rebuke for the same misbehavior would, we suggest, have a minimal effect because the rebuke is not in sufficient contrast to normal parental action and therefore not sufficiently different from the child's adaptation level. The rebuke does not attract much of his attention and hence elicits little or no reflective interpretation.

The attentiveness of a two-year-old, who is just beginning to impose categories on experience, will be drawn to nodes of contrast between himself and others. He will notice differences in physical size, capacity to coerce, and instrumental competence between himself and his parents. The parents will become salient objects, and the qualities of contrast (size, power, competence) will invite categorization. Since the degree of contrast between self and other children of the same age in these dimensions is minimal, one would expect another child to be a much less salient event, and there is some indirect evidence that this is in fact the case.

The infants attending the day-care center described earlier were in the company of a dozen or so other children their own age five days a week from the age of 3½ months through their second year. Signs of apprehension to an unfamiliar adult typically emerged at about 7 to 8 months of age and peaked at 12 to 13 months. Signs of apprehension to an unfamiliar peer did not emerge until a few months later and did not peak until about 15 to 20 months of age.[6] We regard the apprehension to a stranger at seven months to be the result of uncertainty over the stranger's actions toward the child and the child's proper reactions toward the stranger. The temporary inability to resolve those sources of uncertainty produces apprehension. We think that apprehension when faced with unfamiliar adults appears a few months earlier than apprehension toward other children, even among infants who are exposed daily to many peers, because attention is not often directed toward children of the same age during the first year of life, and knowledge of peers is less firm during early infancy. This is, in part, because the peer is not a source of strong contrast in size, power, and competence. After the first year, when social interactions with other children become more frequent and seizing property and parallel play emerge, peers generate more contrasts and consequently become important sources of information. Now the child becomes vulnerable to apprehension in the presence of unfamiliar peers.

The effects of the actions of parents on the child may also be better understood if one pauses to ask: What are the background experiences of the child, and what will be treated as a signal against that background? The potential utility of this conceptual stance toward social experience is best seen when one contrasts an American family with one from a different culture. We shall take as an example the Utku of Hudson Bay. When a child is two or three, Utku parents begin to inhibit his aggression and anger with a form of silent treatment: they consistently ignore him when he displays these actions. The child thus learns to expect this response to aggression. Since all children are treated this way, the five-year-old does not witness much aggression in other children, nor, for that matter, among adults. This experience combined with the adult shaming of aggressive behavior is effective, and one rarely sees aggression among children over four or five years of age.[7] A Western adult may have the impression that such a society is repressing its anger and hostility. Yet none of the theoretically expected symptoms of repression occur. We interpret this to mean that there is no fixed effect of prohibitions on aggression and anger in children. Since the American child is exposed to peers and adults who are occasionally aggressive, he is uncertain about social reactions to, and permissiveness toward, aggression. An American parent who continually punished anger and aggression would probably create symptoms in the child, but only because the punishment was interpreted in a particular context. The American child is in conflict; the Utku child is not.

These special cases lead us to conclude that it may be impossible to state the principles underlying functional relations between specific parental practices and particular behavior in the child, except, perhaps, in the extreme, where consistently harsh physical abuse creates serious physical distress. Although there may be few functional relations between concrete experiences and the child's growth, it is possible that lawful relations exist between the child's conceptualization of experience and his subsequent psychological structures. But those conceptualizations are not tied in a simple way to experience. The categorizations depend on nodes of contrast, ratios, and relations between background experience and the figural present.

The Child's Sense of Virtue

In addition to being a source of identification, a target of attachment, and a haven in times of distress, the family communicates to the child its value or virtue, which in our culture depends to a great extent on the child's belief that he is competent and capable of attracting parental love. Children, like adults, cannot avoid evaluating the self on a dimension of virtue, and their always uncertain decisions are functions of different classes of experience.

One source of information comes from the child's evaluation of how good or bad he believes his actions, thoughts, and motives to be, a judgment based on the congruence between behavior and standards, as well as the evaluative reactions of others toward him. Every child learns standards of actions and thought which the local culture regards as morally proper. Although items on the list will vary with the society, a universal list is likely to contain obedience to parents and the absence of aggression, excessive selfishness, dishonesty, and irresponsibility within the family.

A second component of virtue rests on the child's perception of his value in the eyes of his parents. The young child awards extraordinary wisdom to his parents. If they behave as if he were valuable, he takes these actions as evidence of his essential goodness. If they behave as if he were without worth, he begins to question his capacity to be valued by another. Initially, the child does not question his parents' ability to value him, but assumes instead that something about him prevents a positive reaction. It must be noted, of course, that there is no absolute set of parental practices that will inform the child of his value; the child imposes that meaning on his parents' actions.

Some American psychologists have assumed that one specific set of parental behaviors always signifies acceptance or rejection, for there is remarkable agreement among investigators about the maternal behaviors designated as indicative of these parental attitudes.[8] Inflicting harsh physical punishment and lack of social play and affection were typical signs of maternal rejection in these studies, and consequently it would be almost impossible for an American psychologist to categorize a mother as being both punitive and loving.

But in the seventeenth century, European and American colonial parents were advised to beat their children in order to tame the evil inherent within them. Otherwise respectable and well-educated parents inflicted severe punishment upon their dependents—punishments that would be classified as extreme abuse today. Samuel Byrd of Virginia, for example, made a dependent of his drink "a pint of piss" because he wet his bed.[9] Then, as now, many children of upper class English families rarely remained at home with their parents. After birth they were sent to a wet-nurse in a nearby village until weaning, perhaps at two years of age: then they returned home, but briefly, before again being sent out, this time to boarding school.

Plumb[10] notes that Sir Robert Walpole (born in 1676) rarely spent more than a few weeks each year in his home between the ages of 6 and 22. But since this pattern was common, it is unlikely that parents regarded themselves as cruel or children as being rejected. Evaluating a parent as rejecting or accepting cannot be based solely on the parent's behavior, for rejection, like pleasure, pain, or beauty, is not a fixed quality; it is in the mind of the rejectee. It is a belief held by the child, not an act performed by the parent.

After the age of two, an important discontinuity arises in the child's interpretation of parental behavior, for he begins to evaluate the actions of others in symbolic terms. The five-year-old is conceptually mature enough to recognize that certain resources parents possess are often difficult to obtain. The child views these resources as sacrifices, and interprets their receipt as signs that the parents value him. The child constructs a tote board of the differential value of parental gifts, whether psychological or material. The value of the gift depends on its scarcity. This position would lead to solipsism, were it not that most parents are sufficiently narcissistic not to want to give the child long periods of uninterrupted companionship. Consequently most children place a high premium on parental company. Parents are also reluctant to provide unusually expensive gifts, so that they, too, acquire value for many youngsters. Finally, the American child learns that physical affection means positive evaluation and is persuaded to assign premium worth to that experience as well. Therefore, some uniformity among children in our culture can be found with respect to the evaluation of parental acts that indicate acceptance or rejection. But the point of reference is within the child.

It is possible that the child's perception of value in the eyes of his parents assumes a prominence in our culture that it may not have had in earlier periods, or may not have in other contemporary societies. Many American children are uncertain over whether they are valued by their families, and many parents are eager to communicate to their children that they love them. Unhappiness, failure, and psychological symptoms in adolescence and adulthood are often explained as being the result of the absence or withdrawal of parental love during early childhood. But prior to the mid-seventeenth century, Europeans rarely referred to the importance of the love relationship between parent and child when they speculated on the conditions that promoted optimal development.[11] The child's future was more dependent on Divine than parental love. The child needed a good education and faith in God; parents provided physical care, consistent discipline, and a model for proper behavior.

By the end of the seventeenth century, however, explicit recognition of the significance of the love relation between parent and child, while not un-known earlier, had become more commonly recognized. Locke advised parents to love their children, noting: "He that would have his son have a re-spect for him and his orders must himself have a great reverence for his son."[12] Rousseau warned that, if parents—and he meant both mothers and fathers—did not establish affectionate ties with their children, vice was inev-itable. Anticipating Bowlby's emphasis on the infant's attachment to a single caretaker, Rousseau advised against the mother having a wet-nurse or sub-stitute caretaker. But if that decision had been made, then "the foster child should have no other guardian, just as he should have no teacher but his tutor. . . . A child who passes through many hands in turn can never be well brought up."[13]

This increased emphasis on the love relation between socializing adults and children was paralleled by an emerging self-consciousness about the child's independence, individualism, and personal motives. The child was being differentiated as an entity separate from the family. Unquestioned loy-alty and acquiescence to God and family were losing their moral force to au-tonomy and narcissism. Rousseau and Pestallozzi both anticipated the mood of the twentieth century: Rousseau wrote that "the only natural passion to man is the love of himself"; Pestallozzi that "consciousness of your own per-sonality is the first object of Nature." From the beginning of the eighteenth century until the present, the emphasis on the importance of the child de-veloping an articulated, differentiated, autonomous ego has continued to grow. The spread of that ideal is correlated with the attribution of formative power to parental love. Is this correlation causal, the joint product of more fundamental factors, or an accident? We favor the second of these positions and shall try to support that view.

As the urban middle class grew in size, children became less obvious economic advantages. Since fewer youth were needed to help with agricul-tural work or to care for infants and young children, the role of many chil-dren gradually changed from an object of utility to one of sentiment. Al-though children contributed less to the family's economic position, they could enhance the family's status by mastering academic skills and attaining prestige in the larger community. As a result, more parents began to identify with their children because of the latter's potential for accomplishment.[14]

This change in the child's function in the family could have produced an enhancement of the attitude we call parental love. If a farmer needs his horse for plowing, he worries about the animal's health and takes precau-tions to prevent injury or escape. But it is unlikely he will identify with the animal, for the horse is only an instrument to be used by the competent adult to attain a goal. The farmer who enters his thoroughbred in a show in order to gain status is more likely to identify with the animal, for it possesses qualities the owner lacks. The emotional state that follows a successful plowing is one of satisfaction and perhaps reduction of apprehension, but the state that follows public accolade is one of self-enhancement. The object responsible for that good feeling can generate the emotion we typically label "love." As middle-class families began to regard their children as emerging objects of art who would enhance a parent's sense of self, feelings of love were amplified.

An additional basis for an increased consciousness regarding affectionate relations between parent and child rests on the assumption that seventeenth-century parents began to recognize that an aloof, authoritarian attitude, which seemed to be effective in producing obedience and conformity in children, was not conducive to autonomous achievement. The latter profile requires a different set of parental attitudes. Fear of authority is a potent incentive for inhibition, but it is far less effective as a goad for continued striving toward goals which require the invention of ideas and actions. The desire to maintain the positive regard of parents is a more appropriate incentive for the latter, and it is possible that the seventeenth-century middle-class family recognized that principle, or at least became more conscious of it, as the stereotype of the ideal child changed from passive conformity to active, autonomous mastery.

It is also possible that when families moved from rural areas to the city the child was more often outside the supervisory influence of a family member for some part of the day. Hence it became necessary to use the threat of withdrawal of favor as a source of disciplinary control. When the child is continually surrounded by adults or older siblings, each of whom is within several hundred yards of his action, mischievousness is constrained. When the child is alone or more distant from the home, the policeman must be symbolic, and the society may have discovered that parental love and its potential withdrawal can play the supervisory role at a distance.

We recently collected extensive observations on the location and activity of Indian children growing up in two small neighboring villages on Lake Atitlan in the Guatemalan highlands. During the first five years of life, the children were within 100 yards of their home more than 80 percent of the time and under direct or indirect surveillance by a family member on at least two-thirds of the occasions when our observers appeared on the scene. Under these conditions it is not only difficult for a child to misbehave but it is also clear to all members of the community that there is no reason for any child to be uncertain about the availability of human resources to provide care or control when it is needed.

The economic and social changes that led to new parental attitudes may have also created new nodes of uncertainty in children. The preadolescent in a fifteenth-century farming village had an opportunity, each day, to realize that he was an object of value, since his work made a material contribution to the family's welfare. His virtue was evident in the results of his work. It was more difficult for the 13-year-old son of a middle-class official in eighteenth-century London to enjoy that advantage. His sense of virtue was based less on the products of his labor and more on his psychological qualities. He could not point to a plowed field or a full woodpile as a sign of his utility. As a result, this child may have been more uncertain about his value, more dependent on parental communications assuring him of his worthiness, and more preoccupied with parental attitudes toward him.

Thus the correlation between the emphasis on the child's independence and autonomous achievement (and the decreasing concern with conformity and the child's economic contribution to the family) and the awarding of formative power to attitudes of parental affection may have theoretical substance. It reflects, in part, the growth of a folk theory implying that confidence, independence, and the desire for accomplishment require a belief in one's value and potency and a reluctance to lose parental love. We do not know whether the folk theory is valid empirically or merely believed to be correct by the community.

The power that modern Western society attributes to parental love—or its absence—has an analogue in the theories of illness held by some non-Western communities. (By illness, we mean consciousness of a source of physical disability or psychological discomfort, not the physical locus or material cause of dysfunction.) The possible causes of illness include spirits, loss of soul, sorcery, sin, accident, God, witchcraft, or failure to live a meritorious life. Rarely are the actions or attitudes of one's family considered to be a possible source of illness in most of these non-Western societies. By contrast, twentieth-century Western society assumes the family can be a primary cause of a small set of illnesses that we normally call psychiatric—depression, phobias, obsessions, autisms, schizophrenia, criminality, and, in the infant, failure to thrive. Since phobias, depression, and madness are also present in non-Western societies, why does the modern West believe that the family's practices toward the child—excessive rejection, restriction, or aloof authoritarianism—can produce psychiatric illness during childhood, adolescence, or adulthood? We are not talking about the strong emotion a parent feels toward a young child, but rather the belief that a child's perception of the favor in which he is held can exert a profound influence on his present and future state. Modern parents are convinced that if the child believes he is loved, he will be free of a major source of distress—to be out of favor is to be vulnerable to anxiety.

Adolescents learn of scientific theories that articulate unformed premises about parental rejection and psychic illness. They learn that a person must feel loved in order to be psychically healthy. Occasions for anguish in adulthood are interpreted as delayed reactions to lack of parental love during childhood, rather than the results of the wrong zodiacal sign, being born on the wrong day, or invasion by evil spirits. Our books, magazines, and television dramas all announce the healing and prophylactic power of parental love and the toxicity that follows closely on its absence.

American adults seek out psychiatrists, new love objects, or peers who they hope will love them and dissolve their anguish. This faith in love is not unlike the faith in the curative power of the potion or incantations of a shaman. If the person believes in the curative power of the ritual—be it love or potion—he will feel less anguish after participating in the ritual. As no one would quarrel with the real power of prayer or potion to alleviate disquiet, we do not quarrel with the healing power of love. Both are real and not metaphysical events. But the potency of both depends on a prior belief in their effectiveness.

Recent inquiry into the dynamics of the relation between native healer and patient in Taiwan provides a model for the healing functions of the family.[15] The patient holds a set of hypotheses regarding the possible causes and cures of his particular state of distress. He then seeks a healer who he thinks shares his beliefs about etiology and treatment. That state of mind makes the patient receptive to the healer's diagnosis and prescription and increases the likelihood that he will leave the healer feeling better.

Kleinman notes that a well-educated Taiwanese would not visit a native healer, and, even if he did, he would not be helped because he would have no faith in the shaman's powers or in his theory of illness. Similar results have been found for modern forms of psychotherapy in the West. The patient who believes in psychoanalytic theory is not likely to be helped by a behavior therapist; the patient committed to Reich's ideas will be resistant to the counsel of a nondirective Rogerian. Thus, the necessary conditions for being helped psychologically include not only a state of distress which the person feels he cannot alleviate, but a concomitant conviction that the healer possesses psychological power and shares the patient's beliefs regarding the causes and cures of distress.

Let us assess the child-parent relationship in these terms. The child begins to construct simple theories of the reason for his psychic anguish some time after four to five years of age. The child's sources of distress include uncertainty about possible harm, task failure, and parental disfavor, as well as guilt and shame over violations of societal standards. The child's theory of cause is partly a product of the parents' communications. Hence, the child automatically shares some of their beliefs about etiology and views the parents as having a special power that derives to some extent from their greater size, competence, and prior success in alleviating his distress. Before the age of two, parental actions of comforting, feeding, and attention have become goals to seek when in distress: in most parts of the world, young children who are frightened or in pain approach their caretaker to be touched, fed, or reassured. Even among chimpanzees, a subordinate chimp will approach and hold out a hand to a dominant member, who will touch the subordinate as if to indicate reassurance. (Recall, also, that before the Enlightenment, the touch of a king was believed by some to have potent healing powers.)

A special power to persuade and heal is awarded to the person who has attained to an extraordinary degree a valued quality or competence. During the child's early years, parents have this power. During preadolescence, older siblings and peers can earn a similar respect, if they possess the desired qualities. During adulthood, this power is held by the members of the community who have attained whatever qualities are prized. The child has been told by his family what qualities are admired, and he recognizes that his parents possess them in greater abundance than he. Consider a six-year-old middle-class American child who is afraid to play with other children in the neighborhood. His parents provide an explanation for his feelings and offer some advice. In a middle-class suburb, the mother tells the child that the boys outside are basically friendly and that he must fight his anxieties; it is his responsibility to initiate contact with them. But if we shift the location to an inner-city ghetto, where a particular family views most of the children on the block as a polluting and dangerous influence, the mother may give the opposite advice. In each situation, each set of suggestions is viewed as wise, and each can reduce the child's apprehension.

When the American child in a nuclear family experiences distress, the parents remind him that they will take care of him—he need not worry because the family is present. Both child and parent share the belief that attentive nurture from a sympathetic adult has healing power and that its absence is a major source of anxiety. In many small subsistence-farming villages where the child is cared for continuously by the mother, older siblings, aunts, or grandparents, the psychically alleviating experiences are not parental presence, but obedience and hard work. Indeed the capacity for work holds as central a position among the Mayan Indians of Guatemala as the capacity to give and receive love does in the West. An investigation of the Indian view of valued human qualities revealed that wealth and hard work were the most valued adult characteristics. Adjectives describing the capacity to love children were not among the qualities named as being characteristic of adults, suggesting that this attribute is not viewed as important in the Mayan's construction of reality.[16]

Now we must ask whether lack of parental affection in childhood does indeed make a serious contribution to future psychic illness. Is that proposition valid?

It is not easy to answer that question for reasons that are not strictly empirical. When we ask whether temperature contributes to the probability of snowfall we need only gather easily obtainable objective data to answer the query. But in the case of the contribution of parental rejection to psychic illness, we are in difficulty because we are asking whether a mental state in the child (the belief that one is not favored) makes a contribution to a future mental state (fearfulness or hostility) in the adult. That question has two quite different forms.

The first form is phenomenological and concerned only with the adult's belief in the validity of the functional relation. If a person believes that an early set of experiences (or mental states) is influencing his present state, he will act as if it were so. The second form of the question is public—or scientific; it asks if there is an empirical relation between the child's perception of favor or disfavor and later adult sequellae. At present, the second question has not been answered satisfactorily because, as indicated earlier, parental rejection is not a specific set of actions by parents but a belief held by the child. The only way to avoid this frustrating position is to determine whether there is a lawful relation, in a given culture, between certain parental actions and communications and the child's belief that he is, or is not, favored. There are no data to our knowledge that have demonstrated unequivocally that there is a relation between specific parental actions and the child's belief. Working-class American parents punish and restrict the child much more than middle-class parents do, yet there is no evidence to indicate a class difference in perception of parental favor. When we look at other cultures, we find that Kipsigis mothers, for example, have older siblings care for their young children, while Israeli mothers on kibbutzim use *metaplot*. Again, there is no evidence to indicate that one group of children feels more in parental favor than the other. We are tempted, therefore, to suggest that each child contructs a theory regarding those actions that he thinks imply parental favor or disfavor. The content of the theory is based on local conditions and will not necessarily generalize to other communities in any detail.

The possibility that one might *not* be valued by one's family is common in Western society. Historical events may have been responsible for making this possibility a major source of anxiety and, therefore, of illness, just as they have been responsible for anxieties about nuclear waste, racial violence, and municipal defaults. Mayan villagers worry about hunger, slanderous gossip, and the action of the gods. A society can create a source of distress by introducing a new belief, just as it can create new hazards to lungs by inventing cars and factories, or hazards to viscera by adding carcinogens to food and water.

The Child's Sense of Competence

The child also needs information on his profile of talents. Naturally a child focuses on the instrumental competences that the local society values, whether they be physical endurance, ability to fight, eloquence, or mathematical skills. Each community promotes a valued set of skills, a preferred vocabulary, a style of problem solving, and a standard of adequate performance. Initially the child has no absolute definition of what constitutes skilled behavior and is forced to look to other children—peers and siblings—for standards by which to judge his abilities. Only much later, perhaps by late adolescence, will he have incorporated some standard sufficiently firmly to allow him to judge his competence by performance alone.

The families who have power and feel they are an integral part of the society are more effective in promoting the socially valued skills with their children than are those who feel disenfranchised. They communicate to the child their optimism about his eventual mastery. Hence the family's social class exerts a major influence on the child's sense of competence, not only because the lower classes use and encourage a slightly different style of language and strategy for solving problems, but also because they treat the children differently and communicate more tenuous expectations of success regarding those skills promoted by the dominant class. Lower-class parents may communicate their sense of helplessness and inadequacy to the child, leading him to a more pessimistic view of his chances for success in the larger environment.

The Influence of Social Class

The power of class can be observed as early as the first birthday. About a decade ago, we initated a longitudinal study of 180 Caucasian firstborn children living in the Boston area whom we followed from 4 to 27 months of age.[17] During the four assessments—at 4, 8, 13, and 27 months—we quantified the child's attentiveness to a set of interesting, meaningful, visual events. The four- and eight-month-olds varied dramatically in their attentiveness, but no relation could be found during the first year between the child's attentiveness and the family's social class. However, at 13 and 27 months of age, level of attentiveness to representations of faces and human forms was correlated with the social class of the child's family, but it was unrelated to the degree of attentiveness displayed at four months. If we assume both that temperamental factors exert an influence on attentiveness among the four- and eight-month-olds and that these factors remain somewhat stable, then it appears that their influence had been subdued through experiences in the home by the time the child was two years old. We recently evaluated the intelligence and reading ability of 68 of these children when they were ten years old. Their qualities as infants were unrelated to either their IQ or their reading scores, while the social class of their families had the expected positive relation to both attributes.[18]

We have also completed a study of lower- and middle-class Chinese and Caucasian children, half of them attending a day-care center regularly, the other half raised only at home from 3½ to 29 months of age. The infants differed markedly in their attentiveness, vocalization, and smiling to interesting visual and auditory events during the first year. These differences did not vary with social class. But by 20 and 29 months of age, the class of the child's family had become a major predictor of attentiveness, vocalization, and smiling. Thus, in two independent studies with different families, the effects of social class emerged clearly by the second year and appeared to subdue the inherent dispositions displayed during early infancy.[19]

Observations of working- and middle-class American families consistently reveal that lower-middle-class Caucasian mothers talk less to their infants, are less likely to encourage cognitive development, especially of language, and are more intrusive and autocratic in their discipline. This is not a recent trend. Thirty years ago, Alfred Baldwin and colleagues[20] observed working- and middle-class Caucasian mothers and their young children in rural Ohio and reported that working-class mothers were more autocratic and restrictive in their practices with their children. They intruded more often into the activities of the child and were less disposed to explain punishments or give reasons for their prohibitions. Several years ago, we observed 90 firstborn Caucasian children at home over a five- to six-hour-period on several occasions and quantified the encounters that involved maternal commands, prohibitions, and children's requests. There was an inverse relation between the educational level—and, by inference, social class—of the mother and the number of prohibitions she issued, a rate of one every five minutes for lower-middle-class parents versus one every ten minutes for middle-class parents, a finding in complete accord with Baldwin's data gathered 30 years earlier.[21]

We can only speculate about the psychological consequences of this kind of upbringing, but it is not unreasonable to suggest that the greater autonomy awarded the middle-class two- and three-year-old accustoms him to a freedom from psychological restraint and leads him to expect that he will play the role of initiator. This belief, when wedded to the middle-class tendency to remind the child that victories and defeats are the result of his efforts or deficiencies, rather than the vicissitudes of fortune, creates a mental set toward problems in which the self is supposed to generate plans and fulfill ambitions. Obstacles can be met in one of three ways—an attempt to cope, a retreat or denial, or an expectation that someone or something will intrude. Although both the child and the adult often wish to shift the responsibility of decision or action to another entity—be it person, group, or transcendental force—the middle-class child's socialization, at least in America, appears to make it more difficult for him to do so. Questionnaire studies of middle-and-lower-class children reveal that the former are a little more likely to believe that effort leads to success and lack of effort to failure, while the lower-class child is somewhat more prone to explain success and defeat in terms either of chance or of benevolent and malevolent social forces.[22]

The power of social class experience is seen in dramatic form in the results of an extensive study of more than 27,000 children who were followed from birth to age four in an investigation of the effects of maternal health and pre- and perinatal trauma on the intelligence-test scores of four-year-olds. Despite the fact that the investigators had quantified many biological variables, including birth weight, maternal illness during pregnancy, and difficulties in delivery, the major predictor of the child's IQ at age four was the mother's social class. After the variance associated with class had been accounted for, the remaining biological variables added very little predictive power—only a few points—to the multiple correlation.[23] Indeed, more than 25 percent of the variation in the verbal ability of 11-year-olds can be accounted for by the father's occupation and the number of children in the family.[24]

A family's social class is associated with degree of risk for biological and psychological deficits at birth, specific practices toward the child, projection of parental views of self onto the child, and, finally, the child's identification with his class. These factors lead the typical ten-year-old lower-class child to question his ability to possess the talents and instrumental competences that the middle-class child commands. One of the firmest facts in psychology, a discipline with few replicable pieces of knowledge, is the positive relation between a child's social class and a variety of indexes of cognitive functioning, including IQ or achievement-test scores, grades in school, richness of vocabulary and memory, and inferential ability. Additionally, the middle-class American child typically has a greater expectation of success in intellectual situations, is more reflective, and is less likely to take extreme risks when given a variety of alternatives. Some of these differences are very similar to the differences noted between later- and firstborn children within the same family.

This relation between social class and cognitive performance in America and Western Europe can also occur in small, isolated subsistence-farming villages in Latin America, where the difference in wealth and education among the very poor and the less poor is minimal. In many of these villages, the poorest do not own the land upon which their thatched hut rests, while the less poor do. But from the perspective of an American, all the villagers live in abject poverty. Nonetheless, village parents who perceive themselves to be somewhat better off that their neighbors have children who perform better on tests of memory, perceptual analysis, and reasoning. The correlation between the amount of land held and the size of the house—a good index of class in these villages—and test performance is often of the same magnitude as it is in the United States,[25] implying that the families of the very poor are implementing practices and communicating values to their children that are different from the actions and values of the less poor. It is also likely that these children are identifying with their families' social position in the community, as middle-class children do in America.

We do not believe that the relation between class and cognitive ability in these small villages can be attributed solely to the poorer health and nutrition among the impoverished. A recent study of a modernizing Mayan Indian village of 5,000 people located in the highlands of Guatemala showed that the most traditional Catholic families, whose practices are highly restrictive of the child, have more land and are wealthier than the less traditional Catholic families, and their children therefore better fed and healthier. Yet the performance of these children on difficult memory tests were the lowest in the village, resembling those of children living in a much more isolated and impoverished setting several kilometers away. We interpret this to mean that psychological experiences within the family are responsible for lower expectations of success on cognitive problems, less motivation to perform well, and a more suspicious attitude toward the examiner—all of which lead to poorer performance.

The child's identification with the class of his family is difficult to change, for it is not simply an opinion imposed by another or a habit produced by specific experiences in the home—although these are important—it is the product of a profound inference which is continually supported by evidence that strengthens the original belief. Many human qualities can only be known by reference to another person. We usually say a man is tall and heavy, not six foot three or 250 pounds. "Tall" and "heavy" derive their meaning from reference to others. A child can not know how smart, brave, handsome, or frightened he is unless he has a set of peers available to define his position on the scale. The lower-class child during the years prior to adolescence gradually comes to realize that he possesses little of what the culture values. That insight, which is a component of his class identification, carries with it a sense of impotence—not unlike the mood of the soldier in Stravinsky's *L'Histoire du soldat* after the Devil persuades him to trade his violin for a book that will give him wealth. Not surprisingly, there is a readiness to hide or deny that impotence.[26] The desire to conceal the psychological weakness he imputes to lower-class membership leads to a readiness to take risks, an easier disposition for aggression, and a tendency to assign responsibility for failure to external events.

The Effect of Ordinal Position

The differences between middle- and lower-class children, on the one hand, and first- and later-born children, on the other, show some striking similarities. It is possible that some similar mechanisms mediate these differences because members of a social class or ordinal position use the other class or position to define the self. The influence of an older or younger sibling on the child is probably felt most keenly when the child is between two and ten years of age.[27] The arrival of the second child represents a threat to the firstborn's relationship with the parents. For the later-born, those same years are the time when the oldest is perceived as an omnipotent and invulnerable competitor with special privileges and enviable talents. Since each sibling position has its own set of advantages and disadvantages, let us try to specify some of the psychological consequences associated with each particular ordinal position.

Research suggests that the firstborn has a stronger tendency than the later born to turn to the parents for his values and to use them, rather than his peers, as models.[28] Parents award the firstborn a position of privilege because of his greater competence and age. But the firstborn experiences anxiety over loss or dilution of parental care when the next infant arrives. The firstborn has become accustomed to the exclusive affection of the parents. Since he is not required to share that resource before the next child appears, he comes to expect a certain amount of "attentive care." The disruption or attenuation of that care is a contrast to the past adaptation level and is thus treated as a salient event. Marjorie Konner reports that among the Bushmen, who are excessively protective of their children and who nurse them into the third and fourth years, the most terrifying nightmares of adult women refer to the anger and uncertainty that had surrounded the arrival of the next infant and their subsequent displacement.

The firstborn experiences guilt over his hostility to the later-born child, for he is naturally jealous of the infant's special status, but has no way to rationalize that resentment. Since he knows—and is reminded—that babies are entitled to extra attention, the anger cannot be justified, a condition that predisposes the firstborn to guilt. The later-born, on the other hand, can more easily justify his resentment toward older siblings because they are in fact aggressive and domineering toward him and enjoy privileges he does not.

The combination of identification with parental models, perception of "privileged" status which the child wants to maintain, and apprehension over rejection by adult authority leads the firstborn to adopt higher standards surrounding the competences and attributes that are valued by the parents. Firstborn children of middle-class American parents who value school success adopt and practice that value with greater vigor than do later-born children, as indicated by the disproportionately high percentage of eminent men who are either firstborn or only children. Firstborns are predominant among Rhodes scholars and those listed in *Who's Who among Distinguished Scientists*.[29] A disproportionate number of firstborns also attain very high scores on intelligence and aptitude tests and matriculate at colleges with high admissions standards.[30]

An examination of the scores of almost 800,000 participants in the National Merit Scholarship Program during the period 1962–65 revealed that firstborns had higher verbal scores than later-borns and that these differences could not be attributed to the education or income of the families of the two groups. The advantage of being the oldest was restricted to verbal talents, for no comparable difference occurred in the case of mathematical skills.[31] A similar study of a random sample of 2,523 high school students who were administered a reading-comprehension test revealed that the higher scores of only- and firstborn youths were restricted to students whose fathers had at least graduated from high school. Among adolescents from less well-educated families, the ordinal difference disappeared.[32] This fact suggests that the firstborns are likely to excel in those characteristics valued by the family. If the parental standards stress obedience, the firstborn will be more obedient. If parents promote academic excellence, the firstborn will obtain better grades; if parents value a religious attitude, the firstborn will be more comitted to the family's religion.[33] Among Episcopalians, firstborns were more likely to be committed to the church and to be members of the ordained ministry than were later-borns.[34]

The arrival of the later-born is an incentive to the firstborn to differentiate himself from the younger child. The firstborn cannot ignore the new sibling's presence, and he is pushed to differentiate himself from the younger and associate himself with the values of the parents in order to retain his favored position. The firstborn is propelled to adulthood by the presence of the younger sibling.

Since the later-born is exposed to the less competent talents of the firstborn, along with those of the parents, he has more realistic and pragmatic standards. The combination of a firm commitment to the standards of adults and an affinity for coherence, consistency, and order among standards leads firstborns to adopt more idealistic philosophical positions and to prefer single, unifying principles in both morality and science, in preference to ones that are pluralistic or expedient.[35]

One disadvantage of the later-born position is the sense of inadequacy in comparison with the older sibling, especially if the age difference between the two is not large, say two to four years. The later-born is apt to regard himself as less competent in those qualities prized by the family and actualized by the firstborn. He does not excuse these inadequacies by acknowledging the differences in age but concludes that he is less adequate. As with the lower-class child, this decision can lead, especially in middle-class children, to attempts to deny that conclusion. Later-born children are less cautious; they tend to get involved in physically more dangerous activities. Later-born adults are more likely than firstborns to participate in dangerous sports, such as football, soccer, or rugby, but no more likely to participate in less dangerous sports, such as crew or tennis.[36] In November 1965, during a major East Coast power blackout, 100 adult men and women in a New York hotel were asked the question, "How nervous or uneasy did you feel during this experience?" The firstborns admitted to greater distress and anxiety than the later-borns.[37] Teachers were asked to nominate the two physically most cautious and the two most incautious children in their classrooms. The relation to ordinal position was striking. Children with older siblings were more likely to be classified as motorically impulsive; those with no older siblings were physically more cautious and inhibited.[38] The data imply a more conservative and cautious attitude among firstborns: they are reluctant to provoke rejection by authority or its abstract surrogates, and they seem less ready to alter established attitudes.

If this rather speculative generalization is applied to scientists, one

would expect ordinal position to be associated, at least among active, eminent scientists, with the likelihood of promoting or opposing a theory that
seriously questioned a dominant paradigm. This possibility was first put
forward by Irving Harris in a book entitled *The Promised Seed* (1964). Recently, Frank Sulloway[39] has discovered a remarkable relation between ordinal position and attitude toward new scientific ideas. He argues that
among eminent scientists, later-borns would more likely be ideologically
rebellious, while firstborns would be more reluctant to disagree with a dominant theoretical position. It has already been demonstrated that there are
more eminent firstborn than later-born scientists than one would expect
from chance, given the normal distribution of first- and later-borns in the
population. Sulloway suggests that since evolutionary theory opposed the
strong nineteenth-century belief in the Creation that theory should more
likely have been discovered and amplified by a later-born than a firstborn,
and in fact both Darwin and Wallace were later-borns. Of 98 scientists who
publicly opposed Darwin or the earlier evolutionists from 1750 to 1870 (and
for whom birth-order information is available), only 35 were later-borns.
Among 30 pre-Darwinian evolutionists, including Darwin himself and Wallace, only two were firstborns, and one of these, Isidore Geoffroy St.-
Hilaire, was also the son of an earlier (and himself later-born) evolutionist,
Étienne Geoffroy St.-Hilaire. The other firstborn exception, Henry Bates,
turns out to have been a close friend and scientific colleague of Wallace, who
was himself largely responsible for Bates's pre-1859 conversion to the evolutionary point of view. Of the total of 69 who were either proevolution prior to
1859 or converted after 1859, 56 were later-born and only 13 were firstborn.

Sulloway also examined the three revolutions promoted by Copernicus,
Bacon, and Freud. Of 20 major opponents to the three new hypotheses, 80
percent were either firstborn or eldest sons, 20 percent were later-born
(and, more specifically, younger sons). Of the 43 early proponents, 84 percent were younger sons and 16 percent firstborn or eldest sons. Sulloway's
findings, therefore, point to the special importance for later-borns of having
an older *male* sibling within the family constellation.

Finally, Sulloway examined three other modern revolutions—
Lavoisier's hypothesis regarding the role of oxygen in combustion, relativity
theory, and continental drift. For these three, the scientists were divided
into those under age 40 and those over age 40 when the theories appeared.
Of 51 opponents to these theories over age 40, 84 percent were either
firstborn or eldest sons, 16 percent younger sons. Of 28 proponents over
age 40, 93 percent were younger sons and only 7 percent were firstborn. Scientists under the age of 40 can be presumed to have had less of a

personal or professsional commitment to the older, established paradigms that were then under attack; hence the relation to ordinal position was not present. In fact, as Sulloway also points out, those major revolutions in science that do not simultaneously challenge deep-seated religious or social beliefs are often first promulgated by *young* firstborns (e.g., Newton, Einstein, and Lavoisier), even though an ordinal-position effect separates their older scientific peers in a highly divisive manner.[40] These results imply that the degree to which a scientist is ready to promote or oppose a major ideological system is related—and remarkably so—to his ordinal position in his family.

These theoretically consistent correlates of sibling position remind us that, despite the importance of parental behavior, the mere existence of a younger or older sibling in the family is a salient force in the psychological development of the child. The mechanisms that account for these differences do not rest only with the practices and communications of the parents, and, therefore, they are not solely a function of what is normally meant by "direct family experience." Rather, the catalyst of change is simply the introduction of "another," like the introduction of a crystal into a cloud to precipitate rain. The "other" is the catalyst that creates uncertainty in the child. In response to that uncertainty, the child alters his beliefs, behaviors, and roles.

Like later-borns, the lower-class six-year-old comes to conclusions about his qualities after recognizing the existence of the middle-class child. The middle-class child, like the firstborn, is pushed to differentiate himself from the lower-class youngster once he recognizes his presence, probably during the early school years. Thus, although direct practices issued by parents can shape the child's behavior, we will not completely understand the child's development unless we also take into account his cognitive classification of others. Each individual lives in a social structure and is aware of his position in that structure. That knowledge molds his attitudes toward himself and others, his vulnerability to anxiety and ambition, and his interpretation of the degree to which he is responsible for the outcome of his efforts.

The Modern Western Family

Although the family is a haven and a source of identification and information for all children, there are important differences between the modern Western nuclear family and the less modern, subsistence-farming-village family. Let me use for comparison a village I know best, a small isolated Indian community in northwest Guatemala. The major difference between nuclear families in this community and those in modern America is the more central role played by the Guatemalan family in the life of the child, in part because the child makes an instrumental contribution to its survival. There is no strong peer group available to promote a set of values that competes with those of the family; the child does not have to choose between two value systems. The sex typing is more rigid, and the child's future is inextricably tied to the resources of his family. It is not possible for the adult to have an identity in the village independent from that of the family that reared him.

One of the most important consequences of the increasing geographical and psychological mobility of modern Western youth away from their families is that the identification with family has become weakened and, in some cases, nonexistent. Since there are no other institutions—college, employer, religion—to replace the family, he has no choice but to regard his beliefs and products as the primary locus of the sense of self or, in Eriksonian terms, "Identity." He is psychologically alone. He has no other group or entity to rely on—a position that seems to have the advantage of freedom from coercion and minimal constraints on autonomy of action but which exacts the prices of loneliness and the unavailability of any person or group in which to invest strong emotion. It is for this reason that marriage and the creation of a new family are likely to experience a recrudescence in the West. We take as an axiom that the self resists depersonalization. As modern environments make a sense of potency and individual effectiveness more difficult to attain, freedom from all affective involvements becomes more and more intolerable. Involvement with a family is the only viable mechanism available to satisfy that hunger. The forces that initially weakened the family—urbanization and industrialization—have produced conditions a century later that are now likely to strengthen it. The situation is not unlike the cycle of growth in a cell: the forces that temporarily distort the cell boundaries and chromosomal material eventually produce two new healthy units.

ELEVEN

THE MEANING OF MATURITY

THE DESCRIPTIVE adjectives we apply to human beings fall into two large classes—those that are objective and do not change their definition with time, like "blue-eyed" or "bald," and those whose definitions are continually subject to change and whose meanings are only understood in relation to the specific place and historical period in which they are used. The adjectives "intelligent" and "mature" are two obvious examples of this second class. During the last decade of the nineteenth century, Sir Francis Galton defined intelligence as the possession of extremely sensitive vision and hearing. Today intelligence is defined as possession of verbal, mathematical, and reasoning skills. The rural Guatemalan Indian rejects both definitions, for he views intelligence—or *listura*—as the ability to learn practically adaptive lessons quickly and to take advantage of unusual situations.

This dependence of meaning on locality and historical period is also characteristic of the concept of maturity. After we make the important distinction between physical and psychological maturity—a distinction not always made—we must recognize that the popular definition of maturity as the last phase of a set of progressive changes from infancy to adulthood carries with it the tacit assumption that the traits of the mature adult are stronger, wiser, and more adaptive—better—than those of the child. The mature traits are those the adult "ought to" have. Attainment of adult stature, reproductive fertility, and complete myelination of the central nervous system are some noncontroversial signs of physical maturity. Because many believe in a close parallelism between mind and body, it is assumed that each of man's psychological qualities can and should be arranged on a continuum that proceeds from less to more mature. This ordering is possible for a very small set of psychological attributes, like memory capacity, ability to detect logical inconsistencies in an argument, and inferential reasoning skills. A 20-year-old can remember a longer string of numbers and reason with greater speed and accuracy than can an 8-year-old, and we believe that the better memory and more profound reasoning capacity are adaptive attributes to possess. However, it is less clear that personality characteristics—patterns of interaction with people, the content of beliefs, emotional experiences, and wishes—can be similarly ordered on a scale of maturity that is the same for all societies for all time. Stated more simply, it does not seem possible to list a set of motives, attitudes, and feelings that are absolutely more mature than another set. During the early years of this century Sigmund Freud believed that a mature adult was capable of a deeply gratifying, sexually based love relation with a member of the opposite sex. If a person was not capable of that form of liaison—or did not prefer it—he or she was, by definition, immature. That view is difficult to defend in contemporary America as increasingly large numbers of young adults reject Freud's vision. It strains reason to label as immature the thousands of adults who prefer other sorts of relationships.

Once we acknowledge the relativistic nature of the concept of maturity, there remain two different solutions to the problem of defining maturity. The first, the one preferred here, assumes that each society promotes a normative set of beliefs, motives, frames of reference, and styles of behavioral and emotional expression that maximize adaptation to that community. That set of attributes defines maturity for that particular place. Most Japanese women are conforming, quiet, and passive. Such women are mature in Kyoto, but not in San Francisco. Modern Japanese men strive for status and derive their personal identity from the institution, be it industry or university, for which they work. A Japanese man who took his personal sense of satisfaction, status, and accomplishment from his working for SONY rather than a small electronics company would be regarded as mature in Tokyo but not in Boston. However, many people are bothered by this shifting definition of maturity. They are made uneasy by an approach that allows one to say to a friend that he was mature in early September in Tokyo but immature in late December in San Francisco.

As a reaction to this tension, many psychologists and psychiatrists have insisted that maturity be absolutely defined in terms of deeper, more disguised psychodynamic processes, rather than by the temporary profile of behavioral characteristics and beliefs. The most popular strategy defines maturity in terms of an optimal set of beliefs about the world and the self that are in such harmony that the individual experiences minimal anxiety and is, most of the time, affectively at ease—and will remain so regardless of where he lives. That solution seems theoretically reasonable on first inspection. On reflection, though, it does not seem possible. Eskimo adolescents are trained from early childhood to inhibit all forms of anger and aggression to others;

any display of hostility provokes social rejection and isolation from family and friends. A mature 18-year-old Utku Eskimo living near Hudson Bay does not display any sign of resentment and seems to be at peace with himself and others. If we fly this Eskimo 18-year-old to New York City, he would be exposed regularly to many instances of anger and hostility between others and toward himself but would be unable to retaliate. He would soon experience intense distress for which he would be psychologically unprepared. In a few months he would have to be classed as immature by those who favor the psychodynamic definition based on anxiety and affective ease. There are many other examples that point to the frailty of the absolute view.

Prior to the Civil War, a mature adult in rural Massachusetts or Pennsylvania unquestioningly accepted the moral dicta of the church. The hero for young children was a person who was dedicated to principles of truthfulness, spiritual purity, and devotion to family and to friends. He behaved in accordance with his ideals and proved his self-reliance and dedication by going through trials and ordeals in which he mastered his temptations and acquired the virtues that the child could find listed in almost any manual of conduct—"conscience, justice, honesty, faithfulness, truth, obedience, industry and patience." In most parts of the developing world, whether it be a village in the Himalayas or western Kenya, the woman who feels most mature cooks and cares for her husband and wants and has as many children as possible. That definition provokes pity in the hearts of mature American women.

Early in this century Eleanor Roosevelt wrote an essay as an adolescent which few upper-middle-class contemporary adolescents would write. She said:

> Some people consider ambition a sin, but it seems to me to be a great good, for it leaves one to do and to be things without which one could never have been. Ambition makes us selfish and careless of pushing others back and treading on them to gain our wish, it is true. But we will only be able to push back the smaller souls, for the great ones we cannot tread on. Those who are ambitious and make a place and a name in the great world for themselves are nearly always despised and laughed at by lesser souls who could not do as well, and all they do for the good of men is construed into wrong, and yet they do the good and they leave their mark upon the ages, and if they had no ambition, would they ever have made a mark? Is it best never to be known and leave the world a blank as if one had never come? It must have been meant, it seems to me, that we should leave some mark upon the world, and not just live and pass away. (Quoted in Joseph Lash, *Eleanor and Franklin*, p. 110)

We are driven therefore to the less satisfying conclusion that psychological maturity must always be local in its definition. Like beauty, it is determined by the standards of the viewer, and its denotative meaning is restricted to particular places at particular times.

One reason for the increased concern with "who is mature" is the recent proliferation among young adults of dramatically new value systems that are not just different from those that dominated the first five decades of this century but, in some cases, inconsistent with the more traditional understanding of what is appropriate for mature persons.

Since the meaning of maturity, like the meaning of morality, is always based, in part, on some factual realities in the society, we should expect that social changes will lead to alterations in the definition of maturity. Many such changes have occurred during the last half-century.

There has been, for example, a dramatic decrease in the number of European immigrants to America who share the value system of the indigenous American group. In the early decades of this century, these adults occupied lower social class positions and encouraged their children to attain the status that they lacked but wanted. As these numbers have declined, the numbers of adolescents and young adults with this special motive for upward mobility have also declined. That fact has altered our emphasis on the attainment of status roles as a characteristic of maturity.

Second, the public dissemination and subsequent exaggeration of Freud's views have led to the belief, now widely held, that frustration and anxiety are inimical to physical and psychological health. We used to believe that tolerance of frustration and coping with distress were good for character; we now believe they are injurious to the mind. The existence of psychoanalytic theory and encounter groups have affected, in a serious way, our view of maturity.

A third incentive for change derives from the altered ratio of bureaucratic to entrepreneurial vocational positions over the last quarter-century. The adult in an entrepreneurial job is more likely to develop the belief that he can influence his future life. The person in a bureaucratic position soon comes to believe that forces outside his skill and effort determine future consequences. This assumption weakens the force of the maxim, "Today's effort will be rewarded in the future."

In sum, changes in our patterns of social class distribution, our theories of human nature, and the structure of our economy have transformed our view of reality. Neither our conception of morality nor maturity can be independent of the sociology, economy, and theory of human nature held by the community. And as our moral propositions have changed as a function of new facts, so too has our concept of maturity been transformed. These transformations can be summarized under three major headings—changes in time orientation, changes in source of direction for decision, and changes in our attitude toward emotional freedom.

When Americans believed that the mature adult tried to attain and maintain benevolent status positions, it was necessary for an individual to resolve the conflict between seizing short-lived pleasure now versus more intensive and sustained joy later in favor of the latter. But as the attainment of status *qua* status lost some of its glamour and moral imperative—in part because of the changing social class distribution of the white population, increasing egalitarianism, and new theories of human nature—daily decisions began to be made on the basis of the pleasure they gave in the present rather than the ease they promised in the future. Hence many 18-year-olds who must select a college are likely to choose not the collegiate community that will best prepare them for a job or graduate school, but rather the one in which they believe they will feel good each morning.

Man has only two places to look for direction when he must act—either externally, to maxims announced by authorities, or to internal feelings. When the former sources lose some of their legitimacy—as they now have—then we turn inward for guidance.

A second, related, change has to do with whether sovereignty of decision is given to a benevolent external authority (or ideology) or to the self. As hinted above, since authority has lost some of its legitimacy, the self must now assume the ascendant role. Many people believe, and some psychologists agree, that the most moral adult consults his own conscience and acts in accord with self-generated principles. This catechism leads us to regard Daniel Ellsberg and Thoreau as modern heroes, but we ignore—or repress—the fact that Sirhan Sirhan and Adolf Hitler also behaved in accord with their autonomously generated principles.

The most profound change in America and Western Europe during recent decades does not involve attitudes surrounding sexuality, permissiveness toward drugs, or the celebration of sensuality, but rather the assumption that authority is tainted and is not to be awarded any special wisdom, virtue, or benevolence.

A final force behind the construction of the new maturity derives from promotion of the premise that emotional freedom is more mature than emotional constraint. Marital therapists encourage couples to yell shrilly at one another; parents tell day-care teachers not to suppress their four-year-old's temper tantrum; and Fellini, Bergman, and Antonioni continually remind us of the unhappy, and by implication, childish quality of emotionally suppressed adults.

The push to be true to one's feelings has led to the belief that the slightest temptation to insincerity and dishonesty, even if necessary for harmonious social relations, is immature; honesty, regardless of the context, must always be served first. Couples confess secret resentments, jealousies, and affairs in order to serve that doctrine, even though the confessions occasionally destroy the relationships they were intended to preserve. It is reminiscent of the U.S. officer in Vietnam who reported, "We had to destroy the village in order to save it."

These shifts in our values have led us to replace one set of heroes with another. Daniel Ellsberg replaces William Jennings Bryan; R. D. Laing replaces Freud; Vonnegut replaces Emerson. We do not intend to award a maturity quotient to these men. Each lived in a society during a particular slice of history. The members of every community are aware tacitly, if not self-consciously, of the metaphysical questions each must answer and the qualities each must possess—much like the heart, courage, and brain of Dorothy's three friends in *The Wizard of Oz*. Every adult wants to feel virtuous, not evil; competent, not incompetent; mature, not childish. Each society tells its members the definition of those abstract ideas and the rules by which each searches for possession of those treasures. The treasure hunt begins somewhere between a child's first word and his first articulate question.

Fortunately, there is little danger that changing definitions of the prize once or twice a century will destroy a society, for man would rather love than hate and would rather live in order than in disorder. So we in middle age, who cannot control the change in code, can at least assimilate it and celebrate the hybrid vigor it injects into the social fabric.

TWELVE

ON EMOTiON
ANd iTS developMENT

Words . . . are the wildest, freest, most irresponsible, most unteachable of all things.
Of course, you can catch them and sort them and place them in alphabetical order in
dictionaries. But words do not live in dictionaries; they live in the mind. . . . Thus to
lay down any laws for such irreclaimable vagabonds is worse than useless. A few
trifling rules of grammar and spelling are all the constraint we can put on them. All
we can say about them, as we peer at them over the edge of that deep, dark and only
fitfully illuminated cavern in which they live—the mind—all we can say about them
is that they seem to like people to think and to feel before they use them, but to think
and to feel not about them, but about something different. They are highly sensitive,
easily made self-conscious. They do not like to have their purity or their impurity discussed. . . . Nor do they like being lifted out on the point of a pen and examined separately. They hang together, in sentences, in paragraphs, sometimes for whole pages
at a time. They hate being useful; they hate making money; they hate being lectured
about in public. In short, they hate anything that stamps them with one meaning or
confines them to one attitude, for it is their nature to change. (Virginia Woolf, *The
Death of the Moth*, p. 131)

Introduction

THIS philosophical essay is a critique of some popular views of the concept
of affect. It is neither a theory of emotion nor a synthetic review of the
extensive literature on this topic—excellent reviews can be found in
Mandler (1975), Izard (1971), Plutchik (1962), and Reymert (1950). Its aims
are far less ambitious: to suggest a new way to conceptualize the phenomena
that have traditionally been called affective. Although I am critical of some

From *The Development of Affect*, ed. M. Lewis and L. Rosenblum (New York: Plenum Press,
1978).
    Preparation of this paper was supported in part by grants from the Carnegie Corporation of
New York and the Foundation for Child Development.

current work in this area of inquiry, I do not wish to imply that the phenomena that have been called emotional are unimportant. Quite the opposite; these events must be represented in the unwritten propositions that eventually will describe and explain human behavior. Hence the critical tone is meant to be constructive and not derogatory.

There are two obvious issues that surround this domain of investigation. One controversy concerns the relation between the changes in somatic and visceral discharge to an incentive event, which are the essential features of most theories of emotion, and the central representation of those patterns of afferent impulses. Some believe the relation is reliable, even fixed; others contend it is always changing relative to cognitive evaluations of the situation and the incoming afferent sensations. At one extreme are those who assume that even when cognitive evaluations are absent, as is true of early infancy, special states of consciousness, or when the changes are not perceived, it is still appropriate to talk of the existence of affect.

The second issue is semantic; what is the relation of the words we use to name our feelings and objective assessments of the material bases of those experiences? Stated simply, is there a common envelope of phenomena that occurs every time a person says he is afraid, and is that envelope different from the one that accompanies a declaration of anger? Since both issues engage the classification of psychological phenomena, it seems useful to begin this essay with a discussion of the problems that surround classification. This section will be followed by a brief history of the concepts of affect and finally by some modest suggestions as to how future investigations might be structured.

The Problem of Classification

The parsing of human experience has been the subject of philosophical essays for centuries, and the variety of classification systems reflects the profound presuppositions of the classifier. Nature presents us with an infinite number of discrete events, each of which shares some qualities with another. That experience seems sufficient to lead humans to group the envelopes of events which appear to share common dimensions and to classify them.

A central legend of the Mayan Indians who live in the villages that border Lake Atitlan in northwest Guatemala concerns the final battle between the great Indian warrior, Tecun Uman, who was on foot, and the Spaniard Pedro Alvarado, who was on horseback. After hours of battle, Tecun Uman inflicted what he thought was a fatal wound to the horse. Since he had never seen a man on horseback, he thought the horse and rider were an organic entity and so turned away, believing that he was victorious. Alvarado dismounted and killed Tecun Uman, winning the Guatemalan territory for the Spaniards.

Although the risks we run in misclassifying phenomena are not as serious as those taken by Tecun Uman, scientists are always vulnerable to misdirection if they do not categorize phenomena in a way that is faithful to nature. A potentially serious error in the study of emotional (and motivational) phenomena is the acceptance of the validity of old categories and the attempt to define them in the best way, rather than first detecting the covariances that exist in nature and composing class names after the coherences have been discovered.

The mind seeks to understand events through the generation of propositions filled with categorical terms. The categories chosen to represent the phenomena of interest differ in their utility, validity, and mode of generation. In the mature sciences, categories are typically invented a posteriori to name a new phenomenon (new particle names are invented each time a physicist discovers a unique and reliable energy function in an accelerator), or, in the case of the quark, to point to a potential, as yet undiscovered, phenomenon that might mediate events that are believed to be meaningfully related. In both cases, reliable phenomena led; the categories followed.

Unfortunately, that script is followed less frequently in the social sciences, where reliable relations are less common and the categories that are treated as theoretical terms are too often everyday words borrowed from the language of the larger society. This criticism is especially relevant for the category *emotion* and the terms that constitute the members of that superordinate class, for psychologists often assume that categories like fear and anger exist and try to locate their essence.

Hence, before we turn to the central mission of this paper, which is a psychological discussion of affect, it may be informative at the outset to ask a purely philosophical question—namely, what do we do when we classify events? What factors determine our classifications? Reflection on this issue may clarify the reasons for controversies and misunderstanding.

1. We begin with the assumption that each real event can participate in more than one category (by category we mean a set of shared dimensions) because each event possesses more than one dimension. Theoretically, an event can participate in as many categories as it has dimensions. Consider, as a simple example, the natural event we call a cow. The dimensions of that event include, on the one hand, leather and meat, but, on the other, the fact that a cow carries its young internally and nurses its infant. The first set of attributes leads one to classify cows with alligators, peacocks, and chickens

because they produce marketable commodities. The second set of dimensions leads one to classify cows with weasels, wolves, and gazelles under the superordinate category *mammals*. The category selected depends on the purpose of the classifier.

Consider an event more closely related to the topic of this paper: "The one-year-old child runs crying to his mother upon seeing a stranger." Presented with that event, we can focus on the "crying" and classify it as an instance of an emotion, or focus on the "running to the mother" and classify it as motivational. It may not be useful to decide whether the child runs to the parent because he is "afraid" or because "he wants his mother's solace." Each classification is correct; the one we select depends on our purpose. We shall return to this issue in a moment.

2. Psychological events have as their major dimensions:

> an overt action
> a change in feeling state
> cognitive representations of past, present, or future events
> an incentive event
> an historical or genetic component
> a physiological component
> a context (social as well as nonsocial)
> ease of alteration . . . and perhaps many more

An observer can selectively emphasize any one or more of the above dimensions in his classification, depending upon the use he wishes to make of the classification.

3. Some of the uses (or purposes) of a classification of an event include:

> to describe (the child cried)
> to explain by relating the event to inferred states in the present (the child is anxious; the child wants his mother)
> to explain by relating the event to the product of past experience (the child is attached)
> to include the classification as part of a larger logical or theoretical system (the child is in Stage 4 object permanence)
> to maximize communication with the largest number of people (the child is scared)
> to generate an aesthetic reaction in another through use of poetic terms (the child is psychically vulnerable)
> to relate an event normally classified in the language of one discipline to the language of another discipline (the child's reticular formation is physiologically aroused).

Each of these classifications is potentially legitimate if one saw a 12-month-old child cry following departure of the mother. The one chosen would depend on the purposes of the observer.

4. There is disagreement among psychologists and philosophers with respect to the events that are classified *affective* because scholars have different purposes. As a result, the observers selectively focus on different dimensions of the same event. Those who emphasize a change in feeling state as the central dimension of an affect may treat hunger and thirst as emotions. This position was popular during several historical eras when emotions were regarded as epiphenomenal to more fundamental physiological events.

Another group which emphasizes the afferent feedback from the muscle movements that accompany facial expressions do not regard hunger and thirst as affects. Since hunger has deprivation of food as a dimension, while sadness does not, it is reasonable at least to suggest that hunger and sadness be placed in different categories. But the reasons for insisting on that distinction are largely intuitive. A five-year-old does not regard a mosquito as a member of the class "animal," while a 15-year-old does, because the younger child focuses on the differences and is not yet aware of the similarities between insects and mammals.

Too much psychological classification rests on an intuitive base in which investigators selectively focus on certain qualities following hunch rather than theory.

The naturalist's classification of animals was originally guided by an atheoretical, descriptive morphology but gradually changed following Darwin's writings because evolutionary theory led biologists to focus on reproductive complementarity, common enzyme and blood groups, and even behavior. The theory of evolution replaced concrete morphological attributes as the basis for classification with more dynamic and less public dimensions that included potential behaviors and physiological characteristics.

Since the domain of phenomena we call psychological lacks strong theory, classifications have not been based on sophisticated foundations. Since action, feeling, and thought are so different in their objective and phenomenological qualities, it has been almost impossible for philosophers or psychologists to conceive of any other way to parse human psychological functioning. Although most contemporary investigators regard action and cognition as merely arbitrary envelope categories, that is not the case with emotion. That is, psychologists are not likely to define action in a formal way, attempt to discover, through rational analysis, the primary actions, or posit a group of secondary actions that are blends or derivatives of the primary ones.

Similarly, few psychologists argue that there is a hierarchy of significance among the cognitive processes. Yet some scholars continue to approach the domain of emotion with the twin ancient prejudices of defining essences and hierarchically ordering them into pure and less pure categories.

The distinction between overt behavior, on the one hand, and cognition and affect, on the other, is the most obvious. The first is public and can be pointed out; the other two are private. The more subtle distinction between cognition and affect seems due to the latter experience's having greater phenomenological salience than the former. The change in feeling that accompanies an insult to our dignity is far more distinctive than the change that occurs when we are planning the day's work. That simple fact of experience has led most to declare that emotions must be a special category different from action, on the one hand and thought on the other.

The contemporary separation of affect and cognition resembles, and is likely to be a derivative of, the older division between body and mind, or the ancient distinction between spiritus and animus. Although such remarkable historical consensus might normally be taken to reflect the wisdom of that separation, it might also reflect an enduring historical error. It may be useful, therefore, to suspend prior prejudices, at least temporarily, and pretend that the terms we have used with such confidence for so long do not exist.

Emotional terms have been used in three quite different ways. They have been used most frequently to label conscious experience, less often to name physiological states (either objectively quantified or inferred), or to serve as hypothetical constructs to explain covariation between incentive events and behavioral consequences. To illustrate, there is typically a brief period of temporary inhibition of action accompanied by detectable changes in patterns of muscle and autonomic nervous discharge when a person encounters an unexpected external event. Scientists want to carve out the reliable coherences among incentive events, physiology, and subsequent behavior and assign them to some superordinate category. Hence they have applied the name "surprise" to that coherence. However, "surprise" is not always the term used to describe the coherent set of events that follows the reading of an unexpected piece of new information on the world's fossil-fuel reserves, nor the concept a physiologist chooses when his polygraph records reveal discharge in the reticular activating system.

5. At present, many psychologists, but certainly not all, regard the category *affective* as being characterized by a change in feeling state that is derivative of internal physiological events, produced by an immediate incentive event, short-lived in duration, linked to cognitive structures, and not related to physiological deprivation. There is a general, but implicit, agreement that those five dimensions are central to the category *affective*.

6. The dimensions of events that are classified as *motives* (in contrast to affects) are less clear but often include anticipation of a future goal that was acquired as a result of past experience.

7. The dimensions of those events that are classified as *cognitive* (in contrast to affective or motivational) are even less clear but appear to include mental manipulation of schemata, symbols, concepts, and rules in the present with no necessary change in feeling state or outward behavioral manifestation.

8. The above discussion implies that the popular use of the classification *affective*, *cognitive*, and *motivational* tends to be correlated with the past, present, and future components of a continuous and dynamic unitary event.

Consider the event: "The child who has just insulted a friend apologizes." If we focus on the child's evaluation of his act of insulting, we classify the event as cognitive. If we focus on the change in feeling, we call it affective. If we focus on the child's wish to make amends and apologize, we call the event motivational. The event "The child apologizes after insulting a friend" has thought, feeling, and wish as components. The classification imposed on that event announces the dimensions we wish to emphasize; in the same way the first adjective we use to classify a woman—beautiful, arrogant, intelligent, or educated—reflects the dimension we wish to award primacy.

9. The main purpose of a classification is to package a great deal of information efficiently. When we call an event a star rather than a planet, we communicate a great deal about the event. The classification *star* summarizes a great many qualities including distance from the earth, light source, probable size, age, and temperature. If we call the same event an astronomical object, we communicate only the fact that it is not located on the earth. Similarly, if an observer calls an event emotional, he implicitly announces that he wants to emphasize an incentive that produced a change in feeling state. If he calls the same event cognitive, he wishes to emphasize the evaluation and manipulation of information. If he calls the event motivational, he wishes to emphasize anticipation of a future state.

Many, but not all, psychological events are whole units with an incentive, a feeling state, a mediating cognitive process, and a consequent intention. When we wish to draw attention to the incentive and feeling state, we use classification words like fear, guilt, and sadness. When we wish to draw attention to the child's organization and processing of information, we use cognitive categories like reflect, compare, infer, and evaluate, which share the manipulation of schemata, images, symbols, concepts, and rules. If we wish to draw attention to future aims and potential actions, we use motivational terms like affiliation, achievement, and hostility.

If an observer says, "The man is sad," he tells me of a likely incentive and a present feeling state. If the same observer says, "The man is thinking about his wife at home," he informs me of the content of his present thought. If the observer says, "The man wants to be with his wife," he informs me of his anticipations and likely future behavior. Each classification communicates something different about the same event.

10. There is potential utility in using separate affective, cognitive, and motivational categories, even though these categories are not normally explanatory. The classifications inform us of the qualities of an event the classifier wishes to emphasize.

11. This discussion implies that states like hunger or thirst can be included or excluded from the category *affect*. If one could demonstrate that these drives shared a quality that the other affects did not, it might be potentially useful to separate them. Similarly, the affects accompanied by special facial feedback patterns might be separated from the others. But those who promote that view would have to show first that the classification of the states accompanied by facial feedback is theoretically useful; that is, it leads to predictions and/or principles that are more powerful than those generated when the states with and without facial feedback are pooled. But this is not yet proven. Birds have many qualities that mammals do not, although both share some dimensions. Biologists find it useful at times to distinguish between these classes. But no biologist would argue that birds are a primary class of vertebrates, while mammals are secondary. That is why it is not clear why Tompkins and Izard want to claim that the affects associated with feedback from facial muscles are primary, and all others are secondary. There is reason to believe that the affect states accompanied by facial feedback may be a special category, but it is less obvious that these events should be declared, a priori, the primary emotions.

12. There is a potential relation between affects and motives. The category *motive* refers to complementary representations of future and current states—a comparison of present and future. For example, the category *motivation for friends* implies the generation of a future experience with others that is different from one's current state. The specific motive category named often depends on the affect experienced, the one to be experienced, and the substantive goal sought. Hostility is placed in a different category from sexuality because of the differences in feeling and content of the anticipated goals and state. Hence affect and motive are related, since affect states contribute to the classification of motives. Assuming the validity of the categories: (a) incentive events, (b) change in feeling state, and (c) anticipated goals, a combination of *a* and *b* makes up the superordinate category *affect*, while the combination of *b* and *c* makes up the superordinate category *motive*.

Since motive categories are influenced, in part, by the discrepancy between present state and an ideal state in the future, the motive categories that predominate in a society will be influenced by local conditions, for societies differ in the magnitude of discrepancy between present and desired future for the varied goals humans seek. Wealth is a dominant motive in the West because many individuals experience a large discrepancy between the ideal and the present; food, on the other hand, is not. The opposite profile exists in a Chilean concentration camp. This is another way of saying that nodes of uncertainty within a culture influence the hierarchy of motives.

The discussion thus far has been analytic and critical rather than constructive. We believe the category *affective* has been used in a loose way to denote the universal but complex experience of detecting a sudden change in one's feelings or, by extension, inferring a similar change in another as a result of the recognition of certain unusual action patterns.

Since the occurrence of that class of event is relatively infrequent (the proportion of our waking hours that we are alerted by a serious discrepancy from our normal feeling-tone is probably less than 10 percent), we naturally try to classify that experience. It is generally the case that the observer is initially tempted to base his classification on the dimension that is most discrepant from his corpus of knowledge. Hence most classifications of affect award primacy to the changed feeling state. This cognitive disposition can also be noted when the Western anthropologist categorizes an African society as polygynous even though less than a third of the families in that society practice polygyny. But since a household with several wives is so discrepant from the observer's norms, he is drawn to a classification based on that unusual quality and led away from other attributes that might be more critical to the functioning of the social group. We believe that this egocentric perspective has guided much theorizing on affect. But, as indicated earlier, there is a second strategy. One can first search for covarying phenomena and, if successful, invent categories to provide coherence. There is an important difference in the use of the term "fear" to explain the regular empirical relation in the one-year-old between departure of the caretaker and subsequent crying, in contrast to its use to name my sudden tachycardia following a near-accident on a highway or to suggest the reason why a three-year-old child suddenly put his thumb in his mouth and lowered his head. Scientific progress in the study of emotion will be stalled as long as we fail to stipulate how we want to use affective terms.

What Have We Wanted to Understand—An Historical Survey

What phenomena do we wish to understand and/or predict that require the postulation of a concept like emotion? One popular answer is that we wish to explain the sudden changes in ongoing action and/or subjective experience that are lawfully yoked to certain contexts. A person is talking quietly with a friend when the former suddenly begins to wave his arms and raise his voice. From these data we infer a change in internal state and perceived feeling. How shall we classify those phenomena? When one's progress in solving a problem is stalled, it is occasionally helpful to ask how scholars in the past approached the same problem. We believe it will be useful, therefore, to present a brief historical survey of the concept of emotion. I have borrowed a great deal in the pages that follow from an infrequently cited book entitled *Feeling and Emotion: A History of Theories* (Gardiner, Metcalf, and Beebe-Center 1970).

GREEK OPINION: A SAMPLER

Plato's interest in emotion was guided by a transcendental concern with what was good. Affects either hindered or helped attainment of that precious state and were never ends in themselves. (As we shall see, Kant viewed affects as hindering rationality—the modern West's symbolic substitute for virtue.) The feeling of pleasure, which is regarded as a final goal in modern writing, was only a "way station" in one's progress toward the more transcendental state.

Aristotle, like Plato before him and writers prior to the European Renaissance, viewed emotions the way chemists regard catalysts. The focus of concern was man's movement toward the good. Emotions helped or hindered that process. Thus emotions were typically evaluated as good or bad depending on their ability to move a human toward or away from morally proper action.

Aristotle divided man into three parts: faculties (potentialities to be actualized), formed habits, and passions; but he avoided defining the passions and merely gave examples. Like the writers of the Middle Ages after him, he thought the passions did not belong to the soul but influenced the soul. Aristotle's classification of the passions, found in the tenth book of Nicomachean ethics and the second book of the Rhetoric, was composed of paired opposites that described an evaluative dimension: anger and the ease of being placated; love and hate; fear and confidence; shame and shamelessness; benevolence and churlishness; pity and resentment, emulation and contempt. He did not imply that the list was complete.

Like Plato, Aristotle was concerned primarily with pleasure and pain, but he conceptualized pleasure as the concomitant of the normal exercise of human abilities. The actualization of any natural attribute was a source of pleasure, the degree of pleasure being proportional to the degree to which that talent was realized. It should come as no surprise that frustration of that human effectance, as Robert White might put it, was felt as pain. Unlike later writers, Aristotle did not analyze affects. The affects were epiphenomena—something added to the normal functions of life, like the smile that follows a joke. Like most writers, Aristotle classified the affects by external incentives and associated cognitions. Anger was "an impulse attended with pain to avenge openly an undeserved slight openly manifested to ourselves or our friends." Love consisted in "wishing a person all the things you consider good, not for your sake, but for his and readiness, so far as in you lies, to bring them about." For Aristotle, as for most who followed him, drives, needs, feelings, and passions all had something in common—namely, a distinct and salient subjective experience. Although he speculated on the role of bodily heat and blood in emotion, the key to Aristotle's classification was the context and associated cognition; in that sense it resembled the approach of the modern social psychologist.

The Stoics postulated four basic passions—desire, fear, pleasure, and pain—which were the result of a belief regarding the degree of good or evil inherent in the objects. The Stoics also defined emotion in terms of situation and target and acknowledged the contribution of cognitive factors. Although modern social scientists would reject those classifications in detail, they would at least be able to understand them.

THE MIDDLE AGES

By contrast, the scholars of the Middle Ages generated a classification of emotions that contained presuppositions that are more difficult for the modern mind to comprehend. Thomas Aquinas wrote one of the most systematic expositions in the thirteenth century. Aquinas believed that soul and body were connected and that passions could run in either direction. The consequences of a painful wound ran from body to soul; the results of anger from soul to body. Aquinas differentiated the purely intellective from the sensory and affective and divided the latter into concupiscible and the irascible. The former concerned appetites, needs, and drives in the present with strong sensory components that could be gratified; the latter referred to future goals that were more difficult to gratify. (See Table 12.1.)

It is doubtful that any modern scholar would ever classify the affects in

Table 12 · 1   Aquinas' Table of Passions

Concupiscible		Irascible	
Good	Evil	Good	Evil
Love	Hate	Hope	Fear
Desire	Aversion	Despair	Courage
Pleasure	Pain		Anger

this manner. Like the Greeks, Aquinas made an ambiguous differentiation between what we call affect and drive or motive. The primary passion, and the source of all the rest, was love, which was viewed as an aptitude to move toward the good. If one loves an object, one will move toward it. If one attains it, one will experience joy or pleasure. Although this medieval classification is based on presuppositions about good and evil that are alien to most modern psychologists, it served Aquinas and those of his century who held a different set of a priori assumptions and had different purposes than Cannon, James, Schachter, or Tompkins. It is, in this sense, that we say that the Schachter and Tompkins' positions are complementary and not inconsistent. If the purpose of the classification is to predict behavior, then Schachter's theory is more useful. If, on the other hand, the purpose is to understand the biological contributions to affective experience, the Tompkins and Izard propositions seem more useful.

Aquinas named 11 passions but argued that there are only four major affects; namely, pleasure and pain, on the one hand and hope and fear on the other. Pleasure and pain were states in the present; hope and fear anticipations of the future. Aquinas believed the bodily changes were due to the appetite's being excited by the expectation of good or evil. But mind was the origin of a passion—a movement of soul in the body. "The affections of the soul are not caused by changes in the heart," Aquinas wrote, "but rather caused them." Thus both the Greeks and medieval scholars placed psychological factors, be it in the form of soul or thought, as the origin rather than as the consequence of biological changes.

THE RENAISSANCE

Renaissance writers introduced an important change in the classification of emotions. The rise of science and the hints of the church's eventual decline led scholars away from inquiry into the purpose of affect and toward an attitude of analysis, even though the purpose of the analysis was left ambiguous. Gradually the term *affectus* replaced *passiones*. Philipp Melanchthon, for example, defined pleasure not as the seeking or the attaining of good, but in physiological terms: "The perception in the nerves or nerve coating of a congruent object, a perception not injuring or lacerating the nerves but totally adapted to their conservation." This definition would have been foreign to Plato, Aristotle, and Aquinas, and is not unlike defining "libido" as a recursive polypeptide chain with four methylated hydroxyl groups. Morally neutral description and analysis were becoming the criteria for classification of affects and have remained so for more than 500 years. Soul and body were now seen as less isolated, and a synergism between mind and biology was assumed. The actions of the heart were less eiphenomenal and played a more causal role. In a remarkably prophetic essay, Scipio Claramontius (1565–1653) argued that the most reliable signs of affect were to be found in the pulse and respiration because these two systems reflected the "heat of the heart." Modern writers have moved the site from the heart to the face and brain.

A subtle but important change in the Renaissance attitude toward affective phenomena is captured by the contrast between the medieval concern with pleasure and grief and the Renaissance concern with laughter and weeping. The latter are objective behaviors, not inferred states. Antonius Laurentius wrote two books on laughter in the first decade of the seventeenth century, and even though the explanations are absurd ("Tears flow when the brain is filled with moisture"), the form of the questions is modern, and the dependent variable is a public event, not a hypothetical, evaluative universal. Francis Bacon brought these threads together in "Advancement of Learning," emphasizing the need for accurate description and analysis.

By the middle of the seventeenth century, the empirical spirit was accelerating, and Descartes treated emotions in "Les Passions de l'âme" in psychophysiological perspective. The original element in Descartes' discussion was to award biological forces a status independent of the soul, but in a relation of influence to the soul, as one might conceive of a mother and child as separate and distinct entities, influencing each other. But Descartes was still close to the Greek view, for he regarded passion as an experience in which the soul was the subject, even though the source of the experience was the movement of forces in the body, in the spirit of James and Lange.

Descartes speculated on the physiology of the passions. His view that the body was the source of changes which, via the medium of animal spirits, influenced the soul, is not unlike the statement that the discharge of cones in the retina via the ganglia in the thalamus eventually leads to the perception of color. Note that Descartes' concern was primarily with explanation, not with evaluation or purpose. Whatever teleology was present was distinctly modern in tone. The purpose of passions was survival, to dispose the soul to will the things that nature declared to be useful—an early version of the modern evolutionary biologist's view that the major purpose of behavior is to insure reproduction of the next generation. The change from a "good" emotion to a "useful" one is profound! Unlike those of his predecessors, all the affects proposed by Descartes are in the immediate present, not in the future. They are not potential states or wishes, but the consequence of bodily changes in the here-and-now. Descartes listed six primary emotions: admiratio (alertness, attentiveness, and surprise), love, hate, desire, joy, and grief.

All others were derivative (one notes the absence of fear and guilt and the rejection of Aquinas' division of concupiscible and irascible passions).

Descartes' more empirical, pragmatic, and materialistic view of affect is accompanied by a concern for the first time with the development of emotions. Descartes believed the first passions were joy and sorrow (apparently Descartes called the crying of infants at strangers and caretaker departure sorrow, whereas we call it fear). Sorrow subsequently was transformed into hate later in development. Thus Descartes shares with modern theorists the assumption of an epigenetic relation between the affects of infancy and those of later childhood, as some modern writers posit a relation between infant attachment and later dependency. Descartes is also the first major associationist, for he believed a person could learn a contiguous association between an idea and some bodily change—a conditioned link between visceral reaction and thought. He speculated that individual differences in the emotional reaction to roses, for example, were probably due to differences in prior experience.

THE SEVENTEENTH AND EIGHTEENTH CENTURIES: HOBBES, SPINOZA, AND KANT

Descartes' view of affects as natural phenomena to be explained was amplified by Hobbes, who carried Descartes' fragile materialism much further. For Hobbes, psychological life consisted of mechanically propelled motions of particles within the organism, and body and soul became one unity. Hobbes made the passions more important than any earlier writer. Passions were necessary for life: "To have no desires is to be dead, so to have weak passions is dullness." Affects sustained thought, determined intellectual and moral character, and were the sole incentives for action. Since Hobbes believed passions guided thought, individual differences in behavior could be traced to emotions, especially the emotions related to the desires for power, wealth, honor, and knowledge, which Hobbes believed were environmentally determined.

Hobbes completed the change in philosophical attitude that gradually replaced Plato's transcendental good as the criterion for evaluating an affect with individual survival by anticipating Darwin's assertion that the greatest good was the conservation of the individual. Self had replaced virtue as the entity to the preserved. Appetite and aversion were the primary affects, but Hobbes also posited desire, love, joy, and grief as simple passions. Contempt was a derivative emotion produced by an immobility of the heart in resisting the action of certain things, where the heart was already otherwise moved. Hobbes was concerned primarily with explaining man's behavior in society, not analyzing physiological correlates.

Although Spinoza agreed that emotions were natural phenomena whose aim was self-conservation, he tried to reduce the enormous variety of experience to the smallest number of elementary units, and pleasure, pain, and desire became Spinoza's elemental trio.

Kant provided the next important set of changes in conception, for affect was again separated from cognition (Kant rejected Hobbes' attempt at unification), and motives were differentiated from emotions. The three faculties were knowing, feeling, and appetite; hence, Kant distinguished affects from what we call motives and drives. Kant believed both feeling and appetite hindered rationality and, therefore, were potentially bad. Affect was evaluated once again, as it was much earlier, but this time the evaluation depended not on the relation of emotion to the seeking of an ethical or transcendental good, but rather on the degree to which an emotion hindered or facilitated attempts at rationality, the West's version of virtue. Kant postulated a new set of primary emotions. For the first time, the innate passions were declared to be an inclination for liberty, love of life, and sexuality—all of which placed the self in the center as both subject and object of action. Once again we note that nodes of uncertainty become the basis for classification. As it would have been impossible for Plato to have made "an inclination for liberty" a primary passion, so too it would have been impossible for Silvan Tompkins or Stanley Schachter to declare "love of God" as a primary emotion.

THE MODERN ERA

During the late nineteenth century, there was for the first time an interest in emotional states that might not reach conscious experience. That novel idea was a result of the increased reliance on physiological factors as the criteria for emotion (Reymert 1950). Scientists turned from phenomenology and observation of overt behavior to the quantification of physiological states. It was reasonable now, but not earlier, for James and Lange to assert that emotions were merely the perception of changes in bodily states, and for Spencer to argue that consciousness was due to physiological discharge. The enslavement of psychological products by physiological forces was carried to an extreme when Gall and Spurzheim postulated 35 faculties, each yoked to a specific cerebral organ, with more than half of these faculties being affective in nature. Thus by the late nineteenth century, conscious experience of a feeling became subordinate to biological events, a complete reversal of the views of Plato, Aristotle, and Aquinas, who saw the affective experience as origin rather than consequent.

That reversal has profound implications for our contemporary view of the origins of man's actions, especially those related to morality. When consciousness is the source of passion and motivation, it is reasonable to argue that a person is responsible for the actions that spring from strong feeling. When consciousness is merely the end of a series of physiological events, it is easier to defend the premise that a person does not have total responsibility for all of the actions that are derived from passion. And during the last 100 years, we have seen an increasing friendliness toward the view that entities beyond the person's control—be they genes, neurotransmitters, madness, or poverty—can be the "causes" of behaviors that harm the self or another.

The Present

We have several choices open to us if we still wish to classify affective phenomena. But we must first ask what our purposes are. What uses do we want to make of emotional phenomena? We suggest that an important use of an affect category is as a hypothetical construct to unite contemporaneous relations between incentives and resulting reactions or to serve as a conceptual entity to unite past with present—to explain how present behavior might be derived from the distant past. We suspect that most modern psychologists, or philosophers for that matter, want to use emotional categories in this manner, and not as terminal states to seek or avoid or labels for phenomenological states. Unlike the Greeks, we do not want to posit an ideal telos for all actions and therefore are not burdened with a commitment to an evaluative veneer for emotions. Nor do we see emotions, as Kant did, as inimical to reason. But there is still detectable disagreement among those scholars who believe emotion is an essence that will yield to definition.

Sartre (1962) regards emotions as a manner of apprehending the world. This cognitive view of affect is dictated, in part, by Sartre's philosophical agenda. Since consciousness is central to Sartre's philosophy, and emotion is a form of consciousness, it was necessary that he define affect as a form of understanding.

But a psychologist like Plutchik (1962) cannot help but be influenced by the modern commitment to physiological reductionism and evolutionary theory, and so he makes physiological arousal and adaptive value fundamental criteria in his list of primary emotions. Nonetheless, his final definition of emotion is so inclusive that it admits almost any behavioral reaction to an incentive event: "Emotion is a patterned bodily reaction of either destruction, reproduction, incorporation, orientation, protection, deprivation, rejection, or some combination of these which is brought about by a stimulus" (p. 151).

In addition to the complementary views of Tomkins (1962, 1963) and Izard (1971), to which we have referred several times, Mandler's (1975) recent attempt to tame the many-headed entity of emotion also reflects the belief that although emotion is the result of an interaction of physiological changes and cognitive interpretations, the physiological arousal, which is not viewed as cognitive, is the quintessential first event.

"The particular human behaviors and experiences of interest to us occur subsequent to the activities of the autonomic nervous system, particularly its sympathetic division. I shall refer to this activity as arousal" (Mandler 1975, p. 60). "Arousal, as used here, refers to specific measurable events that occur external to the mental system; in a more ancient language, arousal is stimulation" (p. 111).

Mandler seems to side with Descartes in hinting at the independence of mind and body, but with James and Lange in making the former reactive to the vissicitudes of the latter—as most scholars have done since the early nineteenth century. The primacy of physiological arousal is seen most clearly in his discussion of the ontogeny of anxiety, where Mandler asserts that it is not necessary to specify the incentive for the fundamental distress state of the newborn, which he views as a combination of arousal and helplessness: "The schematic model suggested here for the occurrence of anxiety . . . is the cyclical distress of the human newborn. There may be antecedent events that could account for the crying and increased activity we recognize as distressful in the young infant . . . but it is not necessary to specify or even to assume such a specific antecedent event" (p. 194).

This statement by a leading contemporary theorist reflects the popular presupposition that emotions are theoretically useful entities whose essences are to be found in autochthonous, physiological processes.

Since most theorists—including Mandler, Ekman, Izard, Plutchik, and Tomkins—view emotional terms as hypothetical constructs, they approach the classification of affect, as they do other concepts with this epistemological status, by asking what are the links to empirical reality.

THE CENTRAL CHARACTERISTICS OF AFFECTIVE PHENOMENA

The phenomena that have been called emotional by contemporary scientists generally share one quality. They always involve a change, usually perceived but for some theorists inferred, in internal milieu. We believe there is a profound difference between the state of consciously perceived feeling changes and the state produced by bodily changes that are not detected. We shall consider only the first and postpone discussion of the psychoanalytic notion of "unconscious affective states" for another time.

CHANGES IN FEELING-TONE

Every person is aware of a typical feeling-tone (or normal feeling state) to which he has become accustomed. The perception of a change in that tone has several consequences. The perceived change (1) alerts the person (the "admiratio" of Descartes), (2) may be accompanied by changes in bodily posture, facial expression, visceral reactions, or an alteration of the hierarchy of probable responses that might be issued, or (3) may be an incentive event for a cognitive interpretation. These are three quite different phenomena.

The phenomena that are associated with a change in facial expression more often have as their incentive a real external event in the present, rather than a thought or image. The primary emotions of Tompkins and Izard are typically triggered by seeing, hearing, smelling, or experiencing an external event. In a sense, they are special classes of orientation reactions. Since facial expressions produce afferent feedback to the central nervous system that might subsequently influence the feeling state, it is not unreasonable to regard those states produced by such real events and accompanied by changes in facial expression as a special category. But the decision to call those states the basic emotions, and to imply that a feeling of emptiness in a hotel bedroom 1,000 miles from home on Christmas Eve is not a primary emotion because there is no necessary facial change, has the flavor of theoretical imperialism. Nonetheless, the "face as seat of emotion" hypothesis is helpful, for it names two correlated events that can accompany a change in feeling-tone; namely, an external incentive and a facial expression.

QUALITY OF FEELING

Let us now examine more closely the quality of the change in feeling state. The change in state can vary in intensity, salience, perceived locus in or on the body, duration, and rise time. The change following an hour of exercise or a near-accident on the highway is more intense than the change that follows violation of a standard on politeness. The locus of the change in feeling state can be the heart, chest, trunk, face, legs, stomach, or genitals. The change in feeling-tone also has a salience, duration, and rise time which may provide important information. If a change in feeling-tone is the essential event in emotion, it may be useful to specify, in a way that has not been done, how the combination of these five qualities might influence thought and action.

As we have indicated several times, we should differentiate between the use of emotional words to label conscious experience, to name physiological states, and to "explain" the relation between a set of incentive events and subsequent outcomes.

Since all changes in behavior are likely to be accompanied by changes in the central and autonomic nervous systems, theoretically all behavior change is accompanied by an affect. As we understand each new functional relation, we assign it a name, be it hunger or pain, and remove it from the larger, unknown category called affect. One might conceptualize the task of scientific work as that of trying to empty the term "affect" of any content because we will have eventually grasped the more specific meaning of each of its exemplars. This view implies the wisdom of separating those changes in state we know something about, like hunger, thirst, pain, warmth, or cold, from those we know little about. We might also eliminate the state of continued attention, for we are gaining understanding of those events that control attention, and they differ from those related to hunger and thirst.

But we are still left with a large set of psychological events that are characterized by an incentive in thought or external events, accompanied by a perceived change in feeling state, and associated with a special set of reactions.

If one announces explicitly that one function of a classification of affective phenomena is to relate classes of incentive events to internal changes (acknowledging the legitimacy of other purposes), then the following discussion might be regarded as an initial attempt at categorization.

External Events as Incentives

There is one class of external events that typically produces alerting, attention, and occasionally inhibition. These events are often called *discrepant*. This class of incentives includes all external events that require acquired knowledge for the change in state. These events are to be distinguished from those that innately produce a change in state, like a flash of bright light or a very loud sound. We are concerned here with those events that produce a changed state because they engage knowledge. This category would be closely related to the affects of surprise, fear, and interest postulated by Tompkins and Izard. We believe these to be among the first incentives for state change in the infant and have suggested that they are the origins of the phenomena that in modern terms are called stranger and separation anxiety.

A second class of external events that is linked to changes in state is caused by loss or absence of a target object toward which the child has established behavioral dispositions. These target objects can include care-takers as well as inanimate objects. When loss of a target object is recognized, a special state is created, different from the one created by discrepant events. If the target object remains absent, and there is no coping response available, a different state is generated. A third class of external incentives with a special state involves some agent's interrupting a person's ongoing response routine—an incentive Mandler awards great power.

Thought as the Incentive

When reflections on the past or anticipations of the future are the primary incentives, there are important differences in the physical qualities of the change in state. The change is apt to be less intense and have a slower rise time but a longer duration. We suspect these factors may be critical. For example, Kearsley (1973) has shown that a slow rise time for an auditory event leads to interest in the newborn, while the same signal with a fast rise time leads to a defensive response.

One important class of mental incentives occurs when the child recognizes that his behavior or the behavior of others deviates from a standard. When the child recognizes that deviation, there is often inhibition. When the child is mature enough to anticipate or infer the psychological reactions of another to that deviation, another state is created. This state typically does not occur before three years of age because it requires the ability to infer the psychological state of another. Typical deviations are a failure to meet standards for a task and violation of parental prohibitions. When a standard becomes generalized across many contexts, the reaction to the violation may have a special quality.

There is a complementary state created when the child meets a standard following behavioral effort. In this sequence the child generates a representation of a performance to be attained and invests effort in order to match his behavior to that ideal. If he is able to meet the standard, there is an internal state that some label joy, pride, or happiness.

Thus far it has not been necessary to postulate a construct of self separate from the reactions of the child. By "self" we mean the psychological function that evaluates alternatives and integrates the child's qualities into a coherent category. But by age three and maybe earlier, this new function has emerged. Now the child is aware that he has alternative actions or choices. The two-year-old dirties himself, recognizes that a standard has been violated, and anticipates a reaction from others. Although the two-year-old does not appreciate that it could have been otherwise, the four-year-old considers the possibility that perhaps he could have avoided that misdemeanor. Hence the reaction has a different quality.

The emergence of a construct of self also permits the child to detect similarities and differences between himself and others. Since the self is old enough to evaluate those qualities, the child can categorize himself in desirable or undesirable terms, depending on the pattern of similarities. This process has been called *identification*. Additionally, if the child perceives that he is valued by another who possesses desired qualities, the child feels enhanced.

When either of these external events or thoughts are the primary incentives, we must posit a previously established structure. The incentive event is related to the knowledge in some way. The event can be discrepant from possessed knowledge, absence of a target one has oriented toward, violation of or meeting a standard. This approach to classification of affects makes cognition and cognitive structure necessary components of emotion. The perceived change in internal state—the phenomenon of interest—is due to the interaction of the incentive event and the cognitive structure, as radiation is the result of the interaction of an accelerating electric charge in an electromagnetic field. This position is incompatible with a division of affect and cognition, for affect is the phenomenon that emerges from the operation of cognition on information (see Sroufe 1977 for a similar conclusion).

We have tried to avoid, as much as possible, using the common emotional terms found in textbooks because we are not sure how useful they are. But we might see how this discussion is related to two of those ancient categories. When an unassimilated discrepant event leads to a salient change in state that is intense, has a fast rise time, and is associated with special facial and postural reactions, many might use the word "fear." The term "anxiety," on the other hand, is often applied when an anticipation of the future leads to a change in feeling that has a slower rise time but no necessary sequellae in face or posture.

We suggest that affect states be characterized as classes of coherence among the nature of the interpreted incentive, quality of the resulting feeling state, and cognitive and behavioral sequellae. Trios of phenomena with a high degree of covariance might be grouped together. Consider the classification of the drive state *hunger*. Physiological psychologists have demonstrated the utility of taking into account the incentive, the state change, and the subsequent reaction. For example, the incentive for hunger is deprivation of food, the state change involves alterations in the lipid and glucose levels in blood and liver, and the reaction is a signal to the brain that prompts the organism to seek food. All three constitute a definition of hunger. The hunger state is not to be found in any one of these phenomena, and reliance on any one of these events may provide a misleading definition of hunger. One could be deprived of food for ten hours but not be hungry, because of high fat and sugar reserves. Or one might have a lower level of blood glucose owing to "shock" rather than food deprivation. Or one might seek food and eat in order to be friendly. The coherence of a set of events seems to be a useful way to classify this concept and may be useful for affects as well. Note that this conceptualization implies a continuously dynamic state, not a static one. A person is not either hungry or not hungry, but characterized by a position on a set of potentially quantifiable dimensions. We experience hunger in degrees. It is unfortunate that our affect words—fear, sadness, anger—have such a static, dichotomous connotation. Perhaps research on their referents would have been more profitable had the terms implied a continuum like fearing, saddening, or angering.

It is likely that there is a small set of incentive conditions, as interpreted by cognitive processes, which guarantees that certain states are likely to occur (perhaps must occur) in all settings in which children are raised by and live with human beings. The universally appearing incentives that will contribute to these states include (1) encounter with unassimilable discrepant events; (2) encounter with assimilable discrepant events; (3) detection of inconsistency or deviation among acquired standards or between standards and behavior; (4) loss of a target object to which the person has established a response routine; (5) anticipation of danger, harm, or an event with which the subject cannot cope; (6) an agent blocking a goal or threatening ego's values and standards; (7) the meeting of a standard following effort or the realization of an anticipated state; (8) genital stimulation or the anticipation of genital stimulation; (9) the experience of a person requiring nurture; (10) the experience of a person violating a fundamental standard; (11) release from a distress state.

Some of these incentive events fall into an approximate developmental sequence. For example, discrepant events are an incentive very early in development. Since the 12-month-old child can anticipate the future, he is vulnerable to a new feeling state. He can also hold a future goal in short-term memory for a longer time. Since that goal can be thwarted, a capacity for another state can occur. By two years of age a child can reflect on the past, take the role of another, and make inferences. As a result, he can reflect on his own past behavior and the violation of standards and experience a special state. By four or five years of age, he is able to realize he had a choice with respect to a prior action and is therefore vulnerable to still another state. By seven years of age he has acquired some absolute standards that generalize across many contexts, and events that violate those standards elicit still additional feeling states.

The above incentives, and there are likely to be more, probably occur in all humans who live with others. We believe that each of these is linked to changes in states (we acknowledge that there may not be distinctive changes in feelings linked to each incentive) and with sets of cognitions. These coherences might be called affect states. However, the name to be applied to each coherence is the least important consideration. We could number them from 1 to n.

Since some cultures present unique incentives not present in all locales, some affective states will be unique to a community. The state that results from living alone in a foreign city for a year, or the recognition that one shares few beliefs with others in the community in which one lives, does not happen to millions of people who spend their lives in isolated, endogamous villages of fewer than 1,000 people. The affects we call isolation, alienation, or depersonalization are probably not actualized in these closed settings. However, the villager in these settings has a capacity for those affect states— many genetic predispositions are not actualized if the proper environmental conditions do not occur.

Some Final Suggestions

Since the category *affect* is so broad, it may have outlived its usefulness. Changes in feeling state are such a basic quality of human existence, as are interpretation, storage, and manipulation of information, that it is likely that the use of one term to cover the entire domain distorts nature's plan. Perhaps we should proceed on the assumption, as Guilford does for intelligence, that there are many theoretically independent classes of phenomena with different developmental functions, monitoring factors, and physiological correlates. Our task is to discern the most useful way to crack the domain so that the pieces that fall away are most faithful to the lines of coherence nature drew in initially, and then trace their structures ontogenetically.

If emotions have an internal state change as their essential attribute, it may be logically impossible to be in other than an emotional state, since each living creature is continually changing its state. Plutchik's definition of emotion has this inclusive quality. Perhaps this is one reason why, in practice, psychologists have been concerned with a very limited class of incentive-state change combinations. By popular consensus, these incentives have involved the relations between cognitive structure and experience in the form of recognizing either novelty, deviation from a standard, the meeting of a standard, anticipation of the future, or reflection on the past. These cognitive structures in conjunction with state changes—we avoid implying that the cognition occurs before or after the state change—make up the coherence we wish to understand. The indifference to the temporal order of cognition and state change may strike some as cowardly and others as simply wrong, but it has precedent in other natural phenomena. The introduction of an accelerating electrical charge into a field produces an effect similar to the one produced by creating a field around an accelerating charge; radiation develops in both cases. A sudden ridge of cold air moving into a humid atmosphere produces snow, as does the sudden introduction of moist air into a frigid high-pressure system. A fertilized zygote can result from introducing an ovum into a sea of sperm or introducing the sperm into a location where the ovum is present. Either sequence is effective, and we do not ask about the temporal order. Our ancient commitment to a temporally linear causality may have prevented us from recognizing that in some cases (obviously not all) it is not too important to ask, "Which event occurred first?" and assign that incentive priority. In this sense, Aristotle, Descartes, and James are all guilty of seeking to assign primacy on the basis of temporal priority, rather than looking for coherences. Changes that result from discharge in heart, muscle, or thalamus are necessary but insufficient for the state with which we are concerned. Each is a participant in an event that must involve cognition, and it may be that the temporal order of contribution is less relevant— though we hesitate to say irrelevant—than the elements that are combined.

What practical suggestions for the empiricist emerge from this essay? We should begin to invent categories that summarize replicable functional relations or generate constructs that are necessary to render a set of empirically based propositions logically coherent. Rather than begin with the assumption that affects like joy or sadness exist and we must find their best definition, it may be more useful to search first for coherences among incentives, changes in state, and cognitive and behavioral reactions. We should also expect that some of those coherences will change over time. It is likely that loss of a parent in adolescence is associated with a reliable feeling state and a certain class of cognitions. It is just as certain that loss of a parent at one year of age does not produce the same state.

Let us consider two illustrations of the potential utility of this suggestion. After a half-dozen separate investigations of children living in the United States as well as other cultural settings, it appears that the occurrence of serious inhibition of play and crying in response to the incentive of a primary caretaker's leaving a child alone in an unfamiliar setting or with an unfamiliar person follows an inverted, U-shaped growth function over the period 7 through 36 months of age (Kagan 1976). Here is one of the replicable functional relations we have been urging. Before suggesting a hypothetical state that might be applied to the child during this era, let us examine how some investigators have used this phenomenon.

Some had postulated an emotional state called "attachment" and subsequently tried to find some reactions that would define that construct. An early decision, now rejected, was to treat the protest following caretaker departure as indicative of the state of attachment. We can now see the problems with that assertion. Although protest begins to vanish after two years of age, no psychologist believes that the intensity of the attachment state is decreasing.

An older alternative was to declare that the emotional state "anxiety to anticipated loss of the mother" was indexed by the protest at separation. Again, no one wished to claim that the three-year-old, who does not typically protest parental departure, does not experience a change in state following anticipation of the loss of a parent.

But suppose John Bowlby (1969) had first charted the developmental function for inhibition of play and fretting to maternal departure to see what course it took before inventing a name. He would have discovered the inverted, U-shaped growth function and, we suspect, would have concluded something like, "During the period 7 through 30 months of age, the infant is made uncertain/anxious/fearful by the incentive event of parental departure in an unfamiliar context." Such a statement acknowledges the emotional quality of the young child's reaction but specifies both the incentive and the era when it is potent.

Consider a second, perhaps less persuasive, example. Nightmares are more frequent between the ages of four and eight years than during the preceding or succeeding four-year period. It is less clear, in this case, what class of incentive is producing the sleep disturbances, and much more inference is required than in the case of separation protest. (We choose this example because we do not want the reader to be misled into thinking that we oppose theory; quite the contrary.)

One might infer that a major incentive for the nightmares was violation of standards on hostility to parents, obedience, sex play, masturbation, honesty, and stealing, since this is the time when these standards are being socialized in a serious way by the American family. As in the case of separation protest, even though the nightmares decrease after age nine, one would not conclude that the child does not experience a changed feeling state following anticipation of or committing a violation of those same standards. Nor would it be correct to assert that there is no change in state following violation of a standard on hostility prior to age four, even though nightmares are less common during the first four years of life. As in the case of separation protest, a particular dependent variable (fretting, inhibition of play, or nightmares) bears a very specific developmental relation to a class of incentives. This situation, which is common, suggests at least three possible conclusions.

The internal state produced by the incentive is the same throughout development, even though the manifest behavioral reactions differ. This conclusion places a heavy burden on reasonableness, since it is hard to believe that a ten-year-old who wishes her parents a happy holiday on Barbados as they enter a taxicab is as distressed at their departure as she was at 15 months when her mother walked out of the front door for a minute to allow a visitor to enter. Second, it is counterintuitive to assume that a 15-year-old who swears at his father following paternal insistence that the son stay home that evening is as distressed over his aggression as he was when he swore at his father at age five. The fact that the dependent variable changes probably tells us something important about the emotional state of the child.

A second possibility is that both the incentive and state have been altered because the child's interpretation of the event changed with development. By *interpretation* we mean the cognitive classification of the event. This is a tempting possibility, for psychologists acknowledge that, from a psychological point of view, the incentive is not the objective stimulus but the person's interpretation. However, this posture also elicits some disquiet, since it requires us to assume that the 15-year-old who swore at his father did not regard that act as violating a standard. This is questionable, for if we should ask, "Is it proper to swear at your father?" he would probably reply negatively. Thus it is not clear we can resolve our problem easily by simply declaring that the incentive event had changed.

A third possibility, and one we feel friendly toward, is that incentive events are accompanied by an evaluation of the individual's ability to understand, assimilate, or instrumentally deal with the incentive situation and the resulting state change. When there is uncertainty over assimilation or action, a change in emotional state is most likely. Thus the one-year-old cries at parental departure because of both uncertainty over parental return as well as the absence of coping behaviors that might be issued to deal with the uncertainty that follows departure. Similarly, the 5-year-old is probably more uncertain than the 15-year-old about the possible sequellae of hostile action or thoughts to parents. Hence the change in emotional state may be less intense in the older child.

These suggestions imply that study of the development of emotion must take into account both the altered interpretation of incentive events and changes in the ability to cope with the total event (i.e., control the affect and respond to new information). These two may not develop in parallel fashion. We acknowledge that there are some changes in emotional state whose developmental course will not be handled easily by this last assumption. For example, children show an increased ability to experience a state change following an encounter with another person who is in distress. This phenomenon is not easily explained by referring to uncertainty over coping or understanding the event. Thus the developmental course of this state is being monitored by other factors. Similarly, the likelihood of a state change following an insult is not easily understood by the above assumption. We take this to mean that state changes are influenced by a variety of qualitatively different factors, and the developmental course for each class will follow different principles.

The importance of the child's ability to deal with the change in emotional state brings us to a final characteristic of affects that is often overlooked; namely, the ease with which an affect state can be altered by new information. Some affects are easily destroyed or altered by the introduction of a single fact. A person's anger at someone who failed to return a greeting can dissolve completely or be transformed to sympathy upon learning that the other was ill or blind. But affect states seem to differ in the ease with which they can be changed by new information. Guilt over causing the depression, distress, or death of another usually resists dissolution because the fact of the victim's state cannot be changed easily. The fact that an affect state—even an intensely felt one—can be dissipated by information is perhaps the best support for the statement that affects are dependent upon cognitive beliefs and processes.

It seems easier to alter the affects of young children than of adults because the former's beliefs, not his physiology, are more labile. As beliefs become resistant to change, acute, punctate affect states turn into chronic moods. The adjectives "angry," "fearful," and "joyful" typically refer to acute states; "mean," "anxious," and "happy" are more frequently used to describe the more permanent qualities of a person. As beliefs about self and the world become fixed in adulthood, the occurrence of acute changes in affect state are likely to decrease, while moods become more apparent. There are few dour children or terrified adults.

There is a similarity in the theoretical status of the concepts of affect and intelligence. In the same spirit in which some psychologists reject the usefulness of a concept of intelligence because it is not representative of any unitary process, we suggest that the concept of emotion may be without much utility. For the domain of intelligence, Guilford has suggested that we must take into account the original materials, the cognitive processes, and the subsequent products, and he posits 120 different categories of cognitive ability. We do not know if there are 120 different emotional states but agree in principle with Guilford that there are different classes of incentive events, state changes, evaluation of those state changes, and coping reactions.

In his 1940 William James lectures, "An Inquiry into Meaning and Truth," Bertrand Russell wrote, "All the paradoxes arise from the attribution of significance to sentences that are in fact nonsensical." We have hinted that statements of the kind, "Emotions are ———" fit Russell's definition of nonsense—one reason why many of us have the feeling we are caught in a sticky web. The term "emotion," like the concept weather, must be analyzed if it is to have any meaning.

Summary

Since this essay may read more like a collection of dissatisfactions than a constructive critique, it may be helpful to summarize the points we have tried to make in the preceding pages.

1. Unlike physicists, chemists, and biologists, who frequently begin their theoretical work with a set of known functional relations they wish to explain, psychologists often begin with categories. They assume that certain words stand for something real and try to find their essence. Most of the affect words we currently use in our theories or everyday speech are labels for complex conscious experiences and, in a sense, are analogous to such phrases as "tastes like lobster" or "smells like roses." Sensory physiologists would not have made much progress if they tried to find where on the tongue the taste of lobster lay. For this reason, we suggest it is probably not profitable to try to locate the essence of affects like fear or surprise in the face, heart, or hypothalamus, even though the reactivity of these material entities may participate in the state of interest.

2. Many of the events we call affective are dynamic, continuously changing coherences characterized by a change in feeling state, a class of incentives, and cognitive evaluations and intentions as major dimensions. We tend to classify an event as emotional, cognitive, or motivational depending upon which of those dimensions we wish to emphasize.

3. A change in internal feelings is the one dimension all psychologists agree is central to affective phenomena. But since we are always undergoing changes in feeling state, that criterion is of minimal value. Psychologists have had a tacit understanding that the interest lay in a smaller set of changes in feeling state that were short-lived, provoked by an incentive,

linked to a cognitive evaluation, and not the result of physiological deprivation. We have suggested that it might be useful to carve out trios of coherences that consisted of a class of incentive (either external or mental), a quality of feeling, and cognitive structures, and to treat these as the primary
construct. For example, violation of a standard on aggression by a child who
was able to evaluate his ability to instigate or inhibit the prohibition would
be associated with a particular quality of feeling.

4. Since changes in feeling state are primary, it was suggested that we
analyze the sensory qualities of these feelings, as we do any stimulus event,
and take into account intensity, salience, locus, rise time, and duration.

5. Over the last century we have awarded the physiological events associated with affect states primacy over the psychological ones, owing partly
to the rise of the biological sciences. We suggested that for some psychological phenomena it may not be important to decide whether the physiological or the psychological event occurs first. Temporal priority does not always
imply explanatory primacy.

6. We suggested that some incentives were likely to be universal and a
few might participate in an invariant developmental sequence. Some of the
incentives included: reaction to discrepancy, inconsistency between standards or between standards and behavior, loss of a target object, anticipation
of an event for which there was no coping response, blocking of a goal or a
threat to one's values, the meeting of a standard following effort, genital
stimulation, the experience of a person requiring nurture, the experience of
a person violating a fundamental standard, and release from a distress state.

This discussion has been critical because it is easier to fault existing conceptualizations than to generate a better paradigm. We hope this essay will
provide a stage for discussion that will lead to more constructive ideas, for
we agree with Sroufe (1977) that the child's growth will not be fully understood until we gain greater insight into those aspects of development we call
emotional.

NOTES ANd REFERENCES

ONE / Resilience and Continuity in Psychological Development

Ader, R. 1970. The effects of early life experiences on developmental processes and susceptibility to disease in animals. In *Minnesota Symposium on Child Psychology*, edited by J. W. Hill, 4:3–35. Minneapolis: University of Minnesota Press.

Chess, S. 1967. The role of temperament in the child's development. *Acta Paedopsychiatriac.* 34:91–103.

Dennis, W. 1938. Infant development under conditions of restricted practice and of minimum social stimulation: A preliminary report. *Journal of Genetic Psychology* 53:149–58.

Dennis, W. 1973. *Children of the Creche.* New York: Appleton-Century-Crofts.

Elias, M. F. 1974. Rehabilitation erases behavioral effects of nutritional and rearing restriction in infant monkeys. Paper presented at Federation of American Societies for Experimental Biology, Atlantic City, N.J.

Fiske, J. 1883. *The Meaning of Infancy.* Boston: Houghton Mifflin.

Hess, E. H. 1972. Imprinting in a natural laboratory. *Scientific American* 227:24–31.

Holton, G. 1973. *Thematic Origins of Scientific Thought.* Cambridge, Mass.: Harvard University Press.

Kagan, J., and Moss, H. A. 1962. *Birth to Maturity.* New York: Wiley.

Kagan, J., Kearsley, R. B., and Zelazo, P. R. 1978. *Infancy: Its Place in Human Development.* Cambridge, Mass.: Harvard University Press.

Koluchova, J. 1972. Severe deprivation in twins. *Journal of Child Psychology and Psychiatry* 13:107–11.

Mason, W. A., Davenport, R. K., and Menzel, E. W. 1968. Early experience in the social development of rhesus monkeys and chimpanzees. In *Early Experience in Behavior*, edited by G. Newton and S. Levine, pp. 440–80. Springfield, Ill.: C C Thomas.

Mason, W. A., and Kenney, M. D. 1974. Redirection of filial attachments in rhesus monkeys: Dogs as mother surrogates. *Science* 183:1209–11.

Rathbun, C., DiVirgilio, L., and Waldfogel, S. 1958. The restitutive process in children following radical separation from family and culture. *American Journal of Orthopsychiatry* 28:408–15.

Rheingold, H. C., and Bayley, N. 1959. The later effects of an experimental modification of mothering. *Child Development* 30:363–72.

Rutter, M. 1970. Psychological development—predictions from infancy. *Journal of Child Psychology and Psychiatry* 11:49–62.

Suomi, S. J., and Harlow, H. F. 1972. Social rehabilitation of isolate-reared monkeys. *Developmental Psychology* 6:487–96.

Tizard, B., and Rees, J. 1974. A comparison of the effects of adoption, restoration to the natural mother, and continued institutionalization on the cognitive development of 4-year-old children. *Child Development* 45:92–99.

Winick, M., Meyer, K. K., and Harris, R. C. 1975. Malnutrition and environmental enrichment by early adoption. *Science*, 190:1173–75.

TWO / On the Need for Relativism

Aronfreed, J. 1964. The origin of self criticism. *Psychological Review* 71:193–218

Aronfreed, J. 1965. Internalized behavioral suppression and the timing of social punishment. *Journal of Personality and Social Psychology* 1:3–16.

Baldwin, A. L., Kalhorn, J., and Breese, F. H. 1945. Patterns of parent behavior. *Psychological Monographs* 58.

Bateson, P. P. G. 1964a. Changes in chicks' responses to novel moving objects over the sensitive period for imprinting. *Animal Behavior* 12:479–89.

Bateson, P. P. G. 1964b. Relation between conspicuousness of stimuli and their effectiveness in the imprinting situation. *Journal of Comparative and Physiological Psychology* 58:407–11.

Becker, W. C. 1964. Consequences of different kinds of parental discipline. In *Review of Child Development Research,* edited by M. L. Hoffman and L. W. Hoffman, vol. 1. New York: Russell Sage Foundation.

Brackbill, Y. 1958. Extinction of the smiling response in infants as a function of reinforcement schedule. *Child Development* 29:115–24.

Charlesworth, W. R. 1965. Persistence of orienting and attending behavior in young infants as a function of stimulus uncertainty. Paper read at Society for Research in Child Development, Minneapolis.

Held, R. 1965. Plasticity in sensory motor systems. *Scientific American* 213:84–94.

Helson, H. 1964. *Adaptation Level Theory: An Experimental and Systematic Approach to Behavior.* New York: Harper & Row.

Hernández-Peón, R., Scherrer, H., and Jouvet, M. 1965. Modification of electrical activity in cochlear nucleus during attention in unanesthetized cats. *Science* 123:331–32.

Hess, E. H. 1959. Two conditions limiting critical age for imprinting. *Journal of Comparative and Physiological Psychology* 52:515–18.

Jakobson, R., and Halle, M. 1956. *Fundamentals of Language.* The Hague: Mouton.

Kagan, J., Henker, B. A., Hen-Tov, A., Levine, J., and Lewis, M. 1966. Infants' differential reactions to familiar and distorted faces. *Child Development* 37:519–32.

Kagan, J., and Moss, H. A. 1962. *Birth to Maturity.* New York: Wiley.

Klopper, P. H. 1965. Imprinting: A reassessment. *Science* 147:302–3.

Leuba, C. 1955. Toward some integration of learning theories: The concept of optimal stimulation. *Psychological Reports* 1:27–33.

Melzack, R., and Wall, P. D. 1965. Pain mechanisms: A new theory. *Science* 150:971–79.

Miller, N. E. 1951. Learnable drives and rewards. In *Handbook of Experimental Psychology,* edited by S. S. Stevens. New York: Wiley.

Olds, J. 1958. Self stimulation of the brain. *Science* 127:315–24.

Olds, J. 1962. Hypothalamic substrates of reward. *Physiological Review* 42:554–604.

Rheingold, H., Gewirtz, J. L., and Ross, H. 1959. Social conditioning of vocalizations in the infant. *Journal of Comparative and Physiological Psychology* 52:68–73.

Schachter, S., and Singer, J. E. 1962. Cognitive, social and physiological determinants of emotional states. *Psychological Review* 69:379–99.

Schaefer, E. S. 1959. A circumplex model for maternal behavior. *Journal of Abnormal and Social Psychology* 59:226–35.

Schaefer, E. S., and Bayley, N. 1963. Maternal behavior, child behavior and their intercorrelations from infancy through adolescence. *Monographs of the Society for Research in Child Development* 28.

Sears, R. R., Maccoby, E. E., and Levin, H. 1957. *Patterns of Child Rearing*. Row Peterson.

Thompson, R. F., and Shaw, J. A. 1965. Behavioral correlates of evoked activity recorded from association areas of the cerebral cortex. *Journal of Comparative and Physiological Psychology* 60:329–39.

Thompson, W. R., and Dubanoski, R. A. 1964. Imprinting and the law of effort. *Animal Behavior* 12:213–18.

Tomkins, S. S. 1962. *Affect Imagery Consciousness*. Vol. 1, *The Positive Affects*. New York: Springer.

THREE / The Growth of the Infant's Mind

Bornstein, M. H. 1975. Qualities of color vision in infancy. *Journal of Experimental Child Psychology* 19:401–19.

Fantz. R. L. 1965. Visual perception from birth as shown by pattern selectivity. *Annals of the New York Academy of Sciences* 118:793–814.

Fantz, R. L., and Miranda, S. B. 1975. Newborn infant attention to form of contour. *Child Development* 46:224–28.

Haith, M. M. 1966. The response of a human newborn to visual movement. *Journal of Experimental Child Psychology* 3:235–43.

Hopkins, J. R. 1974. Curvature as a dimension in infant visual perception. Ph.D. dissertation, Harvard University.

Ruff, H. A., and Birch, H. G. 1974. Infant visual fixation: The effect of concentricity, curvilinearity, and number of directions. *Journal of Experimental Child Psychology* 17:460–73.

Scarr, S., and Salapatek, P. 1970. Patterns of fear development during infancy. *Merrill Palmer Quarterly* 16:53–90.

FOUR / The Effects of Infant Day Care on Psychological Development

Barrett, H. S., and Koch, H. C. 1930. The effect of nursery school training upon the mental test performance of a group of orphanage children. *Pedagogical Seminary and Journal of Genetic Psychology* 37:102–22.

Beckwith, L. 1971. Relationships between attributes of mothers and their infants' IQ scores. *Child Development* 42:1083–97.

Blehar, M. C. 1974. Anxious attachment and defensive reactions associated with day care. *Child Development* 45:683–92.

Burlingham, D., and Freud, A. 1944. *Infants without Families*. London: George Allen & Unwin.

Caldwell, B. M. 1964. The effects of infant care. In *Review of Child Development Research*, edited by M. L. Hoffman and L. W. Hoffman, vol. 1. New York: Russell Sage Foundation.

Caldwell, B. M., Wright, C. M., Honig, A. S., and Tannenbaum, J. T. Infant day care and attachment. *American Journal of Orthopsychiatry* 40:397–412.

Collard, R. R. 1971. Exploratory and play behaviors of infants reared in an institution and in low and middle class homes. *Child Development* 42:1003–15.

Decroly, O., and Degard, J. 1910. La Mesure de l'intelligence chez des enfants normaux. *Archives de Psychologie* 9:81–108.

Doyle, A. B. 1975a. Infant development and day care. *Developmental Psychology* 11:655–56.

Doyle, A. B. 1975b. The effect of group and individual day care on infant development. Presented at the meetings of the Canadian Psychological Association, Quebec, June.

Gavrin, J. B., and Sacks, L. S. 1963. Growth potential of preschool-aged children in institutional care. *American Journal of Orthopsychiatry* 33:399–408.

Gesell, A. 1939. *Biographies of Child Development.* New York: Paul Hoeber.

Goddard, H. H. 1975. Bridging the gap between our knowledge of child well being and our care of the young. In *The Child: His Nature and His Needs,* edited by M. V. O'Shea. New York: Arno.

Kagan, J. 1971. *Change and Continuity in Infancy.* New York: Wiley.

Kagan, J., and Moss, H. A. 1962. *Birth to Maturity.* New York: Wiley.

Klein, R. E. 1974–75. Progress report. Guatemala City: Institute of Nutrition for Central America and Panama. Division of Human Development, Contract PH 43—65—640.

Kohen-Raz, R. 1968. Mental and motor development of kibbutz, institutionalized, and home-reared children in Israel. *Child Development* 39:489–504.

Lally, J. R. 1974. The family development research program: Progress report. Syracuse, N.Y.: Syracuse University, College for Human Development.

Leiderman, P. H., and Leiderman, G. F. 1974. Affective and cognitive consequences of polymatic infant care in the East African highlands. In *Minnesota Symposium on Child Psychology,* edited by A. Pick, vol. 8. Minneapolis: University of Minnesota Press.

Lippman, M. Z., and Grote, G. H. 1974. Social-emotional effects of day care. Bellingham: Western Washington State College, Project Report.

Moss, H. A., and Robson, K. S. 1967. Maternal influences on early social-visual behavior. Presented at the annual meeting of the American Orthopsychiatric Association, New York City.

Orlansky, H. 1949. Infant care and personality. *Psychological Bulletin* 46:1–48.

Ramey, T. C., Campbell, F. A., and Nicholson, J. E. 1973. The predictive power of the Bayley scales of infant development and the Stanford-Binet intelligence test in a relatively constant environment. *Child Development* 44:790–95.

Raph, J. B., Thomas, A., Chess, S., and Korn, S. J. 1968. The influence of nursery school on social interactions. *American Journal of Orthopsychiatry* 39:144–52.

Robinson, H. B., and Robinson, N. M. 1971. Longitudinal development in very young children in a comprehensive day care program: The first two years. *Child Development* 42:1673–83.

Schwartz, J. C., Strickland, R. G., and Korlick, G. 1974. Infant day care: Behavior effects at preschool age. *Developmental Psychology* 10:502–6.

Shinn, M. W. 1975. *The Biography of a Baby.* New York: Arno.

Stroud, J. B. 1928. A study of the relation of intelligence test scores of public school children to the economic status of their parents. *Pedagogical Seminary and Journal of Genetic Psychology* 35:105–11.

Tizard, B., Cooperman, O., Joseph, A., and Tizard, J. 1972. Environmental effects on language development: A study of young children in long-stay residential nurseries. *Child Development* 42:337–58.

Tulkin, S. 1970. Social class differences, maternal practices, and infant psychological development. Ph.D. dissertation, Harvard University.

Webster, N. 1965. On the education of youth in America. In *Essays on Education in the Early Republic,* edited by F. Rudolph. Cambridge, Mass.: Harvard University Press.

Werner, E. E. 1969. Sex differences and correlations between children's IQ's and measures of parental ability and environmental ratings. *Developmental Psychology* 1:280–85.

Willerman, L., Broman, S. H., and Fiedler, N. 1970. Infant development, preschool IQ, and social class. *Child Development* 41:69–77.

White, B. L., and Watts, J. C. 1973. *Experience and Environment*, vol. 1. Englewood Cliffs, N.J.: Prentice-Hall.

Winett, R. A., Fuchs, W. L., Muffatt, S., and Nerviano, V. J. 1975. A cross-sectional study of children and their families in different child care environments. Mimeographed. Lexington: University of Kentucky.

Yarrow, L. J. 1964. Separation from parents during early childhood. In *Review of Child Development Research*, edited by M. L. Hoffman and L. W. Hoffman, vol. 1. New York: Russell Sage Foundation.

Yarrow, L. J., Rubenstein, J. L., and Pedersen, F. A. 1975. *Infant and Environment: Early Cognitive and Motivational Development*. Washington, D.C.: Hemisphere.

FIVE / A Conception of Early Adolescence

Jacobson, A. G. 1966. Inductive processes in embryonic development. *Science* 152:25–34.

SIX / Psychology of Sex Differences

Auchincloss, S. S. 1971. Dream content and the menstrual cycle. Honors thesis, Harvard University.

Bardwick, J. M. 1970. Psychological conflict and the reproductive system. In Bardwick, J. M., Douvan, E., Horner, M. S., and Guttmann, D., *Feminine Personality and Conflict*. Belmont, Calif.: Brooks-Cole.

Bardwick, J. M. 1971. *Psychology of Women*. New York: Harper & Row.

Baumrind, D. 1971. Current patterns of parental authority. *Developmental Psychology Monographs* 4:1–103.

Berry, J. W. 1966. Temne and Eskimo perceptual skills. *International Journal of Psychology* 1:207–29.

Brenneis, B. 1970. Male and female ego modalities in manifest dream content. *Journal of Abnormal Psychology* 76:432–42.

Brock, A. J. 1929. *Greek Medicine: Being Abstracts Illustrative of Medical Writers from Hippocrates to Galen*. London and Toronto: Dent.

Cameron, J., Livson, N., and Bayley, M. 1967. Infant vocalizations and their relationship to mature intelligence. *Science* 157:331–33.

Crook, J. H. 1970. The sociology of primates. In *Social Behavior in Birds and Mammals*, edited by J. H. Crook. New York: Academic Press.

DeVore, I., and Hall, K. R. L. 1965. Baboon ecology. In *Primate Behavior*, edited by I. DeVore. New York: Holt, Rinehart, & Winston.

Díaz-Guerrero, R. 1967. Cross cultural studies of personality: Cognitive and social class factors related to child development in Mexico and the U.S.A. Presented at the 10th Interamerican Congress of Psychology. Mexico City: F. Trillas.

Ember, C. R. 1970. Effects of feminine task assignment on the social behavior of boys. Ph.D. dissertation, Harvard University.

Gazzaniga, M. S. 1970. *The Bisected Brain*. New York: Appleton-Century-Crofts.

Harvard Crimson. 1969. Must Wellesley go co-ed to survive? December 16.

Hess, R. D., Shipman, V. C., Brophy, J. E., and Bear, R. M. 1968, 1969. The cognitive environments of urban preschool children. Report to the Graduate School of Education, University of Chicago.

Hesse, H. 1930. *Narcissus and Goldmund.* New York: Farrar, Straus, & Giroux.

Hindley, C. B. 1965. Stability and change in abilities up to five years—group trends. *Journal of Child Psychology and Psychiatry* 6:85–99.

Horner, M. 1968. Sex differences in achievement motivation and performance in competitive and non-competitive situations. Ph.D. dissertation, University of Michigan.

Jensen, G. D., Bobbitt, R. A., and Gordon, B. N. 1967. The development of maternal independence in mother-infant pigtailed monkeys, *macaca nemestrina.* In *Social Communication among Primates,* edited by S. A. Altmann. Chicago: University of Chicago Press.

Kagan, J. 1964. The child's sex role classification of school objects. *Child Development* 35:1051–56.

Kagan, J. 1971. *Change and Continuity in Infancy.* New York: Wiley.

Kagan, J., Hosken, B., and Watson, S. 1961. The child's symbolic conceptualization of the parents. *Child Development* 32:265–36j.

Kagan, J., and Moss, H. A. 1962. *Birth to Maturity.* New York: Wiley.

Kirk, G. S. 1970. *Myth: Its Meaning and Function in Ancient and Other Cultures.* Berkeley: University of California Press.

Knox, C., and Kimura, D. 1970. Cerebral processing of nonverbal sounds in boys and girls. *Neuropsychologia* 8:227–37.

Lancaster, J. B. 1968. Primate communication systems and the emergence of human language. In *Primates,* edited by P. C. Jay. New York: Holt, Rinehart, & Winston.

Lucretius. *On the Nature of the Universe.* Book 4, *Sensation and Sex.* Translated by R. Latham. Baltimore: Penguin, 1951.

Lyon, M. F. 1962. Sex chromatin and gene action in the mammalian X-Chromosome. *American Journal of Genetics* 14:135–48.

Malleus Maleficarum, translated and with an introduction, bibliography, and notes by Montague Summers. 1951. London: Pushkin Press. In Veith, I. 1965. *Hysteria.* Chicago: University of Chicago Press.

Marler, P. 1956. Studies of fighting in chaffinches (3), Proximity as a cause of aggression. *British Journal of Animal Behavior* 4:23–30.

Minton, C. M., Kagan, J., and Levine, J. A. 1971. Maternal control and obedience in the two year old. *Child Development* 42:1893–94.

Mitchell, G. 1968. Persistent behavior pathology in rhesus monkeys following early social isolation. *Folia Primatologia* (a) 8:132–47.

Mitchell, G. D. 1968. Attachment differences in male and female infant monkeys. *Child Development* 39:611–20.

Moore, T. 1967. Language and intelligence—a longitudinal study of the first eight years. *Human Development* 10:88–106.

Moss, H. A. 1967. Sex, age and state as determinants of mother-infant interaction. *Merrill-Palmer Quarterly* 13:19–36.

Moss, H. A., and Robson, K. S. 1970. The relation between the amount of time infants spend at various states and the development of visual behavior. *Child Development* 41:509–17.

Moss, H. A., Robson, K. S., and Pedersen, F. 1969. Determinants of maternal stimulation to infant and consequences of treatment for later reactions to strangers. *Developmental Psychology* 1:239–46.

Osgood, C. E. 1960. The corss cultural generality of visual-verbal synesthetic tendencies. *Behavioral Sciences* 5:146–69.

Paz, O. 1961. *The Labyrinth of Solitude.* New York: Grove Press. Originally published by Fondo de Cultura Economica, Mexico City, 1959, under the title *El Laberinto de la Soledad.*

Poirier, F. E. 1970. The Nilgiri langur (*Presbytis johnii*) of South India. In *Primate Behavior*, edited by L. A. Rosenblum, vol. I. New York: Academic Press.

Robson, K. S., Pedersen, F. A., and Moss, H. A. 1969. Developmental observations of diadic gazing in relation to the fear of strangers and social approach behavior. *Child Behavior* 40:619–28.

Rothbart, M. K. 1971. Birth order and mother child interaction in an achievement situation. *Journal of Personality and Social Psychology* 17:113–20.

Rothbart, M. K., and Maccoby, E. E. 1966. Parents' differential reactions to sons and daughters. *Journal of Personality and Social Psychology* 17:113–20.

Shapiro, L. 1969. A study of peer group interaction in 8 and 28 month old children. Ph.D. dissertation, Harvard University.

Silverman, S. 1970. *Psychological Cues in Forecasting Physical Illness*. New York: Appleton-Century-Crofts.

Simon, W., and Gagnon, J. H. 1969. On psychosexual development. In *Handbook of Socialization Theory and Research*, edited by D. A. Goslin. Chicago: Rand Mc-Nally.

Super, C., Kagan, J., Morrison, F., Haith, M., and Weiffenbach, J. 1972. Discrepancy and attention in the five month old infant. *Genetic Psychology Monographs* 85:305–31.

Tangri, S. 1969. Role innovation in occupational choice. Ph.D. dissertation, University of Michigan.

Werner, W. E. 1969. Sex differences in correlations between children's IQs and measures of parental ability and environmental ratings. *Developmental Psychology* 1:280–85.

Whiting, B. B., and Whiting, J. W. M. 1975. *Children of Six Cultures*. Cambridge, Mass.: Harvard University Press.

SEVEN / Motives in Development

Geothals, G. W., and Klos, D. 1970. *Experiencing Youth*. Boston: Little, Brown.

Iwai, H., and Reynolds, D. K. 1970. Morita psychotherapy. *American Journal of Psychiatry* 126:1031–36.

Prince, R. 1968. The therapeutic process in cross-cultural perspective. *American Journal of Psychiatry* 124:1171–83.

Valins, S., and Ray, A. A. 1967. Effects of cognitive desensitization on avoidance behavior. *Journal of Personality and Social Psychology* 7:345–50.

NINE / On Cultural Deprivation

Balow, I. H. 1963. Sex differences in first grade reading. *Elementary English* 40:303–20.

Broman, S. H., Nichols, P. L., and Kennedy, W. A. 1975. *Preschool IQ: Prenatal and Early Developmental Correlates*. Hillsdale, N.J.: L. Erlbaum.

Dykstra, R., and Tinney, S. 1969. Sex differences in reading readiness: First grade achievement and second grade achievement. *Reading and Realism: Proceedings of the International Reading Association* 13:623–28.

Flavell, J. H., Friedrichs, E. J., and Hoyt, J. D. 1970. Developmental changes in memorization processes. *Cognitive Psychology* 1:324–40.

Gleitman, L. R., and Rozin, P. 1973. Teaching reading by use of a syllabary. *Reading Research Quarterly* 8:447–501.

Guilford, J. P. 1967. *The Nature of Human Intelligence*, New York: McGraw-Hill.

Holtzman, W. H., Diaz-Guerrero, R., and Swartz, J. D. 1975. *Personality Development in Two Cultures*. Austin: University of Texas Press.

Jordan, W. D. 1969. *White over Black*. New York: Penguin.

Kagan, J., Klein, R. E., Finley, G., Rogoff, B., and Nolan, E. 1976. Cognitive development: A cross-cultural study. Mimeographed. Harvard University.

Kreutzer, M. A., Leonard, S. C., and Flavell, J. H. 1975. An interview study of children's knowledge about memory. *Monographs of the Society for Research in Child Development* 40, serial no. 159.

Mattis, S., French, J. H., and Rapin, I. 1975. Dyslexia in children and young adults: Three independent neuropsychological syndromes. *Journal of Developmental Medicine and Child Neurology* 17:150–63.

McCall, R. B. 1978. Development of intellectual functioning in infancy and the prediction of later IQ. In *Handbook of Infancy,* ed. J. Osofsky. New York: John Wiley.

Preston, R. 1962. Reading achievement of German and American children. *School and Society* 90:350–54.

Rogoff, B. R. 1976. A study of cognition in Indian villages. Manuscript.

Rogoff, B. Newcombe, N., and Kagan, J. 1974. Planfulness and recognition memory. *Child Development* 45:972–77.

Satz, P., Freil, J., and Rudegair, F. 1974. Same predictive antecedents of specific reading disability. Mimeographed. University of Florida.

Schachter, F. F., Kirshner, K., Klips, B., Friedricks, M., and Sanders, K. 1974. Everyday preschool interpersonal speech usage: Methodological, developmental and sociolinguistic studies. *Monograph of the Society Research in Child Development* 39, serial no. 156.

Sommer, R. K., and Taylor, M. L. 1972. Cerebral speech dominance in language disordered and normal children. *Cortex* 8:224–32.

Stevenson, H. W., Parker, T., Wilkinson, A., Hegion, A., and Fish, E. 1976. Longitudinal study of individual differences in cognitive developmental and scholastic achievement. *Monograph of the Society Research in Child Development* 39, serial no. 156.

Wender, P. H. 1971. *Minimal Brain Dysfunction in Children.* New York: Wiley.

TEN / The Child in the Family

1. G. Ross, Conceptual functioning in the infant, (unpublished).
2. J. Kagan, B. Hosken, and S. Watson, The child's symbolic conceptualization of the parents, *Child Development* 32 (1961):625–36.
3. J. Kagan, R. B. Kearsley, P. R. Zelazo, and C. Minton, The course of early development (unpublished, 1976).
4. N. A. Fox, Developmental and birth-order determinants of separation protest: A cross-cultural study of infants on the Israeli kibbutz (Ph.D. dissertation, Harvard Graduate School of Education, November 1975).
5. T. G. R. Bower, The evolution of sensory systems," in *Perception: Essays in Honor of James J. Gibson,* ed. R. B. MacLeod and H. L. Pick (Ithaca, 1974), pp. 141–52.
6. J. Kagan, R. B. Kearsley, and P. R. Zelazo, The emergence of initial apprehension to unfamiliar peers, in *Friendship and Peer Relations,* ed. M. A. Lewis and L. A. Rosenblum (New York, 1975), pp. 187–206.
7. J. L. Briggs, *Never in Anger* (Cambridge, Mass., 1970).
8. A. L. Baldwin, J. M. Kalhorn, and F. H. Breese, Patterns of parent behavior, *Psychological Monographs* 58 (1945); W. C. Becker and R. S. Krug, The parent attitude research instrument: A research review, *Child Development* 36 (1965):329–69; J. Kagan and H. A. Moss, *Birth to Maturity* (New York, 1962); E. S. Schaefer, A circumplex model for maternal behavior, *Journal of Abnormal and Social Psychology* 59 (1959); 226–35; E. S. Schaefer and N. Bayley, Consis-

tency of maternal behavior from infancy to preadolescence, *Journal of Abnormal and Social Psychology* 61 (1960):1–6; R. R. Sears, E. E. Maccoby, and H. Levin, *Patterns of Child Rearing* (Evanston, 1957).

9. J. H. Plumb, The new world of children in eighteenth-century England, *Past and Present* 67 (1975):64–95.

10. Ibid.

11. A. Ryerson, Medical advice on child rearing 1550–1900 (Ph.D. dissertation, Harvard Graduate School of Education, 1959).

12. John Locke, *Some Thoughts Concerning Education* (Cambridge, 1913).

13. Jean-Jacques Rousseau, *Emile*, trans. B. Foxley (New York, 1911).

14. Plumb, New world of children.

15. A. Kleinman, The cultural construction of clinical reality: Comparisons of practitioner-patient interaction in Taiwan (unpublished, 1975).

16. M. Kieffer and A. K. Romney, The semantic structure of Tzutujil Maya personal attribute concepts (unpublished, 1973).

17. Kagan and Moss, *Birth to Maturity*.

18. D. Lapidus, "A Longitudinal Study of Development" (Ph.D. dissertation, Harvard University, 1976).

19. Kagan, Kearsley, Zelazo, and Minton, Early development.

20. A. L. Baldwin, J. M. Kalhorn, and F. H. Breese, Patterns of parent behavior, *Psychological Monographs* 58 (1945); The appraisal of parent behavior," *Psychological Monographs* 63 (1949).

21. C. Minton, J. Kagan, and J. A. Levine, Maternal control and obedience in the two-year-old, *Child Development* 42 (1971):1873–74.

22. J. Trotta, Open versus traditional education: Some effects on elementary school children, *Journal of the New York School Board Association*, April 1974, pp. 24–30.

23. S. H. Broman, P. L. Nichols, and W. A. Kennedy, *Preschool IQ: Prenatal and Early Developmental Correlates* (New York, 1975).

24. K. Marjoribanks, H. J. Walberg, and M. Borgen, Mental abilities: Sibling constellation and social class correlates, *British Journal of Social and Clinical Psychology* 14 (1975):109–16.

25. R. E. Klein, *Division of Human Development, INCAP Progress 1974–75*, Guatemala City, Guatemala.

26. The typical reaction to the sense of impotence will vary with the culture. In the antebellum South, it led the slaves to assume a posture of deference and passivity, as it still does among the untouchables in India. But in modern Western societies, where caste and race are being discarded as explanations of differential wealth and power and vicissitudes of economic and psychological forces are awarded explanatory force, the lower-class adult feels more resentful of his status. Moreover, the egalitarian ethic that "all are equal" is taken to mean, "All should feel equal." If one does not feel as potent as one's neighbor, that fact is to be concealed, a state of affairs that leads to a counterphobic reaction to deny disenfranchised status.

27. H. L. Koch, Attitudes of children toward their peers as related to certain characteristics of their siblings, *Psychological Monographs* 70 (1965); The relation of certain formal attributes of siblings to attitudes held toward each other and toward their parents, *Monographs of the Society for Research in Child Development* 25 (1960).

28. S. Schachter, *The Psychology of Affiliation* (Stanford University, 1959).

29. F. L. Apperly, A study of America's Rhodes Scholars, *Journal of Heredity* 30 (1939):494–95; H. E. Jones, The environment and mental development, *Manual*

of Child Psychology, in ed. L. Carmichael, (New York, 1954), pp. 631–96; A Roe, A psychological study of eminent psychologists and anthropologists in a comparison with biological and physical scientists," *Psychological Monographs* 67 (1953).

30. W. D. Altus, Birth order and its sequellae, *Science* 151 (1966):44–49.
31. H. M. Breland, Birth order, family configuration, and verbal achievement, *Child Development* 45 (1974):1011–19.
32. D. C. Glass, J. Neulinger, and O. G. Brim, Birth order, verbal intelligence, and educational aspirations," *Child Development* 45 (1974):807–11.
33. A. P. MacDonald, Birth order in religious affiliation, *Developmental Psychology* 1 (1969):628.
34. A. F. King, Ordinal position of the Episcopal clergy (senior honors thesis, Harvard University, 1967).
35. R. Stein, The effects of ordinal position and identification on philosophy of life, occupational choice, and reflectiveness-impulsivity (senior honors thesis, Harvard University, 1966).
36. R. L. Helmreich and B. E. Collins, Situational determinants of affiliative preference under stress, *Journal of Personality and Social Psychology* 6 (1967):79–85.
37. R. A. Zuckerman, M. Manosevitz, and R. I. Lanyon, Birth order, anxiety, and affiliation during a crisis, *Journal of Personality and Social Psychology* 8 (1968):354–59.
38. L. E. Longstreth, G. V. Longstreth, C. Ramirez, and G. Fernandez, The ubiquity of big brother, *Child Development* 46 (1975):769–72.
39. F. Sulloway, Family constellations, sibling rivalry, and scientific revolutions: A study of the relationship between birth order and scientific temperament (unpublished, 1972); The role of cognitive flexibility in science: Toward a comparative anatomy of scientific revolutions" (unpublished, 1972).
40. Sulloway has also found that individual exceptions to his general findings are themselves usually quite exceptional in terms of having grown up within an atypical family constellation (e.g., one in which there was an early death of a parent or a close sibling). For additional information on these and other findings, together with the criteria and historical documentation upon which they are based, see Sulloway's forthcoming book, *Family Constellations, Sibling Rivalry, and Scientific Revolutions: A Study of the Effect of Birth Order on Revolutionary Temperament in Science.*

TWELVE / On Emotion and Its Development

Aristotle. 1881. *Nicomachean Ethics.* Translated by F. H. Peters. London.
Aquinas, T. 1895. *Summa theologica,* opera editor vives. Paris.
Bacon, F. 1872. *Advancement of Learning.* Edited by Spedding. Boston.
Bowlby, J. 1969. *Attachment and Loss.* Vol. 1, *Attachment.* New York: Basic Books.
Cannon, W. B. 1929. *Bodily Changes in Pain, Hunger, Fear and Rage.* 2d ed. New York: Appleton-Century-Crofts.
Darwin, C. 1872. *The Expression of the Emotions in Man and Animals.* London: John Murray.
Descartes, R. 1825. *Les Passions de l'âme.* Paris: Oeuvre et Cousin.
Ekman, P., Friesen, W. V., and Ellsworth, P. 1972. *Emotion in the Human Face.* New York: Pergamon.
Ekman, P. 1973. *Darwin and Facial Expression.* New York: Academic Press.
Gall, F. J. 1835. *On the Functions of the Brain and of Each of Its Parts.* Translated by W. Lewis. Boston.

Gardiner, H. M., Metcalf, R. C., and Beebe-Center, J. C. 1970. *Feeling and Emotion: A History of Theories*. Westport, Conn.: Greenwood Press.

Hobbes, T. 1839. *Leviathan*. Edited by William Molesworth. London.

Izard, C. E. 1971. *The Face of Emotion*. New York: Appleton-Century-Crofts.

James, W. 1884. What is an emotion? *Mind* 9:188–205.

Kagan, J. 1976. Emergent themes in human development. *American Scientist* 64:186–96.

Kearsley, R. B. 1973. The newborn's response to auditory stimulation. *Child Development* 44:582–90.

Lange, C. 1887. *Uber gemuthsbewegungen*. Leipzig: Theodore Thomas.

Levi, L. 1975. *Emotions: Their Parameters and Measurement*. New York: Raven Press.

Mandler, G. 1975. *Mind and Emotion*. New York: Wiley.

Plutchik, R. 1962. *The Emotions: Facts, Theories and a New Model*. New York: Random House.

Reymert, M. L., ed. 1950. *Feelings and Emotions*. New York: McGraw-Hill.

Russell, B. 1962. *An Inquiry into Meaning and Truth*. Baltimore: Penguin.

Sartre, J. P. 1962. *Sketch for a Theory of Emotions*. London: Methuen.

Schachter, S., and Singer, J. E. 1962. Cognitive, social and physiological determinants of emotional state. *Psychological Review* 69:379–99.

Schachter, S. 1966. The interaction of cognitive and physiological determinants of emotional state. In *Anxiety and Behavior*, ed. C. D. Spielberger. New York: Academic Press.

Sroufe, L. A. 1977. Emotional development in infancy. Mimeographed. University of Minnesota.

Tomkins, S. S. 1962, 1963. *Affect Imagery and Consciousness*. 2 vols. New York: Springer Publishing.